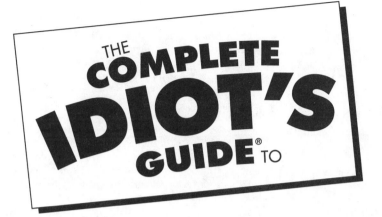

THE COMPLETE IDIOT'S GUIDE® TO

The Pentagon

by Jeff Cateau and Michael Levin

ALPHA

A Pearson Education Company

Michael dedicates this book to his children Chynna, Will, and Isaac, and to the U.S. Military that keeps them safe.

Jeff dedicates this book to the memories of Terry Lynch and Bryan Jack, American civilians on the front line, September 11, 2001.

International Standard Book Number: 0-02-864414-X
Library of Congress Catalog Card Number: 2002113240

04   03   02   8   7   6   5   4   3   2   1

Interpretation of the printing code: The rightmost number of the first series of numbers is the year of the book's printing; the rightmost number of the second series of numbers is the number of the book's printing. For example, a printing code of 02-1 shows that the first printing occurred in 2002.

Printed in the United States of America

Note: This publication contains the opinions and ideas of its authors. It is intended to provide helpful and informative material on the subject matter covered. It is sold with the understanding that the authors and publisher are not engaged in rendering professional services in the book. If the reader requires personal assistance or advice, a competent professional should be consulted.

The authors and publisher specifically disclaim any responsibility for any liability, loss, or risk, personal or otherwise, which is incurred as a consequence, directly or indirectly, of the use and application of any of the contents of this book.

For marketing and publicity, please call: 317-581-3722

The publisher offers discounts on this book when ordered in quantity for bulk purchases and special sales. For sales within the United States, please contact: Corporate and Government Sales, 1-800-382-3419 or corpsales@pearsontechgroup.com

Outside the United States, please contact: International Sales, 317-581-3793 or international@pearsontechgroup.com

Publisher: *Marie Butler-Knight*
Product Manager: *Phil Kitchel*
Managing Editor: *Jennifer Chisholm*
Acquisitions Editor: *Gary Goldstein*
Development Editor: *Jennifer Moore*
Production Editor: *Billy Fields*
Copy Editor: *Cari Luna*
Illustrator: *Chris Eliopoulos*
Cover/Book Designer: *Trina Wurst*
Indexer: *Aamir Burki*
Layout/Proofreading: *Becky Harmon, Mary Hunt*

Contents at a Glance

Contents

Appendixes

Foreword

Until 1947, a pentagon was any figure with five equal sides. The Greek mathematician Phythagoras thought the angles of a pentagon represented the divine order of the universe. Once the 20-acre building squatting on the banks of the Potomac was finished, though, it was no longer possible to think of *a* pentagon without thinking of *the* Pentagon, and what it represented.

Few structures in human history have made the leap from mere stone and mortar to symbol and metaphor. The Parthenon became a symbol of Greek democracy. The Coliseum became a metaphor for the excesses of Imperial Rome. The Pentagon symbolizes the mightiest military on Earth, a metaphor for American power and influence that can be projected across the globe. To Americans, it's a symbol of security. To America's enemies—like the terrorists of September 11, 2001—the building is a symbol of oppression.

Symbolism is simple. Managing the strategy, tactics, affairs, and logistics of a military that ranges across all seven continents is complex. Whether it's Marines in Baghdad, Army Rangers in Afghanistan, sailors in the Persian Gulf, or airmen over Bosnia, the orders, bullets, and billets originate at the Pentagon.

Jeff Cateau is a Pentagon professional who can't use his real name for national security reasons. He and veteran writer Michael Levin have produced a guide that opens up the Pentagon corridor by corridor, explaining how America's defense establishment functions or, sometimes, doesn't function. With a combination of fascinating detail and cheeky prose, Cateau and Levin take you inside the labyrinths of policy and procedure that make up America's military.

Today, more than ever, it's vital for the average American to understand how military police and procedures work. The vast majority of people in the United States have never served in uniform, and so have only the vaguest idea of what the military does. Given the new threats facing America in the twenty-first century, *The Complete Idiot's Guide to the Pentagon* is a necessary introduction to the strategy and tactics of America's peacekeepers and war-fighters.

War, military theorist Carl von Clausewitz observed, is the continuation of policy by other means. American policy has changed and evolved over the decades since the end of World War II. The policy of containing global Communism gave way to the policy of post-Cold War nation building, which gave way to the post-September 11 policy of preemptive action against suspected terrorist organizations and the regimes supporting them. In each of those stages, the U. S. military has been the means and method of enforcing policy.

Protracted land warfare with massed men and machines in World War II gave way to uncertain, political warfare in Korea. That, in turn, morphed into protracted guerilla warfare in Vietnam. The lessons learned in Southeast Asia, in turn, influenced the Desert Storm-era doctrine of striking quickly with overwhelming force. The threats from transnational terrorism have led to new battle doctrines involving highly trained, technologically superior troops moving quickly in small units. On the oceans, a deep water Navy designed to slug it out with the Soviets has morphed into a combat force able to project power forward from the sea, onto coastal areas where most of the world's population lives. An airpower doctrine rooted in protracted saturation bombing has changed into a nimble, precise force using precision weapons guided by satellite or laser.

We have no idea what comes next for either policy or the military enforcing it. All we do know is that the changes will be born in that Pythagorean building on the banks of the Potomac.

—Charles Jaco

Journalist and author Charles Jaco was a war correspondent for NBC and CNN and now hosts the *NightWatch* program for CBS Radio. He is the author of two novels, *Dead Air* and *Live Shot*, as well as *The Complete Idiot's Guide to the Gulf War*.

Introduction

On the Potomac River in Virginia, roughly equidistant from the Jefferson Memorial, the Lincoln Memorial, and the Crystal City Motel, sits a low, sprawling concrete building. It's five stories tall, built of five concentric rings, each with five flat sides. It is called, with simple geometric correctness, the Pentagon.

Built in the 1940s as temporary housing for the suddenly expanded Department of War, the Pentagon is, depending on whether Congress is in session, the second or third most powerful building in the world. It is the nerve center of the American military, headquarters of the most powerful armed forces the world has ever known, and a tough place to get decent parking.

Five Sides, Lots of Angles

But the Pentagon is, first and foremost, an office building. Approximately 23,000 people work there on any given day. Although the subject of what they do may be different from people in other office buildings, many of the jobs and most of the lives are very similar. Yes, some are generals. But far more are accountants, secretaries, and what would in the private sector be called "middle management." Some come in late to work. Others have babysitter trouble. And more than a few think their supervisor is an idiot.

But everyone who works there, from the Secretary of Defense to the servers in the concourse bakery, goes home every day knowing that what they did that day, they couldn't have done anywhere else. Because in this building (referred to as "The Building" by its employees), every memo, every phone call, every cup of overpriced latte helps in the mission unique to the Pentagon—defending America and securing the United States' position in the world.

Which makes that idiot supervisor just a little bit easier to take.

Take Your Pick: Regular, Reserve, or Civilian

Who are these 23,000 people? Well, the American military employs about 3.8 million people, give or take. Of those, 1.4 million are *regulars*—full-time soldiers, sailors, airmen, and Marines. Another 800,000 or so are in the *reserves*, working at civilian jobs but trained and available for military duty on short notice. And almost 700,000 are civilians who help run the services, handle purchasing, and so on.

The regulars need to be fed and housed and given uniforms and guns and tanks. Reservists need to have somewhere to train and to have somebody tell their employer to hold their job while they train or fight. The civilians need to know what their goals are, the mission of their organization, and their unit. Somebody has to work with other countries to keep peace so that American troops don't have to solve every problem. And everybody needs to be paid on schedule. (And, of course, someone has to make sure the 23,000 working in the Pentagon get paid and have desks and pencils, too.)

Oh, and sometimes, somebody needs to decide whether and how to fight a war.

Some of these jobs aren't inherently exciting. Some are also done in other locations by the Department of Defense and the military services. But the direction, the oversight, and the missions come from the Pentagon.

We think of the Pentagon as a single building with a single purpose, as when the news reports that "the Pentagon announced" this or that, or "the Pentagon" took an action. And, to be sure, the building is filled with people working together on national defense. But as with most other office buildings, several major tenants live in the Pentagon. While they all pull toward the same goal (well, most of the time), they are actually different organizations, with different agendas and distinct values. This book will take you on a tour of who these people are, what they do, and how the team is built. But it's only a tour, a visit. To experience the true thrill of the Pentagon, you have to work there.

Perhaps after reading this book, you'll want to. Or maybe you'll just get on with your life. After all, the Pentagon isn't the only place to find overpriced latte.

It's Not an M-16, But ...

We've loaded your pack full of handy weapons to help you battle the enemies—military jargon, classified information, and well, just plain boredom—whose sole mission is to keep you from finishing this book. Use the following boxes wisely, because last we heard Congress was planning to cut the budget for them:

Pentagon Parables

Throughout this book, we share informative tales from the hallowed annals of the Pentagon, very few of which we made up.

Fighting Words

Defense as a Foreign Language: Words your drill sergeant would be proud to hear you use correctly, although Mom might not be so thrilled.

Changes Since 9/11

The Pentagon is rethinking almost everything to do with national defense. This is where we bring you the latest, some (but not all) a consequence of the attacks on the United States.

Basic Training

Amazing facts! Little-known customs! Trivial trivia! And other bits of knowledge that only insiders know, so you might not get shot by security right away!

Disclaimer

The information in this book looks and sounds very convincing, except maybe for the part about the Giant Carnivorous Robot project, but that's secret anyway. Nonetheless, you should not rely on the information in this book to plan or start any actual wars, conflicts, melees, donnybrooks, hockey fights, or professional wrestling matches. You may if you wish, but Alpha Books, Pearson Education, Inc., and the authors have no responsibility whatsoever for the outcome, although the authors wouldn't mind a cut of the gate receipts.

Special Thanks to the Technical Reviewer

The authors of The *Complete Idiot's Guide to the Pentagon* express their pitifully inadequate gratitude to the former Defense Department official who agreed to look through this book and tell us just how many times we had it wrong, which he did on the condition that we not tell anyone his name is David Ochmanek.

Trademarks

All terms mentioned in this book that are known to be or are suspected of being trademarks or service marks have been appropriately capitalized. Alpha Books and Pearson Education, Inc., cannot attest to the accuracy of this information. Use of a term in this book should not be regarded as affecting the validity of any trademark or service mark.

Part 1

The Five-Sided Puzzle Palace

Space, resources, mission, forces, time, and objectives. Know how these six elements apply to a war, and you can construct a winning strategy. Know how they apply to the Pentagon, and you're well on your way to understanding America's military.

The very name of the building defines a space. Inside it, you'll find futuristic systems, dingy paint, and an astonishing array of talented people doing every job you ever heard of—and some you never knew existed. Turn the page and come inside the Pentagon.

The Pentagon Is a Very Big Building

In This Chapter

- ◆ Anatomy of the Pentagon
- ◆ Sluggish and proud of it
- ◆ I Gotta Get to 3D216
- ◆ The military presence around Washington

Before the attack on Pearl Harbor, the Department of War and the Department of the Navy were housed at the President's right hand, in what is now known as the Eisenhower Executive Office Building at 17th and Pennsylvania in Washington. (Until May of 2002, it was called the Old Executive Office Building; and no, it wasn't called that because of all the old executives who work there. Bada-bing.)

Planners decided to bring the War and Navy Departments and 15 other military agencies together in one place for the sake of efficiency. The building they designed is remarkable even 60 years later.

Despite being only five floors high, the Pentagon's office space roughly equaled one tower of the World Trade Center. Its five rings are connected by 10 corridors, two emanating from each corner of the inner, or "A," ring. The structure is concrete, with limestone facings.

The building itself covers 29 acres, not to mention the parking lots, heating plant, and other parts that make up what's officially called the "Pentagon Reservation."

Even more remarkably, the Pentagon was built, start to finish, in *16 months*, at a price of $49.6 million, or what one jet fighter costs today.

How Big Is This Thing, Anyway?

Let's say you wanted to go for a walk around the outside of the Pentagon, starting at the River Entrance. A tenth of a mile later, you'd just have gotten to the first corner. Another tenth, the Mall Entrance. Then it's roughly two-tenths to the helipad. (Getting thirsty yet?) And you're not halfway done. By the time you've passed South Parking, the Corridor 2 entrance, and the Transit Center, and have explained to the guards why you're walking around their building, you'll have covered $^9/_{10}$ of a mile.

That's easy compared to what's inside. Walk every hallway in the Pentagon and you'll have an extra 17.5 miles on your Reeboks. (But you'll have had 284 separate chances to go to the bathroom.) You'll still have had an easier time than walking the same area before the Pentagon was built, when it was a marshy swamp and sometime-airport.

> **Pentagon Parables**
>
> The Departments of War and Navy were merged into a single Defense Department by President Truman in the National Security Act of 1947. The same act also created the Air Force as a separate service. (Historians still debate whether this was Truman's greatest mistake. To be more specific, Army and Navy historians are on one side, and Air Force historians on the other.)

On the walk, you'll have to avoid getting run over by the electric carts that carry supplies, and all the tricycles. (Although they have big wheels, they're not Big Wheels; tradespeople like telephone repairers and electricians get around the building on big tricycles with toolboxes between the rear wheels.) The in-house Army clinic even has an ambulance golf cart. A series of ramps, off-limits to pedestrians, lets the supply carts move from floor to floor.

A classic shot of the Pentagon.

(DoD photo by Master Sgt. Ken Hammond, U.S. Air Force)

Are You a Slug?

The Pentagon is also a significant transportation hub. Bus lines from all over Northern Virginia converge there, both to bring in some of those 23,000 workers and to put more than 30,000 others onto Washington's Metro subway system every day.

Perhaps the most colorful way to get to work is to become a slug. Strategically located around the Washington suburbs are "slug lines," places where workers heading for the Pentagon or downtown D.C. gather to be picked up by perfect strangers in cars. (Apparently, they never listened to their mothers.) Slugging is a good deal all around. Because many major highways in the Washington area reserve lanes for high-occupancy vehicles, the slug driver gets to work faster than he or she would alone, and the passengers get a free ride.

Slugs, as ride-sharers are known, form a whole Pentagon subculture. The building is rife with friendships, marriages, and even bowling teams created when people met while slugging.

Although slugging started informally, it has become a staple of Washington's transportation infrastructure. Virginia has even built park and ride lots, where commuters can park in the morning before reaching the worst traffic, slug in using the express lanes, and reverse the process in the evening. Because this keeps thousands of cars off the already-overcrowded Washington area roads, and because slugging is such a popular way of coming to the building, Pentagon management officially recognizes and endorses it. There's a reserved area for after-work slug lines. Drivers come by and call out their destinations: "Lake Ridge!" "Falls Church!" and slugs jump in.

Often, people who slug in together will arrange their trip home that same evening. Pentagonites who have a choice whether to work late can coordinate through central ride-sharing registries to ensure they have a ride home before accepting overtime. But "Sorry, I slugged in today" is often considered a justifiable reason to decline staying late. (It doesn't work as well for the Secretary of Defense.)

Navigating the World's Largest Five-Sided Office Building

To enter the Pentagon, you come to one of six main entrances. You swipe your ID badge through a reader on what looks like a subway turnstile; the system ponders for a moment, and if it doesn't think you're already in the building, it opens to let you in. This all takes place under the watchful eye of officers from the Pentagon's police force, the Defense Protective Service.

Changes Since 9/11

The Defense Protective Service (DPS) security was augmented after September 11 by uniformed and armed soldiers outside the building, who make sure you have an ID before you actually enter the Pentagon itself.

Also, on May 9, 2002, the DPS was subsumed into a new agency, the Pentagon Force Protection Agency, which adds antiterrorism, defense against unconventional weapons, and other facets to the DPS's basic mission of protecting the people who protect America.

Stop by the ID office and you'll see, on the wall, giant samples of different ID badges. Besides a picture of the person whose ID it is, each badge has a code for what buildings that person is authorized to be in, and at what hours. A badge emblazoned with PNT, for example, is good for the Pentagon only; one that says NCR allows you into all the military buildings in the National Capital Region. The badges also have shaded backgrounds or borders that indicate whether you're an employee, a service member, a contractor, or a foreigner.

Basic Training

The badge office is on the concourse, near the Metro entrance. And yes, it's outside the gate, so you don't have the problem of how to get to the badge office to get a badge if you don't have one in the first place, a problem not unlike trying to find your glasses when you can't see because you don't know where your glasses are.

Once inside, how do you get around? After all, you have 17.5 miles of hallway and no map.

The official line is that it takes no more than seven minutes to get from any point in the building to any other, although if you've blundered into the basement—or the steam tunnels beneath it—it can take quite a bit longer. (Trust us on this.)

The reason you can travel that far in seven minutes without Acme rocket shoes is the hub-and-spoke system. Not all hallways are the same; some are "rings," and some are "corridors." That's an important difference to remember, as you'll see.

I Need to Get to 3D216 ... *This Week*

Say you just came in the Mall entrance, on the E ring at the ninth corridor, and you want to get to 3D216.

First, you have to figure out where you need to be. 3D216 is:

> 3rd floor
>
> D ring
>
> 216—near the second corridor.

Or, in essence, all the way on the other side of a 29-acre office building.

No sweat. Remember that the corridors run *across* the rings—they are the spokes that connect the A ring, the hub, to the E ring, which would be the tire if this were even a reasonably apt simile. So, the fastest way is not to go around the E ring, where some offices are nearly a half-mile away. Instead, take the nearest corridor inward to the A ring. That way, you'll travel a much shorter circle—it has something to do with pi—and, along most of the A ring, you'll enjoy sunlight from the windows looking onto the courtyard.

When you get to the A ring, go around to the second corridor (if you remember which way to turn when you get to the A ring). Take the second corridor back out to the D ring. With 131 stairways, you can probably find one to get you to the third floor.

Changes Since 9/11

Technically, you were always supposed to wear your badge around the building. Military did. Many civilians, trying to avoid the geek factor, kept them out of sight until they were needed. Since September 11, though, your badge must be in sight at all times when you're in the building—and they mean it.

Basic Training

Except for the A ring, few of the hallways have windows, since the ring hallways have offices on both sides and corridors don't have windows. If they did, you wouldn't see much anyway. Indeed, unless your office is on the outside of the E ring, your window looks across at somebody on the next ring's window, with maybe a scrap of sky.

Unfortunately, once you're on the third floor at the D ring, you can't just assume that 216 is between the second and third corridors. One of the few breakdowns in the numbering system is that office numbers relate to the ring they are nearest, not to which two offices they are between. So there are offices beginning with 3D2 on both sides of the second corridor. That's why signs where the rings meet the corridors show which offices are along each segment of the ring.

After a while, you learn where the shortcuts are—the alleys that connect rings between the corridors, which stairways to avoid (they don't all go to the fifth floor, for example, and some are closed off on other floors because they pass through places you'll read about later). But for novices at the Pentagon, it's the old computer game come true: You are in a maze of twisty passages, all alike.

Stuff They Actually Let You See

Throughout the building, one finds memorials and displays honoring various wars, acts of valor, or other militarily significant events. These displays are all a visitor to the building could really observe, apart from locked doors with cryptic nameplates. When tours are allowed, they are given by a cadre of specially trained military guides, whose most significant attribute is the ability—honed through endless repetition—to recite the tour script while navigating a mile and a half of the Pentagon's labyrinthine corridors for 90 minutes, walking only backward. Like Buckingham Palace guards, who aren't supposed to flinch or smile, a Pentagon tour guide never looks over his or her shoulder from when the tour begins until returning to the concourse.

A Pentagon tour, pretty much the way the tour guide sees it.

(DoD photo by Rudi Williams)

Part of the African Americans in Defense of Our Nation corridor.

(DoD photo by Rudi Williams)

Some corridors are named for heroes, displaying memorabilia from their careers. One bears tribute to the life of soldier, statesman, and Secretary of Defense (SecDef) General George C. Marshall, who not only assisted in the defeat of Europe, but even more famously its reconstruction. Another is the ANZAC Corridor, with exhibits commemorating the defense partnership of America, New Zealand, Australia, and Canada. Another celebrates the fiftieth anniversary of the Pentagon, with historical displays. And there's Correspondents' Corridor, decorated with reproductions of famous headlines.

The Correspondents' Corridor is, not surprisingly, where you'll find the office of the Assistant Secretary of Defense for Public Affairs (the PR office). It's also home to the Pentagon offices of the major media, including the television networks. When you see the Jim Miklasewskis and David Martins of the world reporting from the Pentagon, they are probably in one of two places.

If they're sitting down, it's in their Correspondents' Corridor office, a "studio" about the size of a handicapped stall in a bathroom, with a network logo behind them scaled to make it look like a much bigger room.

If they're standing up, it's probably outside the Mall entrance. The bust that's usually out of focus in the background is the first Secretary of Defense, James Forrestal.

Changes Since 9/11

As you go through the hallways now, you see posted on the walls banners, big cards, and other supportive messages from schoolchildren and communities all over the country, like Scottsdale, Arizona, and Plano/Richardson, Texas. Children's crayon handwriting seems out of place here. But it's oddly welcome.

Fighting Words

SOS   Creamed chipped beef on toast. Sometimes it's ground beef instead. A military staple, often found in the field and rather less so in the Pentagon unless one is dining with Marines, who would eat this stuff six times a day, frozen, filleted, or over ice cream. The acronym stands for "(bad word) on a shingle."

Although building tours were canceled after September 11, until they come back, you can take a 24-minute virtual reality version at www. defenselink.mil/pubs/pentagon/virtual.html.

One thing you won't get to enjoy in the virtual tour is Pentagon cuisine. Throughout the building, there are places to get a little something to eat. They range from the formal Executive Dining Room to the Redskins snack bar, a hot dog palace decorated in the burgundy and gold of Washington's NFL team. The largest cafeteria, just off the concourse between the first and tenth corridors, was not unlike a typical college or company cafeteria in quality. But as this book went to press, the cafeteria was closed for conversion to a shopping mall-style food court. (We'll be able to tell you all about it in the next edition!)

The service chiefs and the Secretary each have their own mess, which serves a limited menu of freshly-made dishes and can whip up special requests if you have enough stars on your shoulder. E ring types can get carryout from their mess, although it usually works out that a fretful executive assistant, concerned that the boss is working too hard and not eating right, asks whether he or she can run down the hall to get the boss a salad. (The boss brightens visibly and orders a cheese steak with fried onions.) The messes will also prepare food for working meetings in an E ring office. (We don't know why, but having been through more than a few working breakfasts, it is clear that the services have a fixation with toast. Breakfast can be eggs, oatmeal, *SOS*, or a combination, but regardless, there are always baskets on the table with enough toast to feed the 10th Mountain Division.)

The Pentagon That Visitors Never Visit

Unfortunately, interesting as the live or virtual tour may be, it won't show you things that you couldn't see or read about anywhere else. The coolest stuff—what makes the Pentagon different from any other office building—is what goes on behind secure doors.

A substantial part of the building is taken up by the Joint Staff area, which on some floors even fills in between rings to form a continuous space. This is the nerve center of the Pentagon's military operations. It includes several functions, which we'll discuss now, since you dropped by.

The National Military Command Center

The NMCC, as the National Military Command Center is called, is a room, full of monitors, printers, and overworked coffeemakers (not to mention people). It is where the Pentagon keeps a 24-hour eye on the world. The NMCC receives data from all over the globe: *SIPRnet* messages from Korea, fax traffic from Europe, readiness and regional hotspot reports from the *CINCs*, and intelligence alerts from CIA. NMCC staff can show you the exact position of every ship in the Navy, updated in real time. And often the most valuable input: There's a TV constantly tuned to CNN.

The watch officer in the NMCC is probably the best-informed person in the world about what's happening right now, everywhere. And if not, he or she can be, immediately. And the watch officer needs that information. Because in a crisis, he has an awesome decision to make: Do I wake the Secretary?

> **Basic Training**
>
> In joint areas, the Navy almost always makes the coffee. Navy coffee is known as the most … piquant among the services. Bred of years of midwatches at sea, Navy coffee is strong, it is hot, and it comes with a variety of intriguing additives (depending on who's making it), including salt and pennies in the pot. This ain't cinnamon cappuccino country.

> **Fighting Words**
>
> **CINC** A geographical commander in chief, about whom we'll gossip lots more in Chapter 8. SecDef Donald Rumsfeld abolished the use of the word "CINC," arguing that there's only one commander in chief, the President. "CINC" was the word before Rumsfeld, it will be the word after he goes, and don't look, but lots of people still use it today. SecDefs are transitory, the building rules. So we will use CINC here.
>
> **SIPRnet** The DoD's own secure, classified global Internet. (Okay, the Secure Internet Protocol Router Network, if you have to know.) Unlike the civilian version, it doesn't slow down when school lets out on the West Coast.

The Tank

The Joint Chiefs—all 4-star generals—meet to plan operations and, often, settle differences out of public view in the Tank. While it's actually a fairly unprepossessing conference room with really comfortable chairs, this is the closest thing to a "War Room" in the building.

President-Elect Bush and Vice-President-Elect Cheney receive a briefing from outgoing SecDef William Cohen and Joint Chiefs Chairman Henry Shelton in the JCS Gold Room, unofficially known as "the Tank."

(DoD photo by Mamie M. Burke)

Meetings here are referred to as "Tanks," as in "That'll be decided in this afternoon's Tank." Sometimes Tanks are about operations; other times, to resolve disputes between services on budgeting or responsibilities. While civilians may occasionally attend sessions, this is a service sandbox, where the Chiefs let what exists of their hair down. Because of that, the Tank is the source of much building gossip along the "you'll never believe what CNO said to the Commandant!" variety. And, like most gossip, nobody who passes it along was there.

The Joint Chiefs Briefing Room

The closest the Pentagon comes to having what looks like the public image of a "War Room" is the Joint Chiefs briefing room. It's a two-story-tall auditorium with floor-to-ceiling rear-projection displays that show everything from the inevitable Power-Point slides to maps and live video. During a briefing, the room is usually dark. To the audience's left, audio-visual specialists command a console controlling what appears on the screens.

The OPSDEPS Room

Compared to the Joint Chiefs briefing room, the one-story OPSDEPS (for Operations Deputies—the guys who have to make things work) room feels low-ceilinged, with two tables forming a long V pointed toward the back of the room. The back wall is mostly dark glass, with a multimedia projection room on the other side. Principals sit in high-backed chairs; aides and *horseholders* line up along the walls or in the projection room.

It's really a 3-star version of the Tank. Unlike the Tank, though, the room is used for other purposes. Major decisions are reached in the Tank, or the SecDef's office. But the options and often the conclusions are hashed out here first.

A whole lot of people spend an awful lot of time in the Joint Staff area without seeing the sun. So let's go outside.

> **Fighting Words**
>
> **Horseholder**   The aide who sits outside or silently in the back of the room while his or her star-emblazoned boss meets and plans. From the days when an aide would hold the reins of his boss's horse while he fought a duel. The difference today is that if your general loses the meeting, you don't get to keep the horse.

> **Fighting Words**
>
> **Vice**   A vice-chief. This is why the military recruits for personnel in lower grades. "The Marines are Looking For a Few Good Vices" might not be quite the right message.

Welcome to Ground Zero. Here's Your Corn Dog.

In the center of the Pentagon, nestled within the A ring, is both the safest and most dangerous park in the world. Here, on summer days, hundreds of Pentagon employees enjoy lunch in the sun. They buy ices from a vendor, or hot dogs from a small carryout, and enjoy them on park benches or sprawled on the grass. Apart from the fifth side, it is not unlike a public square in any city, with two exceptions.

First, it is extremely safe, because everyone there has had to pass through Pentagon security to get there. In this park, muggings and purse-snatchings are of no concern.

Second, as September 11 demonstrated, it is one of the most likely targets for enemy warheads in the event of conflict. This fact rarely intrudes into the Pentagon psyche, except for one simple expression: For decades, this bit of sylvan tranquility has been known to its occupants as *Ground Zero*.

Still, it's a really nice park.

Fighting Words

Ground Zero The point on the ground immediately under a nuclear explosion. Called that because measurements of a bomb's effects begin from that point. The Trinity site near Los Alamos, New Mexico, was the world's first Ground Zero.

Changes Since 9/11

North Parking is one of the world's largest weekend skateboard and roller-skating areas. Acres of smooth, unoccupied pavement prove irresistible to locals seeking recreation, although the drainage channels between the aisles could flip the unwary.

The World's Most Powerful Parking Lot

Washingtonians who want to know what's going on in the world watch two indicators. The more obvious is the Pentagon's north parking lot, easily visible from Virginia Route 110. The density of parking at late hours has proven a reliable indicator of the state of world crises. (The other indicator, used often by news organizations, is to call the local Domino's franchise to see how business is. If a whole lot of pizzas are going to the Pentagon, something's up. This is why they pay reporters such big bucks.)

Also, because Route 110 runs so close to the building, the Pentagon Athletic Center, and under some walkways, trucks and tour buses are no longer allowed there. Soldiers in *Humvees* with large weapons make sure you notice the signs.

The spaces in North Parking closest to the building are reserved for shift workers, with passes coded to show the hours they work. That way, folks who start work in the afternoon aren't always stuck 8,700 spaces out.

Fighting Words

Humvee Everybody knows what a Jeep is, right? The most common story of how the Jeep got its name (and there are others) claims that it's a shortening of GP, from its official name, "Truck—General Purpose." When the time came to replace the venerable Jeeps, the Army bought the High Mobility Multipurpose Wheeled Vehicle, or HMMWV. The closest anybody could come to a short name is Humvee. If you hear somebody say "Hummer," they're a civilian. (By the way, the folks at DaimlerChrysler would like you to know that Jeep is their registered trademark. Which makes us want to go Xerox a Kleenex.)

Between North Parking and the Athletic Center is the Pentagon Child Development Center, daytime home to the children of Pentagon workers.

To get into the Pentagon, you pass the Child Development Center and come to a bridge over Route 110. On the sidewalk approaching the bridge is a painted stripe that is small in size but large in effect. It is the line where formality stops. Inside that line, the Pentagon is officially a no-saluting zone. With so many military personnel in one building, saluting superior officers could take a significant portion of the day. It could also be difficult, particularly for an aide carrying a typical overload of documents or briefing charts. But there's another good reason for the no-saluting zone.

The Pentagon, December 28, 2000. You can clearly see the five sets of five-sided rings, with the park in the middle. Let's walk around the picture. At the upper left is South Parking, with a little bit of Interstate 395. Moving clockwise, you see the helipad (the concrete pad with the H on it); the road above that is Virginia Route 27. Arlington National Cemetery is to the upper right of the picture, across 27 from the building. To the right, you can see cars parked in a small lot; that is the Mall Entrance. Farther to the right is the new shipment receiving center, which was still under construction in this photo.

In the lower right, across Virginia Route 110, you see a small scrap of North Parking. The building with four vents on the roof is the Child Development Center. At the bottom of the picture is the River Entrance, with a bit more parking; below that, the parade ground where distinguished visitors are feted. Although the Pentagon is raised above Route 110, it still passes quite close, and you can see why trucks and tour buses are no longer allowed there.

The structure to the lower left of the building is the old transit center, where commuter buses arrived.

(spaceimaging.com)

At an Army base, a soldier is surrounded by other Army personnel. He knows what the rank and other insignia mean. But the Pentagon is full of mysterious uniforms from other services and even other countries. It's easier to tell everybody not to salute than risk that an Air Force captain will fail to salute a Navy captain—or, worse yet, that he might salute the guy selling ices at Ground Zero.

But the lack of saluting doesn't mean all traditional *customs and courtesies* are absent. Rank is no less sensitive in the Pentagon than elsewhere, and in some ways even more so. A base commander might establish a relatively casual working relationship with his staff; after all, in that environment, he is the Man in Charge, and his standards rule. His boss could be six time zones away. But in the Pentagon, any officer knows that a colleague of equivalent rank could be dropping by at any time, and his boss may work two offices away. Worse yet, it's hard to tell an important civilian from the one who's here to fix the clock. So everyone errs on the side of caution. On average, there's a bit more formality here than at a typical military base.

Fighting Words

Customs and Courtesies
The rules that govern military conduct, such as who salutes whom, how to act when the flag is displayed, and how one addresses fellow personnel of various ranks.

North Parking isn't the only lot by a long shot. South Parking, between the building and Highway I-395, has a number of close-in lanes reserved for handicapped persons and for car and vanpools, a common way to get to the building. Visitors pay to park on the other side of I-395, walk a long tunnel under the highway, then across the breadth of South Parking to reach the Corridor 2 entrance.

Bigwigs can park close to the building, in one of very few spaces directly outside the Mall and River entrances. They're taking a chance, though. To drive in, you have to stop at a gate and be ID'd by a guard, who then lowers a sturdy metal barrier to allow your car in. Several times in recent years, the barrier has snapped back up as a car was passing over it. In one case, it was a limousine carrying the Japanese defense minister, who was slightly injured; in another, the same thing happened to his German counterpart. (It pays to have been on the right side in World War II.)

The E Ring: Where the Brass Live

As a rule, the interior of the Pentagon lacks charm and, well, isn't lovely. Although improvements have been made over the years—most dramatically in the recently renovated areas, about which more later—the prevailing atmosphere in the halls is institutional, with drab colors and poor lighting through much of the building. Well-kept institutional, to be sure, but whomever has the brown paint concession will retire wealthy.

Things change when you get to the E, or outer ring. That's where SecDef, other high civilian officials, and chiefs of the services have their offices. Because it's the outer ring, there are plenty of window offices. Of course, the inhabitants don't have a lot of time to enjoy the view.

There's more paneling along the E ring than anywhere else in the building, and offices are finished more nicely. (Well, the principals' offices are; sometimes their personal assistant, their military aide, and their private secretary will be cheek-by-jowl in an outer office intended for one.)

Hallways around the Chief of Air Force Staff's office feature selections from the Air Force art collection. You can tell you're nearing the Chief's office because of all the original Robert Taylors and Keith Ferrises.

Dignified though it may look, the E ring is always hopping. If it isn't preparation for testimony before a Congressional committee, it's resolving a budget decision, deciding whether to deploy more forces to a trouble spot, or whether to give the troops a pay raise.

Basic Training

You may find it reassuring to know that many offices, including the secretaries and commanders of the Army, Navy, and Marines, overlook not the power symbols of Washington, but the rows of headstones at Arlington National Cemetery. Every day's decisions about peace and war are made with the possible consequences directly in view.

Basic Training

The Air Force has a prodigious collection of art, much of which is kept in an archive on the fifth floor. If you work in the building and know the right person to ask, you can check out a piece or two for your office. Oddly, most of the paintings and posters feature airplanes or missiles.

The Extended Pentagon

The Pentagon doesn't just look like a wheel, albeit a clunky one; it is literally the hub of a whole region of military activity in the Washington area. Some related activities, like the Missile Defense Agency, outgrew their Pentagon spaces and others moved to the Washington area to be closer to their top brass. And yet others grew up apart from the Pentagon.

Overlooking the Pentagon, with a prime view of the helipad, is a set of eight oblong beige buildings. This is the Navy Annex, built during World War II to house—you guessed it—naval officials. Like the Pentagon, the Navy Annex buildings were intended to be temporary and torn down after the war, but more than 50 years later, they still stand. The Navy Annex is home, among other things, to the headquarters of the Missile Defense Agency and offices of the Commandant of the Marine Corps.

Basic Training

Program office Each major system—airplane, computer network, whatever—that the Pentagon buys is overseen by a group of people dedicated to getting that system through the procurement process. Together, they are the program office. We'll discuss the procurement process in more detail in Chapter 11.

Across I-395 from the Pentagon, overlooking Reagan National Airport, is a cluster of high-rise office buildings grandly called Crystal City by its developer. Many military functions are housed in leased space there. NAVSEA, Naval Sea Systems Command, the part of the Navy responsible for developing new ships, is there; so are NAVAIR, which does the same for airplanes, and the *program offices* overseeing a number of major procurements. Lots of defense contractors also house their Washington outposts there, to be close to their Pentagon customers and Congressional funders.

But that's not the only place where the military is good for the Northern Virginia office-rental market. A few miles farther south, in Alexandria, Virginia, the Hoffman Building houses several agencies, and Army Materiel Command is just up the street. You can find a lot of Air Force activity in Rosslyn, just on the other side of Arlington Cemetery from the Pentagon; buildings in the Bailey's Crossroads area, south of the Pentagon, are Navy and OSD (Office of Secretary of Defense; see Chapter 3) country. Fort Belvoir, about 15 miles south of the Pentagon in Virginia, hosts the Army Engineer Center and parts of the Army's Computer and Electronics Command, or CECOM. The Defense Acquisition University is here, too, where program managers and people who buy things for a living learn the intricacies of DoD's unique and tremendously complicated acquisition system. (Look, if you need a whole university to understand shopping, it's some serious shopping.) And if your tastes run to gules rampant on a field of argent, the Army's Institute of Heraldry, which creates official seals not just for the military but the whole Federal government, is at Belvoir. At the fort's northern edge, Davison Army Air Field hosts a small fleet of Army transport helicopters and C-12 turboprops for the brass.

Fort Myer, on the other side of Arlington Cemetery from the Pentagon, is home to ceremonial units such as the Old Guard and the soldiers who stand watch at the Tomb of the Unknowns. It has a lot of good housing for brass, but is best known in history as the site of both the first military aircraft flight (by Orville Wright and Lt. Frank P. Lahm, in 1908) and the world's first airplane fatality (Lt. Thomas Selfridge, killed in a crash that seriously injured Wright, a week later). The commissary at Myer is hugely popular with the Washington military community, as is the Class Six (liquor) store. And a number of Pentagon social events, retirements, weddings, and so on take place in the Myer officers' club. When a new SecDef or Chairman comes in, the official farewells and welcomes take place on Fort Myer's parade ground.

Fort McNair, a small post on the Potomac in Washington, is home to the National Defense University, the highest institution for professional military education, and the Industrial College of the Armed Forces, specializing in acquisition and logistics. McNair features a gracious Generals Row, a line of distinguished, albeit modestly sized, brick houses on the edge of the Potomac.

Andrews Air Force Base is most famous as the home of Air Force One, the converted 747 that carries the President around the world. (It also carries a full communications suite, well-appointed staterooms, and more press than the White House would really care to drag along.) Located just outside the Beltway in Maryland, Andrews is also host to the 89th Airlift Squadron, which maintains a fleet of "executive transportation" aircraft. Besides Air Force One, these range from little C-21s (as the military calls Learjets) to Boeing 757s (C-32s) to take Presidential press pools or Congressional delegations overseas. Andrews is thus the closest point of embarkation for military traveling *space-A*, and not a bad one. Across the field, a Navy facility plays host to itinerant P-3s and F-18s, and houses transport aircraft for Navy officials, the F-16s of the D.C. Air National Guard, and support for a Marine reserve F-18 wing.

Travelers waiting for an Andrews flight relax in a well-appointed VIP lounge featuring snacks, newspapers, and magazines, and excellent restrooms. It's like an airline frequent-flyer club, but with much nicer artwork.

The Washington Navy Yard, at the confluence of the Potomac and Anacostia Rivers, includes more offices of NAVSEA, various administrative functions, and a museum. Alongside, visitors can board the destroyer USS *Barry*, named not for Washington's infamous mayor but Commodore John Barry, naval hero in the Revolutionary War and the senior officer of the newborn United States Navy.

> **Basic Training**
>
> Andrews is also the scene of a big annual air show. To keep harmony in the Pentagon family, the headline act alternates each year between the Air Force Thunderbirds and Navy Blue Angels demonstration teams.

> **Fighting Words**
>
> Space-A (space available)   Shorthand for the military benefit of being able to ride along free on a military flight as long as they have a spare seat. Military and some retirees use space-A to go all over the world. It's getting back that's tricky.

Bolling Air Force Base, on the D.C. side of the Potomac, hosts a number of headquarters functions, including the people who handle OSD's payroll. Strangely enough, it has no runway. It is home, though, to a futuristic, shiny silver building housing the Defense Intelligence Agency, about which the less said in these pages the better (but here's a secret: Chapter 9 will have more about DIA. Shh!). Just north of Bolling is the Anacostia Naval Station, which has some really interesting antennas.

Thirty miles south along I-95 brings you to Marine Base Quantico. Join the Marine Corps, and you'll start your training at Parris Island, NC; Twentynine Palms, CA; or Quantico. In addition to the recruit training, Quantico has a large *Hogan's Alley* and large infantry maneuvering areas, and is home to the FBI training academy.

Marine Barracks Washington, better known by its address "8th and I," is barracks for the Marine drill teams and Presidential detail. It's also the home of the Commandant of the Marine Corps. Not his office, his actual home. (Charming single-family white brick house, wooden floors, including parade ground, and very large servants' quarters. Excellent security.)

Barely outside the Washington Beltway, the Naval Surface Warfare Center, Carderock Division, is home to a surprising concentration of naval architects and hydrodynamicists—considering the Potomac is, at that point, navigable only by canoe. Their pride is the David Taylor Model Basin, a quarter-mile-long building that houses what looks like a rather strenuous lap pool. In this long channel, the Navy creates waves and other ocean conditions to test the performance of differently shaped ship hulls. It is excellent employment for anyone who really enjoys boats in the bathtub.

Washington's two famous military hospitals—Walter Reed Army Medical Center in northwest D.C., and Bethesda Naval Medical Center—are where the President gets his checkups. Which one he goes to depends on who's the White House doctor.

And Annapolis, home of the Naval Academy and center of a large number of Navy installations, is not far to the east.

We Get Around

To get from one place to the other, DoD operates a system of shuttle buses that circulate among the installations and offices in the area.

If you rate a little better than the bus, DoD and the services maintain a fleet of nondescript sedans and vans, which senior officials can call on 24-7 for their own needs or to pick up visitors. They are driven by military personnel with specialized training in how to handle threatening situations, similar to the executive protection driving courses offered by many private firms.

But for longer trips, the executive helicopter fleet comes into play. The southwest side of the Pentagon looks out over a helipad with its own fire rescue vehicles and mini control tower. SecDef can call on the executive helicopter fleet, HMX-1, based in Quantico, Virginia—the same unit that operates Marine One to transport the President. Uniformed brass can make use of their own service's choppers.

Changes Since 9/11

The airspace around Washington was closed to all civilian aviation in the days after the attack on the Pentagon, and Reagan National Airport was closed. Once it reopened for business, except for a one-day window when private aircraft were allowed to evacuate National, general aviation has been prohibited within 12 statute miles of the airport, so the only flights in the area (except airliners) are military helicopters.

The Least You Need to Know

- It takes awhile to figure out how to maneuver around the 17.5 miles of Pentagon hallways.

- Slug culture revolves around carpooling, and is an integral part of Pentagon life.

- The NMCC watch officer is probably the best-informed person in the world about what's happening right now, everywhere.

- The Pentagon is the hub of a much larger military community around Washington.

Chapter 2

May the Forces Be with You: The People of the Pentagon

In This Chapter

- ◆ The military and civilians side by side
- ◆ Breaking the insignia code
- ◆ Who should stay and who should go
- ◆ How to think like a tank

It wouldn't be the best use of military manpower to have people in uniform do all the 23,000 jobs in the Pentagon proper, much less the thousands more in the Washington area. With very few exceptions, Washington duty doesn't require experience with weapons or hand-to-hand combat. So even many functions in the military services fall to civilians to perform.

On an expedition to the Pentagon, you'll see many types of personnel, with varied plumage. Think of this chapter as your birdwatcher's guide.

Stars Aligned Randomly: Military Personnel

The Pentagon is a command center, so you have a lot of military folks there with stars on their shoulder. Generals may be rare toucans compared to common crow colonels, but in a 23,000-bird aviary, you see a lot of toucans.

The number of general officers in each service is limited by law. From time to time, the services will ask for more, less because they don't have enough in total than because they don't have enough of the right kind. Certain jobs in the military are reserved for certain ranks; Director of the Joint Staff, for example, is a three-star job, (or "billet" in military talk). It's very important that, especially on joint working groups, a service's representative is of equal rank to the other services' so they can't boss him around. But sometimes fate has all the right people already assigned, or for some other reason the service believes it needs just one more general.

The problem is that even if they *frocked* an existing general to the right number of stars, it would take him away from some other duty. (Although you could frock a colonel to be a general, you'd have to make him a general soon, which would run up against the numerical restriction on generals.)

Many Pentagon generals, especially three- and four-stars, are in their *terminal assignment*. After all, only one gets to be Chief of Staff.

Fighting Words

Frock   No, it's not a peasant's dress. To frock an officer means to authorize him or her to wear one rank higher than he or she actually has earned, if promotion to that grade is forthcoming. They are neither paid for the higher grade nor get any of the other benefits, but they can "pin on" the rank early for purposes of customs and courtesies.

Terminal assignment   Where you go to catch your plane. No, that's not right; how did that get in here? A terminal assignment is your last duty post in the military. Because many military personnel have trouble using all their leave during their careers, they will often use it all up right at the end of their terminal assignment, which means that if you're scheduled to retire in July, you might leave the building in April and just show up for the last day.

Colonels of Truth

Pity the poor colonel. Anywhere else on the planet, he's a god. In the real world, colonels and their Navy equivalents are base commanders, ship captains, and diplomatic attachés. "The colonel wants this done now" are words to fear.

In the Pentagon, however, colonels are the worker ants. Look at any significant task force or study group, and the action officers—the ones who do the lifting—are 0-5s and 0-6s, lieutenant colonels and colonels, Navy commanders and captains. And when they are not on their knees scrubbing at one assignment or another, colonels are horseholding for a general.

The life of an *action* officer at the Pentagon can be quite varied. They can be working with the Chief of Staff of their service in the morning, on a joint project at noon, and representing their service to OSD in the evening. Good action officers—and that usually means those on their second tour in the building, as it takes that long to learn the ropes—have a network of contacts in offices throughout the Pentagon, so whatever needs doing, the officer knows the right guy or someone who knows the right guy. Those contacts usually run within services, the primary exception being for officers who have attended National Defense University or another joint school, for whom classmates become the principal contact web.

Fighting Words

Action   The most versatile clean word in the Pentagon. It can be used as almost any part of speech, with many meanings. There's military action, which means an operation or engagement. There's an action, or action item, as in "The Secretary signed out an action." What he signed could be a decision, in which he was taking the action, or a to-do, requiring action on someone else's part. Ask a question at a briefing, and if the briefer doesn't know the answer, he'll say, "I'll take that for action," meaning "I'll find out and get back to you." And that's before the technical references, like the action of a gun (the mechanism). Also, the person assigned to a task is the action officer (or, in less formal terms, the *stuckee*, from "Who got stuck with this action?"). And there are some less proper uses, too, usually involving weekend activities.

The jobs they do might not be that different from their previous duties. But the effects are much greater. You're not just helping a base commander set policy for the post; you're helping the Chief of Staff set policy for the whole Army.

But talk to any colonel in the Pentagon, and you'll hear the same thing: "I can't wait to get back to the field." Like root-canal surgery, a Pentagon assignment is a wonderful thing to have in one's past. But neither is too pleasant while in progress, or so they'll tell you. Assignment to a senior staff is an honor, and not at all a bad thing for a career. But there's a service ethos that the Pentagon is not the place to be for real soldiers/sailors/airmen/Marines.

Basic Training

Military personnel are paid more and gain more deference as they increase in rank. To keep things equitable among services, there is one scale of pay regardless of what each service calls the rank. An E-1 is a new recruit, even though the Army calls it a private, the Navy a seaman, the Air Force an airman, and the Marines a disgusting maggot. It also helps ease confusion, since services use the same name for different ranks; an Air Force captain is an O-3 and a Navy captain is an O-6. E is for enlisted, O is for officer, and G is for "Gee, what nice stars I have."

Some colonels buck that view, and wind up becoming what's known derisively in the field as "Washington colonels." They succeed so well at staff duties, or in a particular specialty like personnel, that they don't wind up going back to the field, and in truth some don't really mind, not that they'll ever admit to that.

No Time for Sergeants

While the building is understandably brass-heavy, noncommissioned officers (NCOs)—the sergeants and chief petty officers who make the real military work—are underrepresented there. The reason is simple: In the real world, NCOs supervise the enlisted troops, who do most of the work. In the Pentagon, officers do most of the work. The few functional jobs like weather analysis or communications tend to befall to yeomen or specialists. Good NCOs are almost too valuable in the field to bring to the Pentagon when there are so many O-5s available.

Civilians

Most Pentagon employees don't own a uniform (if you don't count red ties with dark suits). Like the military, they come in a variety of grades, with ranks and privileges appertaining thereto.

Do You Have an Appointment?

Every presidential candidate talks about what he would do with defense. That's why a number of the most senior civilian jobs are reserved for political appointees; it's how a president puts his or her own stamp on the building. Any job with "Secretary" in the title, as long as it has a capital S, is appointive, as are many more.

The most visible positions, like Secretary of Defense, are "confirmable," which means the Senate must vote on their suitability for the job following occasionally-entertaining hearings. (Nothing says Saturday night like a coupla brews and a good confirmation hearing on C-SPAN.) Lesser jobs, from the deputy assistant level down, don't require confirmation. But they have to leave when the administration does.

Every Day Is Senior Day

But most civilian positions aren't appointive, since you don't want to have to teach the whole building what defense is every four years, and skills like accounting and systems analysis aren't supposed to be political in nature. The civil service structure of the Pentagon exists to execute guidance and provide answers to whatever questions the appointed leadership asks. And different appointed leaders ask very different questions. (Although they often differ by one word: "not." One administration will ask, "How can we make X happen?" And the next will ask, "How can we make X *not* happen?")

Civil servants come in two flavors. The Senior Executive Service, roughly equivalent to the military's general officer corps, provides the most experience. These are the department heads just below the deputy assistants, the service senior scientists, and the trade specialists. While administrations change every four years and military assignments usually turn over even faster, the SESs provide continuity, institutional knowledge, and professionalism. (Another way to look at it is that "continuity" is the enemy of new ideas, but we're trying to be nice here.)

Like doctors and lawyers, SESs have to keep their professional knowledge current through symposia and schooling. They are professional managers, and many of them take that profession very seriously. (Whether those are the ones you'd want to work for is another question entirely.)

SESs come in six ranks, 1 to 6, although by the time you make an SES-6, you've probably got a building named for you.

Basic Training

At the end of each administration, there's a flap over whether some lower-level appointees are "burrowing," trying to change status from an appointee to a civil servant while keeping the same (or a similar) position. Although not necessarily improper, burrowing is discouraged, especially by the incoming administration that has 15 people lined up for that job.

Are You Being Generally Served?

The bulk of the Pentagon's civilians though, are in the civil service's General Service. GS employees are the analysts, benefit experts, secretaries (with a small S)—in short, the regular office folks. But because they are in the Pentagon for a career, they provide a significant repository of institutional knowledge.

That said, GS service can be confining. Each GS employee is assigned a code that looks something like this: GS-13-0340. The 13 indicates your level, or rank, from 1 to the highest-paid 15; the 0340 is your occupational specialty, whether budget analyst or telephone sanitizer.

The civil service is not a good place for generalists. Positions are advertised for a certain specialty and level. Although you might be promoted to an appropriate level, whether you are qualified to do the job or not, you won't be considered if you don't have the right occupational code. Similarly, although managers have the authority to grant bonuses, compensation is strictly governed. Within each GS level are a series of 10 steps; every GS-13 step 2 makes the same as any other GS-13 step 2 in the Federal government, so you know that that bozo Jenkins up the hall makes just as much as you do even though he has trouble operating the water cooler. To make more money, your manager and personnel chain have to grant a step increase, with formal review procedures—quite a difference from your average dot-com. (Oh, wait, are there any average dot-coms any more?)

Making the Grade

Wage-grade employees are the unsung civilians. They are the day laborers, plumbers, janitors, and other blue-collar civilians without whom any government organization would fall apart. Like GS employees, there are 15 WG steps. There's a separate track for WG supervisors, similar to SES.

All GS and WG hiring policies, job conditions, and grading standards are overseen by the federal Office of Personnel Management. They're the same people who announce whether employees will get the day off when it snows, except it rarely snows in Washington, and closures usually don't apply to "essential personnel," and who—especially at the Pentagon—doesn't want to be essential?

Contractors

Much of what the Pentagon does—particularly its thinking—is actually accomplished by civilian contracting firms. Some, like the RAND Corporation, are well known to the public; others, like BDM or Booz-Allen, less so. But a hefty proportion of those in the Pentagon every day don't actually work directly for the U.S. Government.

A major concern of every service is the "tooth to tail ratio," the number of personnel out there on the sharp end versus those in supporting positions. Support is necessary; someone has to order rations and make sure they get where they're needed, plan for the future of the forces, develop new strategy, and so on. One way that all the services maximize tooth is to turn over many of their tail functions to civilian contractors.

Bandits on the Beltway

How often have you thought that you'd like to just take some time and think, if you could only get past paying the bills and doing laundry and playing Barney videos? That's a big part of what some *Beltway bandits* do, which is why they're also known as "think tanks."

In the field, food service, base operations, and even maintenance might be provided by contractors. In the Pentagon, though, contractors' principal job is thinking. A whole industry has grown up around helping the Pentagon think. Often, these thinkers are retired military continuing to give their expertise to America. A top logistician, for example, may retire and start doing almost the same job for a Beltway bandit. Although he can't give orders, his or her experience can continue to inform and improve the way the service does business. Even though there are some restrictions on what military people can do after retiring, in more than a few cases, someone retiring from a military job on Friday has turned up in the same office on Monday, in a civilian suit.

Fighting Words

Beltway bandit   A firm that makes its living by supplying analytical or other support services to OSD or the services. The name derives from the location of many top firms along the Washington Beltway in Virginia. You may never have heard of BDM, the MITRE Corporation, SAIC, or their kin, but they are the glue in the particleboard of national security.

For proof of this, one need look no farther than the roster of those lost at the Pentagon on September 11, 2001. Lieutenant General Timothy Maude was the Army DCSPER, Deputy Chief of Staff for Personnel. He was in his office on the second floor of the E ring, being briefed on a study of how to improve benefits for the survivors of military personnel. But the briefers weren't from Army Personnel Command; they were from a consulting firm, a major Beltway bandit called Booz, Allen, and Hamilton. The Booz-Allen team included Gerald Fisher, Ernest Willcher, and Terry Lynch. Willcher had done personnel work in the Army; Lynch on Capitol Hill. But now that they were in the private sector, they could devote much more time to thinking about how things should be rather than dealing with implementation.

Thinking for Fun and No Profit?

A very different flavor of think tank is the handful of Federally Funded Research and Development Centers, or FFRDCs. (Say "Eff-eff-ar-dee-cees." You're welcome.) The FFRDCs are nonprofit organizations, with contracts that let them be treated as an extension of their respective services. Probably the best-known FFRDC is the RAND Corporation, home to the Army's Arroyo Center, the Air Force's Project Air Force, and OSD's National Defense Research Institute, each a think tank dedicated to the component's problems. The Center for Naval Analyses performs the same function for the Navy, and the Institute for Defense Analyses for the Joint Chiefs.

Understandably, Beltway bandits dislike the close and at times exclusive relationship between the services and their FFRDCs, believing that all of the analysis business should be open for competition. For their part, Pentagon officials defend the FFRDC relationship, saying that some things just have to be kept within the family.

Think tanks are one example of a *support* contract, in which contractors help with planning, force structure, and other headquarters functions while OSD or the service retains decision authority. In *operations* contracts, firms are actually allowed to make decisions and run something. For example, Brown & Root, a major construction and services firm, operates the home base of Task Force Eagle in Kosovo. Other contractors handle space-launch services, tow targets for aerial gunnery training, or run the Pentagon food courts. Even aircraft maintenance is becoming privatized as manufacturers sell military aircraft with cradle-to-grave logistics and major maintenance support.

> ### Basic Training
>
> As with all government procurement, some of the support contracting in the Pentagon is reserved for individuals with challenges or disabilities. Some of the small newsstands in the building are operated by an organization for the visually impaired. These are known colloquially (and perhaps indecorously) as "blind stands," as in "I'm running down to the blind stand for a Tastykake." Similarly, some building janitorial and maintenance work is performed by a group helping the developmentally disabled.

Political Bandits

Washington being what it is, another set of think tanks also plays in Pentagon planning. These are the more political organizations, like the Heritage Foundation, Cato Institute, Center for Strategic and International Studies, and Brookings Institution, which often issue self-funded studies on military matters from different (but usually predictable) viewpoints. They don't work for the Pentagon *per se*, but their studies play a significant part in political (and especially Congressional) debate on national security.

Finally, organizations focused on particular issues, like the Center for Military Readiness, Servicemembers' Legal Defense Network, and industry groups also issue papers, hold symposia, and stir the political pot on issues important to them.

All of these people—contract and government, consultant, direct-hire, and even Pentagon outsiders—contribute in some way to shaping the defense of the nation.

The Least You Need to Know

- Both military and civilian employees work in the Pentagon.

- Wage-grade employees comprise a significant amount of the Pentagon work force.

- Politically appointed officials must leave their position when an administration ends.

- Think tanks and contractors, while not government employees, also provide considerable support to the Pentagon.

Chapter 3

Going Round in Military Circles: How the Pentagon Is Organized

In This Chapter

◆ Breakdown of each department

◆ Responsibilities of top brass

◆ Historic tidbits of Pentagon organization

◆ Roles of civilians

The civilian leadership of the Pentagon is the Office of the Secretary of Defense, or OSD. Although each of the services has its own civilian secretariat, OSD sets policy for all of them. That wasn't always true, and you read about the reorganization that placed the War and Navy Departments under a SecDef in Chapter 2. (1947, remember? Or were you looking out the window during that part?) But civilian control still isn't an easy fit. Sometimes it shows in a tug of war between services and a reluctant SecDef; sometimes it's shown in bureaucratic rear-guard actions against an overactive one. But there always does seem to be a tension.

Nonetheless, it's the civilians' building; the Constitution says so. These are the people who make the Pentagon go.

The SecDef and His Office

The Secretary of Defense is the senior civilian in the Pentagon and, with the exception of the President, in the entire national security structure. He (and it has always been a he) is appointed by the President and confirmed by Congress. SecDef (as he is known, and not just to friends) has a number of powers reserved to no other Cabinet secretary. By law, the President and SecDef constitute the National Command Authority (NCA). That's an important concept, because some powers, like authorizing the movement of troops, are specifically reserved for NCA. But that doesn't mean the President has to make the decision; the Secretary can, too—up to a point. Unlike the President, he cannot order troops into harm's way.

By the way, when we say the "Defense Department," we're describing all of the Pentagon's tenants and then some. Although "the Department" is often used to mean the civilian side, the Office of the Secretary of Defense (OSD), the services, the Joint Chiefs of Staff, the defense agencies, and more, all fall under that umbrella. OSD does not equal DoD. (Although sometimes it's hard to convince OSD of that.) We'll untangle the bureaucracy of the Pentagon in this chapter.

> **Basic Training** _____
>
> Offices in OSD are abbreviated with the acronym for the rank of the officeholder (USD for Under Secretary of Defense, ASD for Assistant Secretary of Defense, and so on) and the responsibility of the office in parentheses. So the Assistant Secretary of Defense for Special Operations and Low-Intensity Conflict becomes ASD (SOLIC). The whole office is known by the latter part: "SOLIC opposed the position," or "I have a buddy in SOLIC."

The Deputy Secretary

The Deputy Secretary is number two in name, but in many ways number one in the life of the building. Although his role varies from administration to administration, the DepSecDef (no kidding, that's what he's called) usually runs much of the day-to-day work of the building and acts as the chief winnower for the Secretary. The Deputy Secretary chairs many senior task forces, and reports going to the Secretary often stop here for review, or to narrow down the available choices.

The Assistant Secretaries and Under Secretaries—titles that function in the same manner—are the specialists. They initiate and often run the studies that result in new policies. And they are responsible for seeing that the Secretary's decisions are carried out.

As a child might ask, "Where do Assistant Secretaries come from, Daddy?" Some have been career defense civilians. Others come from private industry or academia, particularly in the financial and policy areas, respectively. And more than a few come over (or up or down, depending on your view) from Congressional staffs. It's often interesting to see their view of Congress' proper role in defense change when they get into the building.

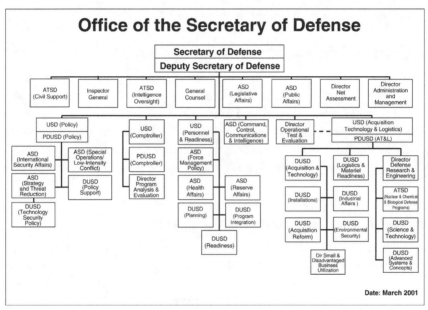

How the OSD is organized. (DoD graphic)

Under Secretary of Defense for Policy

What should our nuclear force structure be? It isn't just a military question. Yes, you need enough warheads to accomplish the mission. But whether the United States should sign treaties controlling the number or type of nukes, or agree to ban landmines, or use bases in a particular country—these are all political decisions as well. The Policy shop exists to help answer those questions.

USD Policy is also on point for some of the biggest debates in military matters. Should the United States be involved in peacekeeping operations? What should be the relationship of international law and the UN to American forces? And, perhaps most significantly, what should America's defense strategy be—what is the U.S. military's place in the world?

> ### Pentagon Parables
>
> For many years, the mission of the nuclear force has been defined in the SIOP, the Single Integrated Operations Plan. The SIOP described where each of those warheads was going in the event of nuclear war. SIOP preparation was among the most strictly classified activities in the Department.
>
> Over time, as nuclear rivals and scenarios multiplied, the SIOP added variations and branches to the point where today it is hardly "Single" anymore.

USD Policy oversees three Assistant Secretaries of Defense:

Assistant Secretary of Defense for International Security Affairs

The ISA office is broken into a number of regional directorates, each under a Deputy Assistant Secretary, that serve as principal military contacts for our allies (and other countries, if they dare show themselves) in Africa, Asia, the Near East, and the Western Hemisphere. These are often countries to whom the United States gives military assistance, which ISA also oversees. One Deputy Assistant Secretary is committed to the search for American prisoners of war and those still missing from Vietnam and other wars.

Assistant Secretary of Defense for International Security Policy

You see the tricky one-word difference: policy versus affairs. ISA is about helping other countries today; hands-on stuff. ISP is about figuring out how America's military should relate to other countries. They help formulate America's security treaties, decide on *technology transfer* rules, and represent DoD in negotiations with other countries. They also handle relations with Europe, NATO, and anybody not in ISA's bucket.

> ### Fighting Words
>
> **Technology transfer**
> The Pentagon is rather cautious about what weapons and technologies American firms can sell to other countries. After all, our stuff is so good that we wouldn't want it pointed at us someday. So every proposed export of militarily usable equipment has to be approved by the State Department and OSD before it leaves the country. (Just put the Palm Pilot down, sir, and back away slowly.)

Assistant Secretary of Defense for Special Operations and Low Intensity Conflict

In the early 1980s, the Pentagon and Congress realized that the military was structured for large, conventional wars. ASD (SOLIC) was created so someone would be able to focus on the unique needs of smaller conflicts. SOLIC also coordinates all DoD special operations.

Under Secretary of Defense for Acquisition, Technology, and Logistics

What is the government's interest in maintaining a viable defense industry? Due to mergers over the last 10 years, the number of major military aircraft makers has shrunk to two. (If you're reading this on a Tuesday, check back Friday; it may have changed again.) There are now six major shipyards, but they are owned by only two companies. The defense electronics market is shrinking almost as fast.

Basic Training

When a major contract is about to be awarded, a phalanx of Pentagon officials begin calling affected Congressmen and Hill staffers an hour or so in advance, since Congress is notoriously averse to finding out anything at the same time their home-state press does. This is in part why there are Congressional ethics laws, because with an hour's notice, you could make a mansion-load of money shorting the loser's stock.

Suppose one aircraft company—we'll call them "Brand LM"—wins a big contract. Should the next contract automatically go to Brand B in order to keep competition in the industry? If Brand LM wins again, will Brand B be able to stay in business? If not, Brand LM will have a monopoly on the aircraft market. The government doesn't like monopolies, in part because they tend to drive prices up. So, shouldn't Brand B automatically get the next contract?

But wait, this is the United States of America. It's a capitalist, free-market country. Awarding a government contract just to keep a company alive is central control of the economy, right? Like they had in the Soviet Union? Do we want Americans to stand in line for fish sticks? And what if Brand B's design is a mutt? Should the American taxpayers buy a mutt just to keep a company afloat? Should American pilots be made to fly a mutt? Isn't that government waste?

Add in the fact that each of these companies has plants in a jillion states represented by about six jillion Congressmen, and spends roughly the national budget of Ecuador on lobbyists, and you can see why the USDs for Acquisition, Technology, and Logistics tend to be sallow, sleepless-looking men.

The USD (AT&L) is also the Office of the Secretary of Defense's lead for reviewing various systems as they hit development milestones. And as if that weren't enough, he also gets to referee one of the nastiest continuous debates in Washington: the war between government employees and private industry for who gets to receive big military contracts. When it comes to fixing planes and ships, or providing base support, this fight makes the one between private think tanks and FFRDCs (discussed in Chapter 2) insignificant.

It started a long time ago. The government built its own shipyards and repair depots when the big private firms were oriented toward production, and didn't seek repair or overhaul work. Similarly, there wasn't a question of who mowed the grass on a military base; that's what privates were for.

Later, though, particularly as government and the military began to shrink, contracting out some functions became attractive. Big hardware makers needed more work, so they got interested in overhauling what they'd built in the first place. And military personnel were needed to go places and carry guns, so base operations contracts seemed like a good idea.

To government employees in the depots, though, this seemed like folly. They argued that a government facility would always be there when it's needed. What if a war came and Lockheed didn't have enough people to do the work, or their people were on strike? Besides, government workers were cheaper.

The contractors didn't agree. Those government workers only looked cheaper because their facilities, tools, and salary benefits were being paid for by tax money, whether there was a contract or not. But the contractor had to pay for all that out of the contract. The total cost to taxpayers was the same, but the amount included in the contract wasn't.

> **Pentagon Parables**
>
> The latest way to resolve the tension between private and public contracting is for private companies to do their work in government facilities, using some government workers. That way, the work gets done without paying for two workforces and two sets of facilities, and the depot or arsenal gets more use out of the taxpayers' existing investment. It just seems vaguely socialist.

It would be like opening a lemonade stand when you bought your lemons but the kid down the street's dad had a lemon farm. So it couldn't be a fair comparison. Besides, wasn't government supposed to avoid competing with private businesses?

Eventually, the government developed a process (called A-76, which we're not going to describe here because we like our readers awake) to decide between public and private bidders for the same work. But it's a fight every year and on every contract, which is another reason USD (AT&L) reaches for the Pepto.

Fortunately, USD (AT&L) has two Deputy Under Secretaries of Defense to carry some of the strain. They are:

DUSD for Installations and Environment

DoD is the world's largest landlord, controlling nearly 850,000 buildings and 30 million acres. (Just be glad you don't have to mow it.) Working for USD AT&L, DUSD I&E is responsible for developing policies for handling those properties and overseeing their management and cleanup.

I&E is also responsible for developing housing at military bases and working with the services. Increasingly, the private sector is getting involved, building new housing for a base in exchange for the right to develop a piece of DoD land elsewhere for private use, for example.

One of the most intensely involving parts of the installation DUSD's job and his or her service counterparts is base closure. Like any firm that is accountable to its shareholders, the Department of Defense tries to be big enough to do its job without paying for excess plants and facilities. As the military changes size and missions, existing bases may no longer be needed.

Until 1988, base closure was a tug of war between DoD and the services on one side, and Congress on the other. The Department would try to close what they considered redundant bases, incurring the wrath of affected Congressmen, who would often reverse the decision or retaliate in another legislative or monetary way.

Then SecDef Dick Cheney made a deal with Congress: You don't trust DoD to pick what bases to close, and DoD doesn't trust you to let us close 'em, so let's put it in the hands of an independent commission.

Congress went along, and the 1988 Defense Secretary's Commission on Base Realignment and Closure approved 16 major domestic closures. (Domestic is an important word. The Department has closed a much greater percentage of its overseas base structure than domestic over the last decade, with nary a peep from Congress.)

But Congress had a different idea on how to proceed. They passed legislation that let the Department choose which bases to close, with an independent commission to check the Department's numbers and ensure that bases were selected for closure for sound analytical reasons, not politics. At the same time, Congress limited its own power by agreeing to vote up or down on the entire list each year, rather than being tempted to take some bases off. Under this system, bases were closed in 1991, 1993, and 1995. Another round, under different rules, is scheduled for 2005.

Base closure is a particularly taxing chore for the DUSD for Installations and Environment, because he or she (and there have been both) lives with the closure process longer than just about anybody in the building. Once the bases are closed, the DUSD takes off the Installations hat and puts on the Environment hat (or, as the case may be, goggles and protective clothing), because by law, any base closed must be completely cleaned up before being sold or given away. As you might imagine, military bases can be real cleanup challenges. While some industries or other entities may have to deal with cleaning up sites used for fuels or solvents, like an Air Force base, rather fewer commercial companies have to worry about unexploded ordnance or former poisonous gas storage sites.

DUSD for Acquisition Reform

Acquisition law is astonishingly Byzantine. In part because of past indiscretions, the rules governing acquisitions have grown to encompass every detail of how an item is made, who may make it, how it is bought, and how much profit the manufacturer may make. One effect of all this is that it takes 10 to 20 years to develop and buy new systems—almost guaranteeing that they will be behind the state of the art in some respects by the time they arrive in the force.

For years, items procured by the Department had to meet exacting military specifications, or MILSPECs. For a jacket, for example, the MILSPEC would detail not just size and color, but materials, what thread had to be used in the stitching, how many stitches per inch—in short, the kind of detail that would make most of us throw down the job and say, "If you're such an expert, do it yourself." MILSPECs applied even to items bought off the shelf; if the services wanted an ordinary T-shirt, they couldn't just buy a $3 one from Wal-Mart. Instead, they would have to develop an elaborate MILSPEC, send it out for concurrence and validation, test candidate T-shirts against the MILSPEC, and likely end up buying the Wal-Mart shirt. But because of the cost and complication of developing and meeting the MILSPEC, the shirt cost $6.

Even worse were the cases where the MILSPEC differed in some tiny particular, like color or thread type, from a commercially available item. Because they were now unique, those shirts cost, say, $15. This, folks, is where $600 toilet seats come from.

The law is also very specific on how procurements are sourced. A certain percentage of procurement spending must be "set aside" for small and minority or women-owned businesses. "Buy American" laws require that many military contracts go to U.S. firms. Under the section of law known as the Berry Amendment, the textiles and food products DoD buys must be grown or produced in the United States.

Part of the job of the DUSD for Acquisition Reform is to make it simpler and easier for companies to do business with DoD, which makes April 15 easier for taxpayers.

Director of Force Transformation

This is a brand new position, created in 2001 to coordinate the efforts of the various services, detailed in Chapter 20, to keep themselves relevant in the twenty-first century, called "transformation." The Director also exists to make sure that OSD has a say in the process, and, frankly, to give a gentle kick in the stern to those services not too happy about the whole transformation thing. Although the Director is part of AT&L for administrative purposes, he reports directly to the SecDef, which is part of why it's a "director" rather than a USD or ASD.

> ### Basic Training
>
> Part of why the Berry Amendment specifies that items must be grown or produced in the United States is that just because a contract goes to an American company doesn't mean that the work is performed in the USA.
>
> In 2001, the Army decided to outfit every soldier with a snazzy black beret. There wasn't enough domestic capacity to make 4.8 million berets in time for the scheduled rollout, the Army's birthday. So the Army received a rare exemption from the Berry Amendment, allowing procurement from foreign sources. Some were bought from Canada, a friendly nation that under free trade laws counts as the United States for some procurements. But some came from China, which aroused such public and Congressional indignation that the schedule was slipped so it could be met by North American production. Your local surplus store probably has a great deal on snazzy Chinese berets.

Under Secretary of Defense for Personnel and Readiness

Building a cohesive force out of regulars, reservists, and civilians is no small challenge. Neither is taking care of those people. And once they've been trained to work together and kept healthy, making sure they're ready to fight might be even harder. All of these jobs fall to USD (P&R).

This is the Pentagon's corporate human resources department. On the personnel side, when increased deployments mean decreased reenlistment, it's up to P&R to figure out how to get folks to stay in the military, and failing that, how to get new recruits in and keep them happy and healthy.

Those jobs fall to five ASDs:

ASD for Force Management Policy

"Quality of life" is an often-heard reservation about serving in the military. ASD (FMP) is OSD's quality of life headquarters. From pay to promotion policy to recreation, if it's about the soldier (sailor, airman, Marine), it's FMP's job.

While the services employ the uniformed folks and carry out policies on P&R's behalf (and not without the usual service versus OSD griping), FMP has more authority over the OSD workforce. P&R sets the labor policies and (when DoD-unique) the pay and benefits. They also set the goals for civilian employee levels, and help decide who gets the pink slips when downsizing is necessary.

FMP also performs the same functions—planning and building the budget for health care, transition assistance, and various forms of support—for military retirees.

ASD for Health Affairs

ASD (HA) sets the direction and budget for the military health care system. This means, among other things, overseeing the ever-popular TRICARE system. (If you haven't heard of TRICARE, consider yourself lucky. To listen to many military and retirees, we should have declared a war on TRICARE a long time ago. And if you have heard of it, by all accounts it's getting better.)

ASD for Reserve Affairs

The reserve community has specific concerns separate from the regulars, like employer support or what happens to their unit if the local base closes. There's a traditional problem of how to optimize the "AC/RC mix"—what jobs should go to the Active Component and which to the reserves, and how many of each there should be. ASD (RA) is the OSD advocate for the reserves, and works to answer these and other questions about the makeup of the force and role of the reserves.

ASD for Readiness

ASD (Readiness) gets to answer the following questions: What can the force do today, what can it not do today, and how do we fix that? He or she is the OSD representative to the Senior Readiness Oversight Council, which you'll learn more about later in the chapter.

Broadly, ASD (Readiness) covers two areas: readiness assessment and training. The assessment function monitors readiness of the forces, and figures out ways to improve it. The training folks design ways of educating troops, helping them get ready for their next assignment without getting in the way of their current work.

ASD for Program Integration

ASD (PI) gets a lot of oddbins jobs, the most significant of which is collecting and managing the data on the force that lets the rest of P&R do its jobs effectively.

Assistant Secretary of Defense for Public Affairs

The most visible assistant secretary is the one who stands in front of the press every day. ASD Public Affairs is the public face of the Pentagon. He or she (and in this case, there is precedent for "she") must deliver just enough information, but not too much; enough to satisfy the press and let the public know what their military is doing, but not so much that enemies learn anything useful. And it all has to be cast in certain terms, whether because of diplomatic concerns and the "meaning" of some words, or to conform with Department policy, which can be very nuanced.

The public affairs staff responds to press and public inquiries of all sorts, and from all over the world. They also have to coordinate their messages with other government departments, lest State announce one thing and DoD another, which in Washington is a big no-no.

> **Basic Training** _____
>
> Perhaps the most popular product of the public affairs office is the Yellowbird. This is a collection of news items of interest from around the world, distributed around the building in early morning. Officially, it's the "Current News Early Bird," but in the days when it was an artfully cut-and-pasted printed folio, the cover page was bright yellow to help it stand out on cluttered desks. Today, the Yellowbird is distributed on the web, but the name has stuck. It's not accessible to the public.

Assistant Secretary of Defense for Command, Control, Communications, and Intelligence

Say "Ay-ess-dee-see-cubed-eye." (No, we just wanted to hear you say it. It's actually ASD (C3I).

C3I is far more than a hardware office. Yes, they set the policies and budgets for DoD's use of computers and communications equipment. And they spend a good bit of money buying them. But ASD (C3I) also has a lot to do with what travels over those communications nets.

Command and control, or how the orders get to the forces and the commanders know the message arrived, is key to running a military. If an enemy can shut down those links, our forces could be isolated and vulnerable.

And don't forget the "intelligence" part of C3I. Knowing what the other guy is up to, and being able to get that information to the right place at the right time is the key to how America intends to fight all of its wars from here on out.

The goal of good *intel* and good *comms* (cool hipster slang, Daddy-O) is to get inside the other guy's *OODA loop*. Go ahead, say it. It feels good. "OODA loop." Not O-O-D-A, OODA. Like "gouda." If you want to know what it is, look in the following box.

> **Fighting Words** _____
>
> **Information superiority** Enjoying an advantage in the speed of distributing data to where it's needed when it's needed there, while denying one's opponent the same ability. The American advantage in information superiority was a very big part of its success in the Persian Gulf War. (The fact that American tanks could destroy Iraqi tanks before they even knew any American tanks were around was a bonus.)

Pentagon Parables

An OODA loop is a basic Pentagon knowledge point. Say "OODA loop" and they'll figure you have your own STU key at least. Say "what?" when somebody else says "OODA loop" and they'll make you for the frosting guy at the concourse bakery.

The OODA loop comes from work done by the late John Boyd, a fighter pilot. He broke down dogfights into a logical sequence that, it turns out, can be applied to almost any competitive situation.

OODA stands for Observe, Orient, Decide, Act. First you Observe the situation: There's two of you in the aisle and only one Mr. Fuzzy doll. Orient yourself: You are closer to the Mr. Fuzzy doll, but he is much bigger than you are. Decide: Your child's happiness is not worth the pounding you will receive. Act: Bribe the store clerk to give you the one they have in back for the manager's grandkid.

Apply the OODA loop to a more serious situation, though, and you can see that the goal is to complete the loop and start over before the other guy does. If you can observe faster, get oriented sooner, make a quicker decision, and/or turn that into action faster, you win. You've pulled the trigger while the other guy's still orienting.

While other countries have reasonable rivals for American military hardware, C3I remains a distinct U.S. advantage. It's the ASD's job to see it remains that way.

Assistant Secretary of Defense for Legislative Affairs

OSD has its own legislative liaison office, as does each of the services. These are two-way operations, making sure Congress understands military priorities while responding to constituent concerns, arranging trips, and so on. If you write a letter to your Congressman asking about your pension, or why your daughter has to wear such a funny uniform, it will probably wind up with the legislative liaison's correspondence branch for an answer.

Director of Operational Test and Evaluation

Created by Congress to make sure nobody fudges when testing hardware, DOT&E oversees and approves the plans for testing systems, advises USD (AT&L) on whether development milestones should be approved, and perhaps most importantly certifies whether new systems are operationally effective (do they do what they're supposed to do?).

Director of Program Analysis and Evaluation (PA&E)

We'll have a bunch more on PA&E in Chapter 6, when you read about how Robert McNamara still runs the Pentagon. The short version is that PA&E is the grandmother who always told you not to buy that fancy sweater when the one at Wal-Mart will keep you just as warm, except PA&E does it for fighter planes. (No, Wal-Mart does not sell fighter planes—yet!)

General Counsel, Department of Defense

Look, you have a building this big, you employ nearly four million people, we don't care if you're Saint Peter, you've gotta have a lawyer. The General Counsel advises SecDef and OSD on legal matters, including whether a proposed policy or the order the President just gave the Secretary is legal. He or she also supervises and sets standards for all lawyers throughout DoD. Each year, the Department submits a package to Congress listing, "Great Laws We'd Like To See"—that's written by the General Counsel. The office has a roster of Deputy General Counsels with specialties roughly mirroring the lineup of USDs.

Inspector General

The IG is OSD's house dick. This office investigates allegations of wrongdoing, whether improper personal conduct or failure to perform on a contract. Waste, fraud, and abuse are the IG's foes, and he has an array of tools, including audits, with which to chase them down. You can help IGman battle these enemies, citizen! Report Pentagon waste, fraud, or abuse at www.dodig.osd.mil, under the Hotline section.

Under Secretary of Defense (Comptroller)

This is Mr. Moneybags. The Comptroller settles the arguments between services for funds. He oversees preparation of the budget, and is the one to whom services go screaming when they think they haven't received their fair share. The Comptroller also decides how money is handled anywhere in DoD, sets the budget process rules for the other departments, and oversees the PPBS (Program Planning and Budgeting System) process, described in Chapter 11 in near-Torquemada levels of detail.

Executive Secretary of the Department of Defense

The Executive Secretariat ("ExecSec") handles paper. They manage the SecDef's in-box, which may not sound like much until you realize the power inherent in deciding which piece of paper goes on top and which doesn't make the take-home reading pack.

ExecSec makes sure reports are appropriately coordinated among all the relevant offices. Reports coming out under the Secretary's name, like the Quadrennial Defense Review, are edited here also. And, in their spare time, ExecSec also handles the (not-inconsiderable) logistics when the SecDef or the DepSecDef goes overseas. The Executive Secretary is a general officer.

DDR&E and DARPA—The Magic Factory

Along with dedicated, well-trained people, the United States' edge in technology is a big part of its advantage on the modern battlefield. Stealth airplanes, unmanned aircraft, nonlethal stun guns—where do these guys get their ideas?

Maybe the coolest job in the building is Director of Defense Research and Engineering (DDR&E). While much of the building is dedicated to paying today's bills and planning tomorrow's wars, DDR&E is looking years and even decades down the road. DDR&E sponsors the development of new ideas, whether by contractors, by services, or in-house.

Each service has its own chief scientist and R&D shop. But the real in-house effort is OSD's own gadget shop. The Defense Advanced Research Projects Agency (DARPA) is working on wars 30 years away.

Every job mentioned so far in this chapter is appointive, so the incumbent changes with each administration. That's true of all ASDs—with two exceptions. One is the ASD for Administration and Management, Doc Cooke, who gets his own section in Chapter 6. The other is the ...

> **Basic Training**
>
> You've probably used a DARPA creation. In the early days of computer networking, DARPA (then ARPA) created a messaging network to help widely scattered researchers work together. It was called the ARPAnet. Today, after some growing pains, ARPAnet has become the Internet. (If you want the authentic ARPAnet experience, go find an old 300-baud modem and hook it to your Teletype. *Then* try downloading that picture of Anna Kournikova.)

Director of Net Assessment

The Office of Net Assessment was set up in 1973 to answer a tricky Cold War question: *Who's the big dog?* We could measure the relative strengths of the United States and the Soviet Union in lots of objective ways. We had more friends; they had more missiles. We had better technology; they could produce huge numbers of weapons relatively cheaply.

The question is, how did that all stack up? Given the various advantages and disadvantages, where did the United States stand, and how could they best advance?

The job of answering that question was given to a top analyst from the RAND Corporation, Andrew Marshall. And today, 30 years and six administrations later, in a geopolitically different world, the Director of Net Assessment is still Andrew Marshall.

> **Pentagon Parables**
>
> The Office of Net Assessment reports directly to the Secretary, is a major player in assessing future threats and how they should be addressed, and has clout far beyond what its small staff might indicate. Yet in the Pentagon phone book, it is relegated to the odds and ends section in the back, along with the Armed Forces Hostess Association and the Pentagon Amateur Radio Station.

Net Assessment's broad role hasn't changed as the world has; their mission is still to figure out who's on top and what keeps them there. But Net Assessment has become more of a future shop, not in the hardware sense of a DDR&E but in divining the politics and shape of future conflicts 25 and more years ahead.

That futuristic task had a current component added early in 2001, when SecDef Rumsfeld tasked Marshall to apply his analytical skills to defining U.S. defense strategy for the future, which takes that future vision and adds the "how are we going to get there" component. Because the review involved the missions of different services, the announcement made many Pentagonites uneasy. Since then, though, they've had other things to worry about.

Each major civilian official has a military aide, who gives advice from the service perspective and coordinates matters with the military.

The Military Component

While civilians are bountiful in titles and in quantity, some military are allowed in the building. Here's who they are.

The Joint Chiefs of Staff

While not every service calls its highest-ranking officer the Chief of Staff, the group of heads of the military services is called the Joint Chiefs of Staff. They are the command council for the military services. With the reorganization of the Department in

1986, described later, the Chairman of the Joint Chiefs is first among equals, acting as the principal voice of the U.S. military.

The Joint Chiefs have a staff to support their endeavors, and the staff is joint, too; not just an amalgamation of various services, but a place in which you'll find Navy officers working for Air Force officers studying a question of import to the Army, all actually pulling on the same oar to a much greater degree than prevails in the rest of the building. (Or so it seems to us. Maybe they're masters of deception.)

Once You Figure This Out, the Rest Is Easy

The organization of the Joint Staff is important to understand when interpreting the Pentagon, because it is basically how all the services organize their senior staffs.

Branches of the Joint Staff are identified by the letter J and a number. The J1 is the personnel section; J2 is intelligence; J3 operations; and so on. If you work for the J3, you get a two-digit number (well, your office does, but it becomes how you are known, too). The Director of Strategic Operations is the J36, for example.

Popular wisdom says that operations types are the top dogs. It's their phones that ring in the middle of the night when the balloon goes up. But to operate, the military needs each branch. Why? *The Complete Idiot's Guide* Table Department was hoping you'd ask that:

Branch	What They Do	Why You Need 'Em
J1	Personnel	No people, no operations.
J2	Intelligence	If we don't know who or where the enemy is, how can we win?
J3	Operations	Ssh. We're talking about everybody else right now.
J4	Logistics	Armies need two things: People and stuff. Logistics guys get the people and stuff where they have to go. Without people and stuff, the operations guys have nothing to command.

Branch	What They Do	Why You Need 'Em
J5	Plans	If the troops don't know what to do whe, where they're going, the ops guys are SOL.
J6	C^4	Without communications, the ops guys are going to have to go do the job themselves, because they can't tell anybody else to do it.
J7	Requirements	Unless the requirements bubbas figure out well in advance how big an Army we need, and how many fighters, and so forth, the Ops guys' larder will be bare when the balloon goes up.
J8	Resources	If we don't pay for the people and their stuff, we won't have any to send.

Fighting Words

SOL (Somewhat) Out of Luck. Except they don't say "somewhat." You fill it in. Indeed, colorful acronyms are a military specialty. The B-52 bomber is known as the BUFF, for "Big Ugly Fat (Feller)." The A-7 fighter became the SLUF, for "Short Little Ugly (Feller)." And that's just what they call stuff on *our* side.

Organization of the Services

We'll look at each service in its own chapter later. While they're arranged pretty much along the lines of the Joint Staff, every service does things a little bit differently, and everybody has to have a different name for the same function.

Take the General Officer in charge of operations:

The Army calls him the DCSOPS (say "dess-ops"), the Deputy Chief of Staff for Operations.

The person with the same job in the Navy is the N3. N for Navy; 3, as you saw with the Joint Staff, signifies operations.

The Air Force Director of Operations is the AF/XO. (The Air Force has this incredibly bizarre way of designating their offices that winds up with some of them looking like manic tic-tac-toe players.)

And the Marine version is the PP&O, the Deputy Commandant for Plans, Programs, and Operations.

In a pinch, though, the real shorthand comes through. Ask a military officer, "What does your 3 think about that?" and regardless of what the service calls their ops head, the question is immediately understood.

Why have office designations in the first place? Why not just use their title, "Director of Operations," or their name, "General Enos Thesia"? Two reasons. First, brevity. If you're sending a military communication, a TO: line that lists everyone's title is MUCH longer than TO: AF/XO, AF/XOX, AF/XOXXO, AF/XTC.

Second, the military is not about individual personalities. Don't misunderstand; they take great care of their people, and any general or service secretary will tell you that their best asset is the men and women in uniform. And since the force became all-volunteer, they *have* to take care of their people in order to keep them out of the clutches of the rapacious private sector, which loves hiring people with skills paid for by the government who know how to dress well, speak politely, and blow stuff up. (Especially Microsoft.)

But the military is based on the principle of interchangeability. Take General Thesia out of one job and put General Bluster into it, and the job should be done just as well. Who the person is doesn't matter; you respond to the requests or commands of the office. People retire; office designators live on.

Basic Training

Look, the Pentagon and the military are organizations of humans like any other, just bigger. And just as in church groups or condominium boards, there will inevitably be cults of personality. Some underlings will want to hitch their wagon to a rising star and follow that superior from assignment to assignment. Others just get along better with one superior than another. But the services do not (and cannot and should not) organize on that basis. That's where you get generalissimos overthrowing El Governemente.

The Services work on some things together outside of the Joint Staff, as part of standing committees and councils. These tend to be high-level, but as usual the real work is done by O-4s, 5s, and 6s. Two will make fine examples:

Joint Requirements Oversight Council

The JROC evaluates new hardware ideas to make sure they make sense, and to keep multiple services from wasting resources developing the same thing at the same time. It's principally made up of the service vice-chiefs and is chaired by the Vice Chairman of the JCS.

Senior Readiness Oversight Council

The SROC monitors readiness of the forces, convening a monthly meeting known as the Joint Monthly Readiness Review (JMRR, or "Jammer") where services and OSD-readiness types look for shortfalls in training, equipment, or any factor that would keep units from being able to carry out their missions, and attempting to find and fix patterns across the services.

While OSD, the Joint Chiefs, and the services are all organized somewhat differently, their offices follow the same broad functional categories. OSD sets policies and goals, and the JCS and services carry them out.

The Least You Need to Know

- The Secretary of Defense is the senior civilian in the Pentagon.
- DDR&E sponsors the development of new ideas, whether by contractors, by services, or in-house.
- The group of heads of the military services is called the Joint Chiefs of Staff.
- The military is based on the principle of interchangeability within ranks.

For Your Eyes Only: Secrecy and Security

In This Chapter

◆ The many classifications of classified information

◆ Background checks

◆ What triggers a red flag in your history

It's no secret that even the best military plans wouldn't be worth a lot if your enemy knew all about them. Consequently, much of what goes on at the Pentagon is secret. Indeed, secrecy is a large part of the building's identity. (But we didn't tell you that.)

If you take a sensitive job in the building, you'll be handed a booklet of forms on which you'll be asked to detail your personal history, financial state, details of travel, military service, medical issues—quite a bit more than you'd tell a first date. They'll ask about your drug use and criminal record, too, although mild errors early in life aren't necessarily disqualifying. And there's a section on affiliations—groups you belong to, especially those that may have had agendas inimical to national policies or which involved explosives. How far back in time you'll have to go depends in part on what kind of clearance you're applying for.

Do Ya *Really* Need to Know That?

We'll discuss the different kinds of clearance a little bit later on, but the basic principle of classification is that information should go to the people who need to know it, and not to those who don't. (Do you *need* to know what's in the cafeteria entree? No. And sometimes you don't *want* to know either.) So you'll only get the level of clearance you need to do your job.

One of the most important parts of the questionnaire is the list of references who can verify different parts of the information. The Pentagon's in-house investigators, the Defense Investigative Service (or sometimes a contractor) spend quality time with those people—usually in person. This can be a nerve-wracking time, as you find yourself thinking about all the bad things you may ever have done to those people, and how this wouldn't be a great time for them to remember that you never did give back that copy of *The White Album*.

What will they ask? First, they'll check the basic data on your form. Can that person confirm you spent the years 1990 to 1993 in a seminary? Do they know you were a member of the Future Defense Geeks of America? Did you really win the Pulitzer Prize at 16?

Then comes the next level of questions. What sort of person are you? Did you get into trouble much? Did you drink or partake in stronger stuff? Did you seem to have a lot of money—or too little? Questions about partisan politics are not cricket. Did you hang out with groups that opposed American policy? What kind? How many? *That* many?!?

> **Pentagon Parables**
>
> Either extreme on the financial scale is a trigger for further investigation, especially if this isn't your first clearance. If you had unexplainably large amounts of money (don't you wish?), they'll wonder what you did to get it. If you didn't have enough, the concern is that you'll sell out cheap.

The third general category is to find out who else they should talk to—and it won't necessarily be people who like you. So be kind on the way up. (And because of this practice of getting names from others they interview, and other names from them, they may sooner or later ask Kevin Bacon about you.)

Once you fill out the form, sit back a bit. Routine security investigations take six months at the best of times, and at particularly busy periods—like changes of administrations, when all the new political appointees have to be checked in addition to the usual load—the process can take a year or more. So you might be helping sort paper clips for a while.

And getting your clearance isn't a license to misbehave. Your clearances will be reinvestigated periodically, and poor judgment is looked at less favorably once you have been cleared.

Basic Training

Over time, some of the criteria and questions have changed. Homosexuality, for example, used to be almost an automatic disqualification for a clearance, because it was thought that you would be vulnerable to blackmail should an enemy intelligence service learn of your proclivities. As society changed and more people became openly gay, the threat of blackmail lost its punch.

Similarly, the prevalence of experimentation with alcohol and drugs has made those issues less prejudicial toward your chances at a clearance, as long as you haven't continued that experimentation into your 50s and don't try to sell the investigator a lid of Sumatran Firecracker.

Secrets in Plain Sight—and Out

Look at a service's budget, and it may be hard to understand what's going on. Sprinkled among the entries for fighters, clothing, and training are items like "Seek Axle" and "Retract Maple." These are classified programs, whose purpose may or may not have anything to do with the programs listed around them, but probably has nothing at all to do with their names.

But if these programs are classified, how can they appear in a budget? Simply, the *name* is not classified, but what the name *means* is. You could run down the street shouting "Retract Maple! Retract Maple!" as many times as you want, and if you don't say it too many times to the same person and keep your clothes on, you wouldn't be breaking any laws. But just tell somebody what installation or technology or operation "Retract Maple" refers to—even if you don't give them a technical drawing, operational plan, or anything that could be used to create a Retract Maple—and you'll be looking at a long time playing dominoes in a poorly-lit room.

Clearances aren't printed on your building pass or tattooed on your forehead. To the contrary, the level of clearance you have may itself be secret. So, how can you share secrets with other cleared people? Each office in the Pentagon—and indeed, throughout the national security structure, government and private sector—has a security officer. That person makes sure you understand how to handle classified material, oversees compliance with security procedures, and maintains your security file. If you need to

Fighting Words

SCIF In a SCIF, the room is the safe. Access is controlled, and the rules about handling documents are different. They have open storage, which lets you leave a classified document out if you leave the room briefly. You'll still see safes in SCIFs, as you do have to lock documents up for the night.

have a meeting on a classified subject, your security officer verifies with the other attendees' security officers that you have the right clearance.

Some of those meetings will happen in Secure Compartmented Information Facilities, or SCIFs (say "skiffs"). As you walk the halls of the Pentagon, you'll see many doors with combination locks or keypad locks on the doors. Many of these are SCIFs. Some people work in SCIFs all day, because so much of what they do is highly classified; other offices have smaller SCIFs attached for meetings, storage, or sensitive projects.

Brown Paper Wrappers: Not Just for Lingerie Catalogs Anymore

Sometimes, secrets need to be portable. You might be bringing back photos from a briefing at the Defense Intelligence Agency, or you are scheduled to present a secret paper at a conference at Strategic Command in Omaha. (Yes, there are quite a lot of classified conferences every year. They're very much like conferences in any business, except all the nametags say "Bob.") How do you keep secrets secret?

Pentagon Parables

You might think the guy with the most access to sensitive documents in the Pentagon is named Donald Rumsfeld. He isn't.

His name is Snake.

Snake is the building locksmith. If you need a combination changed, or an access pad for your SCIF, you call Snake. Whatever you have, he can open it. Snake gets called a lot after vacations, when highly paid public servants responsible for handling secret war plans and billions of dollars can't remember the combination to their own safes.

Secret documents in transit are double wrapped. The outside wrapper has only the name and address of the recipient. The inner wrapper shows the classification as well as the addressee of the document. That way, it isn't obvious to a passerby that you (or whoever the courier is) are carrying anything more interesting than entry sheets for the basketball pool, and a tear in the outer wrapper doesn't show the actual secret material. Couriers who regularly carry classified material also have fancy locked pouches that look like the ones in which banks give robbers cash.

You can't hand-carry classified material without a courier letter from your security officer that tells them what you have, where it's going, and when it should arrive. They don't care whether you make it all right—but you'd better believe they care whether the document does. And yes, they will check with their opposite number on the receiving end. (And don't try the "lion ate my homework" line. Some security officers are kindly, jovial people. But not one of them has a sense of humor about this part of their work.)

Obviously, while you can double-wrap a document, you can't do the same for a telephone call. Discussing any level of classified information on the phone is strictly verboten. So is the practice—and it is not uncommon—of hinting around at secrets on the phone while trying not to provide enough context for a listener to understand.

"Remember that thing we were talking about?"

"The ... ah ... wet thing?"

"The very wet thing."

"Yeah."

"Well, I found what I was looking for. 17."

"17?"

"Yeah."

"Wow!"

This is not a very useful conversation to begin with, but if the number 17 is a classified number in reference to some capability of a submarine, it's a security violation. Even if there's no context for the number 17 in this call, who's to say the same person listening to this call didn't listen to the one before it that left a blank where the number 17 has just been filled in?

Pentagon Parables

In the early '80s, the Soviet Union decided to move out of its dark, gothic embassy on 16th Street in Washington, just a couple of blocks from the White House. They acquired property on Mt. Alto, in the upper Georgetown section of D.C. It seemed a somewhat unusual choice for a location, as it sat at some remove from both Embassy Row and the buildings of official Washington. It seemed that way—until someone noticed that the property was on almost the highest point in Washington, with direct sight lines to the Pentagon; in short, the perfect place to put a listening post to gather telephone and other transmissions. The Soviets were delayed from moving into the new site for years (in part because bugs were discovered in the then-new U.S. Embassy in Moscow). They got in just in time to change the nameplate on the gate as the Soviet Union dissolved.

That's why the rule is never to talk or hint at classified material on the phone or in the presence of unknown or uncleared people. And it's a safe operating rule to assume that every telephone call is being listened to. It may seem paranoid, but when you work at the Pentagon, it's not a delusion—some people really *are* out to get you … or at least your secrets.

The exception to not discussing classified on the telephone is when the phone is a *Secure Telephone Unit* (STU). Typically, your security officer holds on to the STU key. Having your own STU key is a little status symbol; having a STU on your desk means a lot of people salute you.

Fighting Words

STU   (say "stew") Secure Telephone Unit, the most abundant model of which is the STU-III, a white, slightly oversized phone that requires a key to operate.

Yes, as with any other part of life, the classified world has ways to tell who the cool kids are. If you store classified material, for example, geek chic demands that it be stored in a safe with a $3,000 Mas-Hamilton lock that is *very* finicky, caring not only what numbers you dial, but how quickly you dial them. Get it wrong and you won't be able to try again for a while; get it repeatedly wrong and you're in for a visit from Snake, at least.

But the coolest thing an analyst can do is create a "collateral secret." This means that you take a bunch of public information—newspaper articles, sale flyers, Tom Clancy novels—and put the information together in such a way that the result has to be classified, because you are such an analytical stud that you found or created something entirely new and very interesting. This is the Pentagon equivalent of building a working submarine from scraps you have around the house.

If a pile of classified documents fell on your car, you'd know it because the cover page of each is brightly colored, with a couple of words in big capital letters. Broadly speaking, you might see the following words on those sheets:

- **FOUO (For Official Use Only)**   Basically, "Don't hand to *The Washington Post*." The contents of FOUO aren't bomb designs or cipher keys. They may be documents in draft, decision memoranda, or other working papers. It's hard to make decisions in a political atmosphere—and the Pentagon's official address is Washington, D.C., definitely a political atmosphere—if every option is leaked beforehand. FOUO is intended to keep what's inside, inside until it's official.

- **CONFIDENTIAL**   The least respected of classifications. Kinda like "FOUO," but more sensitive. Kinda like secret, but not as important. Confidential documents have to be signed for coming in and going out just like real secret stuff, and you need a clearance to see them, and they must be kept in safes when not in use. But you can't figure out why.

◆ **SECRET** The first category of "real" controlled material. You sign when you get it; you keep it in a safe when you're not using it (unless you work in a SCIF); and unlike most FOUO or Confidential documents, you can see why some of it is secret.

◆ **TOP SECRET** Like "secret," only more so. Everybody calls it TS, as in "There's a TS brief at 1300 in the kitchen with Professor Plum."

◆ **SCI/SAP** This is where you get to find out what Retract Maple is. SCI refers to "Sensitive Compartmented Information," often intelligence data; SAP is Special Access Programs, or things we do that are quite secret. Once in this world, you have to get a separate clearance for each program and each type of information. So, just because you're cleared to know what our next-generation tank looks like doesn't mean that you're allowed to know what it's made of, or what the other guy's next generation tank looks like. And that's about all we can tell you, because we're not too good at dominoes.

In short:

◆ FOUO　A study on whether we can cut the number of airplanes we have.

◆ Confidential　Which ones the Secretary wants to get rid of.

◆ Secret　How many airplanes we really have.

◆ Top Secret　Where they all really are.

◆ SAP　What they can really do.

◆ SCI　How many airplanes the other guys have, where they are, and what they can really do. Oh, and how we know that.

And these comport with the standard clearances: Secret, Top Secret, SAP, and SCI. Polygraph tests are optional for TS, depending on what line of work you're in (you have a "TS" or "TS/Poly"), but go for anything above that and you'll have to talk to the machine.

Although not separate DoD security classifications, some of those colorful papers might also say:

◆ *Q*　Access to Q data requires a separate clearance from the Department of Energy. (This is where they keep the plans for that 100-mile-per-gallon carbure-tor everybody just *knows* is out there.)

◆ NOFORN　No foreigners. Something that's *SECRET NOFORN* means that even if a foreigner has a secret clearance—and lots of allied ones do—you don't tell. This stuff stays with people that know who won the American League pennant in 1956.

- LIMDIS   Limited Distribution. This has always confused us, because all classified information is by definition limited distribution.

- CNWDI   Classified Nuclear Weapon Design Information. As opposed to the other kind.

- BEST BUY   That's a sale flyer that got mixed in with the other brightly colored papers.

The Least You Need to Know

- If you're relatively clean, background checks are relatively painless.

- Information should go to the people who need to know it, and not to those who don't.

- Many factors (e.g., homosexuality) that once precluded someone from receiving a clearance are now considered less relevant.

Chapter 5

A Day in the Life of the Pentagon

In This Chapter

- The importance of handball
- Daily activities at the Pentagon
- Twelve hours just isn't enough
- Rethinking your calendar

With world events constantly changing, 23,000 people having new ideas and different views, and personnel constantly rotating in and out, there is no such thing as a typical day at the Pentagon. Here are just a few of the things that might happen on any day.

Rise and Shine

0530 The Pentagon day starts at the POAC.

Officially, it's the Pentagon Athletic Center, and it's open to all Pentagon employees (so the wait for a locker can be many months). But in less ecumenical days, it was the Pentagon Officers' Athletic Club—and everyone still calls it the POAC (say "POE-ack"). While the exercise and weight machines are modern, chlorine vapors from the indoor pool mix with a constant swirl of sweat and sneaker squeaks from the basketball courts to produce an ambience much more YMCA than Banff Springs Hotel. Pentagon people work hard, and they play hard.

Because the Pentagon is not a nine-to-five building, the POAC is open from 5:30 A.M. to 9:30 P.M. most days, and if it opened earlier, there would still be a crowd. The clientele is a little more military than the actual ratio in the Pentagon, especially in the morning when servicepeople of all ranks try to get their *PT* in before work. The lunchtime crowd is mixed; after five is more civilian.

Fighting Words

PT Physical training; in short, exercise. Because the military has stern standards on fitness, PT is part of most personnel's day. Most of them actually seem to like it. Go figure.

In addition to the weights, pool, and basketball courts, the POAC features a small grill open for breakfast and lunch, a sporting goods shop, and a barbershop. It is not a blond-wood-and-Formica club; the locker rooms sport metal lockers and linoleum. (Well, the men's locker rooms do; we would be ill advised to testify to what's in the women's, even if we knew.)

But with all the attractions here, one stands out: handball.

A military culture includes a large dollop of competition, and while the Pentagon teems with competitive runners and athletes of all sorts, handball is the measure of the Pentagon alpha male. The POAC hosts a series of handball ladders, with tournaments constantly underway and courts oversubscribed. Among the many appeals of the sport: Rank stops at the court door.

More Pentagon trash-talking sessions concern handball than the Army-Navy game, except during the week before and after the game. Then "Beat Navy!" and "Go Army!" bumper stickers appear in inappropriate places (architecturally inappropriate, not anatomically). And afterward, one is apt to find a hallway blocked by wandering choruses of personnel from the losing service singing the winner's service hymn.

Quick Quiz

Match the service with the hymn excerpt.

Army	"Anchors Aweigh"
Navy	"Off We Go, into the Wild Blue Yonder"
Air Force	"The Shores of Tripoli"
Marine Corps	"The Caissons Go Rolling Along"
Space Command	"Ground Control to Major Tom"

0830 The Secretary of Defense, who's probably been at work since 0600, sits down to breakfast in his *mess*. Many of the Secretary's meals are working sessions; this one involves a group of Congressmen interested in the status of women in the military.

0900 Representatives of two contractor teams vying to provide a new missile system meet with the Assistant Secretary of the Army for Research, Development, and Acquisition to find out whether the Army intends to go ahead with the program, and if so, when a contract might be let and for how many missiles.

Fighting Words

Mess   A place where someone eats. Term used because "the Secretary's chow trough" sounds somewhat inelegant.

0930 An OSD analyst needs a map of Eritrea. Fortunately, the Defense Mapping Agency maintains an outlet in the building, with all kinds of maps (aviation maps, nautical charts, street maps, even National Geographic maps) available for free to qualified customers. And what they don't have can often be printed out on the spot, thanks to the miracle of digital storage.

1000 The Under Secretary of Defense for Policy gives a speech at an industry conference in D.C. At the same time, the Assistant Secretary for C3I begins testifying at a hearing of the Senate Appropriations Committee Defense Subcommittee. Officials testifying before Congress are accompanied by at least two horseholders; one notes which questions require follow-up, while the other is a subject expert who sits right behind the principal in order to pass him notes when needed. Service Chiefs of Staff seem to bring at least a squadron of such experts.

1045 A message is received in NMCC: Two soldiers have been hurt in a training accident at Hohenfels, Germany. NMCC notifies the Secretary's office, the Chairman's office, OSD Public Affairs, and OSD Legislative Affairs. They already have contact information for the troops' families in hand.

1100 A study team for the current Quadrennial Defense Review meets. Chaired by an OSD GS-15, the team is made up of colonels and a lieutenant commander whose commander boss just told him that, congratulations, he's now the Navy's representative to this study group, which the commander can't stand going to anymore because the Air Force puke at the meetings doesn't understand that carriers are sovereign bases of the United States that can be moved anywhere, anytime, and nobody's going to let the Air Force have bases in forward areas anymore. (The subject of the study panel is family housing.)

High Noon

1200 The Pentagon concourse is full of Pentagonites looking for sunscreen, a driver's license, or a Nutty Buddy. In the concourse are a drugstore, bank, credit union, bakery, clothing store, motor vehicle office, and other concessions designed to give Pentagon employees everything they need without having to leave the building. A library recently replaced the concourse bookstore, so if you got this book there, please check to see whether it is due back.

1230 Donors line up at the Red Cross blood donation clinic off the A ring, second floor. This is, perhaps not surprisingly, a rather busy place, both because military folks are dedicated to public service and because in their line of work, they never know when they might need to get some back.

1300 ASD for Public Affairs starts the daily press briefing. Sometimes she is accompanied by a military officer to give updates on an ongoing operation; other times, another OSD official could talk about acquisition or policy matters. And some days feature the presence of a Senior Pentagon Official. That's not like a silhouette interview on *60 Minutes*; everybody in the room can see who the person is. But the deal is and always has been that even if it's the Secretary himself (and it usually isn't), anything the person says can be attributed only to a Senior Pentagon Official. In exchange, reporters are graciously allowed to keep their press credentials.

The practice of quoting an unnamed official is not unique to DoD; other parts of the government use it, too. It's done to let the world know of ideas the Department is considering without making them official. That can send a message to others about U.S. interests and intentions without making it seem as if the United States is demanding something. And it can be used to gauge response to a new idea; if it flies, it may become policy, and if not—well, it's hard to fire an Unnamed Official.

Occasionally, you'll hear a reporter quote "an unnamed official familiar with the Secretary's thinking." This is reporter code, and a cheap way to get around the "Unnamed Official" rule. After all, how many people are familiar with your thinking? (Unless you say everything you think out loud, in which case you should *not* apply to be ASD for Public Affairs.)

1330 The retirement party for an SES in AT&L gets underway in the Executive Dining Room. Retirement parties quite often seem to start around 1330 or 1400, which means you get a good party in and wander back to the desk for half an hour before it's time to go home. With an average of 63 birthdays a day in the Pentagon, plus arrivals, promotions, retirements, and so on, it's a good place to have the bakery concession. (The concourse florist also does good steady business, and positively box-office on

Valentine's Day, when Pentagonites, feeling guilty because they spend so much time at the office, attempt to make it up with dead plant matter.)

1415 Sales are picking up at the uniform store on the fifth floor. Close by, the joint services MWR (Morale, Welfare, and Recreation) office sells discount tickets to local attractions and the hot item each year, the Pentagon Christmas ornament. (We are not making this up.)

1500 A flourish of trumpets and a gun salute welcome the Minister of Defense from Poland, as the Deputy Secretary hosts an honor cordon on the parade ground outside the River Entrance. Foreign dignitaries visit the Pentagon almost daily. Sometimes the visits are purely ceremonial, a defense minister visiting perhaps in combination with the visit of a head of state to Washington. Other times, the visits have a very serious purpose, to coordinate on exercises or policy vis-a-vis a common adversary. But the minister's honor cordon is just the tip of the iceberg; a minister or foreign general is usually accompanied by a retinue of lower-ranking individuals who are probably beavering away with their American counterparts on some joint project while the SecDef and Minister smile for the cameras.

1615 The phone rings in the OSD Legislative Liaison office. It's the legislative correspondent from a senator's office looking for the answer to a constituent's letter about their retiree benefits. The matter will be assigned to a caseworker in the office, and the Senator will receive a response within a week.

1730 The Pentagon's own Five-Star Toastmasters Club meets in an OSD Conference Room.

And on into the Evening ...

1800 A team from the Joint Staff meets in the DepSecDef's office to brief him on options for providing forces in Korea. The issue is how many troops would be needed in the event of a North Korean invasion of the South. Three strategies are presented: one high-risk, one medium-risk, one low-risk.

In strategy briefings, "risk" usually doesn't mean the chance of absolute failure; a plan that had a significant opportunity to fail wouldn't make it this far into the process. Commanders and planners speak of risk as the chance they won't succeed *according to their original timeline, with their original forces*. That schedule risk has tangible effects; if, for

Basic Training

The Pentagon is a 24-hour-a-day building, and like most of the government, even the senior levels work long hours. Meetings before 0700 or after 1800 aren't unusual.

example, you were planning to fight in two different places nearly simultaneously, missing the schedule in the first conflict means some of the forces planned to go to the second one won't make it in time. And that becomes a risk of losing.

To reduce risk, you can change the timeline or add forces. But the timing isn't always up to you. In Korea, for example, the capital of South Korea is 45 miles from the North Korean border. So you have to get in the way fast.

But to reduce risk by adding forces isn't easy either. Moving troops, planes, or even ships requires considerable advance planning and lots of logistical support. A service might not want to dedicate so much of its available combat power to one or another theater. (We'll get into more detail about this in Chapter 10.)

Pentagon Parables

"War" isn't a word you hear so much anymore. Planning focuses on "conflicts" or "contingencies." That's partly because the United States hasn't fought a declared war in 50 years. (Korea was a "police action" under United Nations auspices; the Vietnam War was never declared; Congress authorized "use of force" in the Persian Gulf "War," but didn't declare war.)

Why not declare war? Under international law, a formal declaration obligates the parties to certain standards of conduct and settlement practices that the United States may not want to be bound by. And, to be Machiavellian, the declaration of war gives Congress a level of control over the conflict that the administration may not want.

1820 A network reporter does a live report from the River Entrance on the training accident that morning.

1945 The OSD General Counsel finally gets their coordination copy of the proposed rewrite of the rules governing shipment of servicepeople's personal vehicles to their overseas duty stations turned into the Executive Secretary's office, where it will be compared with other comments and melded into a final draft for the Secretary's signature.

2230 Someone familiar with the Secretary's thinking gets into his car outside the Mall Entrance for the ride home. It's an early night, but he has an inch-thick folder of papers to read before bed.

What's with This "2230" Stuff?

To the rest of the world (well, America, anyway), Christmas will come at midnight, December 25, 2003. To the Pentagon, it's at 0000 hours local, 25 December 2003.

That difference isn't just to be contrary. Let's break down that date:

0000 hours. Lots of military communications have numbers in them—target locations in latitudes and longitudes or GPS coordinates, radio frequencies, altitudes, and so forth. By saying "Rendezvous at 1100 hours" instead of "Rendezvous at 11," there's no question that the meeting is at 11 o'clock, not Camp 11 or 11,000 feet.

Instead of "hours," why not say "o'clock" as everybody else does? First, it's less precise. "O'clock" means "of clock." Whose clock? Most soldiers don't carry clocks into battle. Yes, they have watches, but "We meet at 11 o'watch" is just silly. By saying "hours," it means at that time no matter what you're using to tell the time.

Besides, look at the 0000. Does your clock have a 0 on it? Neither do many watches. So you can't say 0 o'clock, or 13 o'clock, because they're not *on* the clock.

And 13? What's this 13 business? Military time is on a 24-hour clock, beginning from midnight, which is 0000. Things proceed pretty familiarly through 1200, which is noon. But then, what you might call 1 P.M. is 1300 to the military. The reason is again precision. On a 12-hour clock, "We meet at 1" could mean 1 A.M. or 1 P.M. But there's only one 1300 on a military clock. Sure, they could say "A.M." or "P.M.," but the whole point of military communications is to minimize the chance for errors or misunderstandings. They follow the principle of KISS: Keep It Simple, Stupid. Using a time system with only one 11 each day keeps it simple.

Local. Pretty innocuous word, right? After all, if you're meeting someone, they have to be in the local area. But remember, the Pentagon is a 24-hour operation, talking to commanders and units all around the world. You probably know whether your house is in Central Daylight Time or Pacific Standard Time, but if you just parachuted out of a C-130 somewhere over Europe after flying for four hours, you might not know what time zone (or even country) you were in. So the Pentagon usually uses one of two times.

Local means wherever the person being talked to is. Christmas doesn't start at the same moment in New York as Los Angeles; it starts at 0000 local. But it wouldn't make much sense to begin an invasion on local time, since some of the targets might be a different time zone. Some things start everywhere in the world at the same instant; the State of the Union address, for example. For those events, the Pentagon uses UTC, Universal Time Coordinates, also called *Zulu time.* (You might know it as Greenwich Mean Time.) Use it like this:

> **Basic Training**
>
> World time clocks aren't used so officials can avoid waking up the field commander in the middle of the night. It's so they know to say, "Sorry to wake you" at the beginning of the call.

"The Super Bowl will begin at 2300 hours Zulu." Major offices in the Pentagon, especially those concerned with operations, have multiple clocks showing the time in areas of current interest around the world. One of those clocks is always on Zulu.

0000 hours local, *25 December 2003*. The date that looks backwards to our eyes actually makes more sense than the way we Americans often tell time. "Christmas starts at midnight, December 25, 2003." Perfectly true, but illogical. It starts with the most precise point, the time; then jumps to December, the month; then gets more specific, with the date; then finishes with the broadest measurement, the year. Or, to be graphic:

TIME MONTH DATE YEAR

… while the Pentagon measurement goes:

TIME DATE MONTH YEAR

… which is both in logical order and puts the most essential data first. (It's a little more likely that you'll need to know what time the invasion is than what year.)

And, yes, while most of the Pentagon's world time clocks are digital, many offices have round clocks with hands and numbers from 0 to 24.

The Least You Need to Know

- Physical fitness, especially handball, plays an important role in Pentagon life.
- Working at the Pentagon is not a nine-to-five job; the building is abuzz with activity all hours of the day.
- Pentagon time is measured on a 24-hour, as opposed to 12-hour, clock.
- Military dates are formatted as day-month-year, as opposed to the common American method of month-day-year.

6

Three Men Who Run the Place (and One's Retired and Two Are Dead)

In This Chapter

- ◆ McNamara's legacy
- ◆ Goldwater-Nichols loves jointness
- ◆ Doc Cooke and his empire
- ◆ Building a better Pentagon

Along the A ring, on the second floor between the eighth and ninth corridors, hang the official portraits of former Secretaries of Defense. While many had profound effects on the Pentagon during their terms, the nature of the building—constant personnel rotation, changes in administration direction, yanks on the Congressional leash—means that over time, the contributions of any particular SecDef can get lost.

But one Secretary, gone from the building for decades, is arguably still running the place. While others focused on personnel, or reshaping military technology, Robert McNamara fundamentally changed the way the Pentagon itself does business. And it still runs largely by his design.

McNamara and His Merry Band

In the 1950s, the services ran the Pentagon; heck, they *were* the Pentagon. Program and budgeting decisions were made with very little input from the civilian side of the house; indeed, the Office of the Secretary was then only a small, ad hoc organization with few staff and little legal authority. Services functioned as separate fiefdoms, with little coordination.

President Kennedy wanted the Pentagon run less like feudal Germany and more like a business. As a top executive at Ford Motor Company, McNamara had reshaped the company to run more efficiently, a goal he achieved by using tough-minded, objective analysts to scrutinize every part of the company for wasted spending or inefficient management structures. Today, major companies like McKinsey and Accenture make good livings by providing these services. In 1960, though, McNamara's approach was new, especially to government.

McNamara transferred his analytical team from Ford, along with analysts from places like RAND (called the "Whiz Kids" for their nerdish youth) to the Pentagon. He established what today is the office of Program Analysis and Evaluation, PA&E, to provide cost estimates for new programs independent of the contractors and services, and to audit existing systems for budget compliance. And he established the planning and budgeting processes to govern how programs begin, the relationship of what services required to what they were allowed to buy, and *metrics* by which an individual program's success could be measured.

Fighting Words

Metric The measurement relevant to a particular decision. At Disneyland, your ability to afford admission is a metric to decide whether you get in the park; your height isn't. Your height is the metric that decides whether you can ride Space Mountain. Alternative example: PowerPoint and handball are the metrics that measure Pentagon studliness.

To be sure, firms like RAND had been in the defense analysis business for years. But at the time, they focused on coming up with or evaluating strategies and policies. McNamara and the Whiz Kids followed the money.

Systems analysis, figuring out need for a program and its total cost in advance, was the first serious financial tool OSD had in its ongoing struggle with the services to decide who shaped the defense budget. By institutionalizing systems analysis on the civilian side of the building, McNamara created an atmosphere in OSD that persists today: That money is the measure of what's important in defense, that OSD's job is to be a watchdog over the services, and that money is the key to doing that. Look at the number of employees and offices dedicated to reviewing programs and managing money *vice* those setting defense policy and strategy, and McNamara wins hands down.

Today, systems analysis is most of OSD's reason for living. PA&E has morphed into far more than its original financial oversight role. It helps evaluate the need for programs before they're bought. It's the referee in disputes. And it has a very significant role in most major studies, like the QDR, as the über-analyst, checking to see whether other study teams got their sums right.

Fighting Words

vice   With a small "v," it's not a vice-chief. When most of the world would say "versus" or "against," the military says "vice." Can't begin to tell you why.

And today, PA&E has lots of help in performing the oversight role from some offices you read about in Chapter 3. There's the Office of Test and Evaluation, which makes sure nobody cuts corners on testing to make underperforming systems look good. There's the Cost Analysis Improvement Group, which wields the financial sharp pencil, preparing estimates of program costs independent from the services and contractors. An Assistant Secretary for Acquisition decides (with PA&E's input) whether programs are performing to standard, and what financial strategy will be used in acquisition. The Defense Acquisition Board (DAB), made up of OSD and service brass, must periodically review development programs and approve their continuation. A stronger DoD Inspector General has the power to audit programs for waste or fraud.

While these oversight organizations were sometimes established by Congress and/or in response to some particular scandal, they all owe their existence to the spirit established by Robert McNamara, that the accounting pen is mightier than the sword.

Changes Since 9/11

Although not related directly to the events of September 11, Secretary Donald Rumsfeld began at about that time to change the oversight culture in the Pentagon. Believing that the oversight burden had grown too heavy, Rumsfeld cut many reporting requirements for some major initiatives, beginning with the missile defense program. He established a "Senior Executive Council" to review major programs; while PA&E, OT&E and other oversight agencies advise the Council, they don't have votes.

How Barry Goldwater Changed the World

Imagine a baseball game in which the first base coach and the third base coach had their own favorite players, their own strategies, and didn't work for the same manager.

That's what fighting a war was like until 1986. Each war had an Army commander, a Navy commander, an Air Force commander, and a Marine commander. Although they all reported to a "supreme commander" for the war, he had no structural authority. In the Second World War, the Army's Pacific commander, General Douglas MacArthur, and his Navy equivalent, Admiral Chester W. Nimitz, coordinated their operations not through the supreme commander, but through the chiefs of their respective services. Running coordinations through Washington may seem absurd for two forces operating in the Pacific, but there was no option at the time. (Certainly, when MacArthur and Nimitz agreed on what to do, it could be implemented locally. But disputes or inconsistencies had to be arbitrated six time zones away.)

Also, interservice command arrangements were put in place only when a war made it necessary. But the rest of the time, the military functioned as many separate entities rather than one.

The experience of interservice rivalries and often-conflicting goals in Vietnam sparked an interest in reforming that structure. However, a more proximate cause was Operation Eagle Claw, the failed Iranian hostage rescue mission in 1980, where Air Force, Navy, and Marine pilots were combined in Marine helicopters in an *ad hoc* effort at *jointness*. Led by legendary Arizona senator Barry Goldwater, known as an ardent supporter of national defense, the reformers were determined to make jointness work. To do so, they completely restructured national defense.

Fighting Words

Joint   The ability to operate together with other services.

Pentagon Parables

The failure of Operation Eagle Claw could be attributed only in part to a failure of joint operations. An after-action report cited unexpectedly bad weather (dust storms) and the fact that the mission had been rehearsed with only half as many aircraft as actually flew as contributing to the debacle at Desert One.

A 1986 law, known as Goldwater-Nichols, wrought the greatest change in the defense structure since the National Security Act of 1947. It had a clear objective: to make jointness paramount. It explicitly stated that the services and Joint Chiefs worked for the Secretary. It made the Chairman of the Joint Chiefs the principal military advisor to the President, where before the Chiefs fought for attention.

The biggest impact in warfighting, though, was the bill's creation of the Unified Command Plan (UCP). The UCP cuts the world up into regions. Each region has a single commander in chief, with *operational control* over all U.S. forces in his or her CINCdom, whatever uniform they wear. The services supply forces to the commander, almost like temp agencies supplying clerks. And even back home in training, units report to a joint command, so they can train and be managed the way they fight.

Fighting Words

CINCdom   A simple way to refer to the territory overseen by a regional Commander in Chief. It also refers to the CINC's near-absolute power in the region.

Operational control (OPCON)   Having the authority to issue orders. An Army unit may be under the operational control of the regional CINC, which means he can assign them missions, but he isn't responsible for paying them or deciding their promotions.

Goldwater-Nichols divided the world into "unified" combatant commands: Southern Command (SOUTHCOM), European Command (EUCOM), Pacific Command (PACOM), and Central Command (CENT-COM). It also created four other functional commands: United States Command (USACOM), later called Joint Forces Command (JFCOM); Space Command (SPACECOM); Transportation Command (TRANSCOM); and Special Operations Command (SOCOM).

Pentagon Parables

While everyone in the defense community calls it Goldwater-Nichols, the actual name of the law is the Department of Defense Reorganization Act of 1986. Barry Goldwater of Arizona led the effort in the Senate and Bill Nichols of Alabama in the House. Many defense-knowledgeable members such as Senator Sam Nunn and Representative Ike Skelton backed the effort.

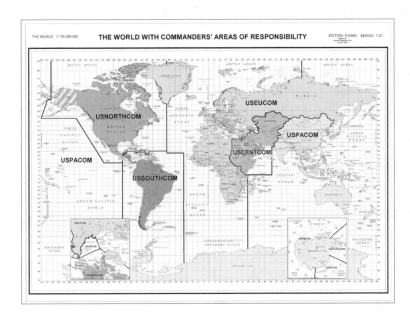

The Magic CINCdoms.

THE WORLD WITH COMMANDERS' AREAS OF RESPONSIBILITY

USACOM, TRANSCOM, SPACECOM, and SOCOM do tasks for all the services, while the geographical commands brought all the services together to perform tasks. Simple, right?

We'll explain the geographical commands in a moment. But first, the oddest duck, USACOM.

USACOM was primarily an administrative command, responsible for overseeing the training and readiness of forces in the United States. A geographical commander preparing for war would ask USACOM for a shopping list of forces—two fighter squadrons, an artillery brigade, and so on. USACOM would know the status of all units, and could put together a package of the most prepared units to send the geographical commander. It was also responsible for defending the United States, although that fell pretty far down on the to-do list.

SOCOM brings together the special operations forces (SOF) from all services. Individually, the special operations forces components are small, with greatly varied capabilities. By bringing them together under the SOCOM umbrella, Navy SEALS can train with Army special forces who jump out of Air Force helicopters—just the way they will fight.

Basic Training

The role of special operations forces is largely misunderstood. Yes, they perform unconventional combat missions. Yes, they have a skills inventory that would make a very interesting resume. But the principal role of special forces is to work with foreign militaries, helping to train them or to aid in coordinating their efforts with the United States. We saw that recently in Afghanistan, where special forces units (and sometimes individual "snake eaters," as they are known) operated with Afghan militias as liaison to U.S. forces.

(That was, of course, only one of their roles. Other SF were in country well before overt U.S. military action, reconnoitering targets, finding out who was really on our side, and trying not to whistle anything from American Top 40.)

The first real test of the Unified Command Plan came during the Persian Gulf War. Kuwait fell in Central Command's area of responsibility, so CINCCENT took charge of the operation. At that time, CINCCENT was Army general Norman Schwarzkopf. Schwarzkopf ordered an array of forces from the services and from SOCOM, and assembled them during Operation Desert Shield.

Schwarzkopf's joint organization included commanders for the air war, ground war, and naval forces. The JFACC, or Joint Forces Air Component Commander, for example, issued the daily orders for all Allied airplanes, whether they belonged to the Air Force, Navy, Marine Corps, or other countries. The United States and its allies fought as one air force, with one set of orders and one military agenda. The same was true for the sea and land components. (Political agendas were another matter entirely.)

> **Basic Training**
>
> Note that CINC started out as CinC, Commander in Chief. However, official orders and other communications are transmitted ALL IN CAPITALS, so the CinCs came to be known by their official names. The same is true for operation names, although we use the civilian version here.

Pentagon Parables

Joint command is hardly a recipe for universal happiness. Just ask the Marines positioned at sea during Operation Desert Storm. Early on, they were poised off the coast near Kuwait City … and stayed there, riding ships, throughout the conflict. The Marines wanted to stage an amphibious landing, which is, after all, what Marines do. Instead, they got seasick. But Schwarzkopf wanted the Iraqis to think the Marines were coming, to keep them from sending more of their forces to the front. And it worked.

To advocates of Goldwater-Nichols, the Gulf War proved that jointness works. And, while his reforms remained controversial for the remainder of Barry Goldwater's life, the debate has since largely ended on the merits of the structure he created.

But Goldwater-Nichols didn't just change the military's organization; it also changed the career of every military officer, again with the idea of making the services work more closely together.

> **Changes Since 9/11**
>
> On April 17, 2002, Secretary Rumsfeld announced the creation of Northern Command, or NORTHCOM. It takes over the homeland defense functions of JFCOM. When the previous UCP was devised, nobody believed that we would need such a command. September 11 told them otherwise.

Before Goldwater-Nichols, you were promoted within your service based on your skills and how you had done in previous assignments. You could become Chief of Staff without ever working with someone in a different color uniform. The problem was, under Goldwater-Nichols, that's not how you would fight.

Goldwater-Nichols broke the service stovepipes by requiring that an officer aiming to become a general or an admiral complete a period of joint service, working within OSD, the Joint Staff, one of the CINCdoms, or in another capacity that put them alongside officers from other services. The point was to learn how the other services did things, thought about things, even used their terminology, so you wouldn't have to learn it on the fly in the event of war. Importantly, this also compels the services to send their most capable officers to joint billets at least once in a while.

Basic Training

The Navy, always on the cutting edge of military fashion, is the only branch offering a choice of uniform color. The debate rages on between what's better/cooler/sexier, summer whites or khakis?

Even though a Pentagon posting isn't a dream for many officers who would rather be in the field, many positions offer the tantalizing possibility of joint service credit, or "punching the joint ticket." Not all Pentagon positions qualify, and it's not uncommon for an officer in a nonqualifying billet to try to find ways to get his time counted. But pollen draws the bees, and the thousands of joint billets in and around the Pentagon make it a must-do tour for ambitious young officers.

Doc Cooke Ain't No Military Chef, and He Ain't a Doctor, Either

Note to readers: On June 22, 2002, as this book was readied for press, David O. Cooke died of injuries suffered in a car accident. We have left this section as written to recognize the profound effect his presence still has on the Pentagon.

You might think the Secretary of Defense was lord and master of this realm. You would be wrong.

For decades, through administrations liberal and conservative, budgets fat and budgets thin, one man has ruled the daily life of the third most powerful building in the world. David O. Cooke, known as "Doc" from his monogram, is officially the "Assistant Secretary of Defense for Administration and Management." He is, in truth, the mayor of the Pentagon. And not only its mayor, but also its landlord, utility provider, moving service, interior decorator—everything that happens here, every service that is delivered, every person or item that arrives or leaves, goes through Doc Cooke or someone in his office.

The late David O. "Doc" Cooke with some of the SecDefs he served. (left to right) William Perry, Frank Carlucci, Harold Brown, Caspar Weinberger, Donald Rumsfeld, Elliot Richardson, Melvin Laird, Clark Clifford, and James Schlesinger.

(DoD photo)

Let's say your organization wants to hire another analyst. You call Doc Cooke for authorization. But that means you need more office space. Call Doc Cooke. And, of course, a desk and computer. Yep, Doc Cooke.

So complete is Cooke's control over the Pentagon's infrastructure, that he has on occasion forced SecDefs to back down from desired policy and personnel changes. Is he subordinate to the SecDef? On the chart, yes. But he was here before most of them were.

The signature of Cooke's tenure will doubtless be the Pentagon renovation.

> **Basic Training**
>
> Among the vendors that receive preference in federal procurement is UNICOR, which supplies Pentagon chairs and desks, among other things. UNICOR is the marketing name for items built in the federal prison system.

A New Building Inside the Old

Like many Washington buildings of the period, the Pentagon was intended to be temporary and torn down after the war. As such, it was not built to the same standards one might find in a structure intended to last the ages, like the Sphinx, the Great Wall of China, or Dolly Parton.

As the building aged, demands on it grew. In 1942, photocopiers, laser printers, and PCs were the stuff of science fiction. Nobody thought there might be a need to run television cables through the building, much less fiber optic computer networks. And the increased size of Pentagon staffs put many more demands on an increasingly tired building. Major systems, like plumbing and heating, just wore out.

Over the same period, building and fire codes changed, as did environmental standards. Accessibility and energy conservation technology improved. And somebody figured out that all that asbestos in the building might not be the best stuff to work near.

The sheer scale of the building and its imminent exhaustion meant a patchwork solution would not be enough. So in 1990, Congress gave the go-ahead for a complete renovation of the Pentagon. While the effort will cost over one billion dollars, building a new structure with the same systems would cost even more.

So Doc Cooke and his contractors began building a new Pentagon inside the shell of the old one. The building is being closed, one-fifth at a time, gutted down to the concrete (and sometimes beyond), and completely rebuilt to modern standards. Offices in the wedge under renovation are moved to Crystal City and other available space in the region. The finished building will include escalators, easily reconfigurable office space, lighting that won't leave you feeling like you forgot to take off your sunglasses, and less brown paint.

Changes Since 9/11

The bulk of the renovation effort has now been channeled into what's called the "Phoenix Project," reconstructing the damaged section of the Pentagon. Working 24 hours a day, 6 days a week, workers had the avowed goal of reopening the building within a year after the attack. The most publicly visible portion, the E ring wall, was back intact in concrete six months after September 11; the last of the limestone blocks finished the outside wall on June 11, 2002. You can follow their progress or celebrate their triumph at renovation.pentagon.mil.

The project began in 1994, with renovation of the basement. The first wedge was started in 1998 and opened in March of 2001. Work on the second wedge was just beginning in earnest when much of the finished first wedge was damaged on September 11.

The first wedge was intact long enough to show what a real difference the renovation made. Like the moment when *The Wizard of Oz* switches from black and white to color, walking into the renovated area challenged the senses. It was hard to believe that you were in the Pentagon. It was just so … *modern*.

You could even tell the renovated offices from outside the building. Windows in the new wedge were yellowish, thanks to reinforced glass. Looking from inside toward Arlington Cemetery felt like looking through a glass of Metamucil, without the fiber bits. (The rest of the windows were strengthened after September 11, so you can't tell the renovated wedge from outside anymore.)

> **Pentagon Parables**
>
> One benefit of the renovation was quite visible immediately after the September 11 crash: While E ring windows in the unrenovated section were shattered along almost the whole southern face, the strengthened windows immediately next to the hole were unbroken.

The Power of Three

Robert McNamara changed what the building did; Barry Goldwater changed how the Pentagon did it; and Doc Cooke is reshaping the building itself. Without them, the Pentagon would be a relic, stuck in the 1950s.

The Least You Need to Know

- Robert McNamara implemented great changes that provided greater efficiency in Pentagon business practices and increased civilian control.

- The Goldwater-Nichols bill made jointness a military reality.

- David O. Cooke ("Doc") was a legendary civil servant who "ruled" the Pentagon for more than four decades.

- Because the Pentagon was meant to be a temporary structure, it is undergoing a complete renovation that will cost about $1 billion.

Part 2

A Little Help from Our Friends

Whaddya got? You can't fight without weapons, without information, without money. The Pentagon is just part of the national security apparatus. And the military services are just part of the Pentagon. Here are some of the other pieces that make defense work.

Chapter 7

Beyond the Uniforms

In This Chapter

- ◆ Reducing the threat
- ◆ Time to make the maps
- ◆ Buying and selling
- ◆ Accounting for change

It may take a village to raise a family, but it sure as heck takes a lot of agencies to run the defense establishment. We've already talked about some of the things that go on in the Office of the Secretary of Defense inside the Pentagon. But just as most of the military works at bases or on ships far from the Pentagon, much of the work on the civilian side is far from headquarters as well.

Under the Office of the Secretary, you find a number of organizations dedicated to specific tasks that make your military run. If you think of DoD as its own country, these would be some of the cabinet departments. Although most of their work is done outside the Pentagon, they are an inseparable part of the national security establishment. We'll take a look at a few of the more significant agencies in this chapter.

Defense Threat Reduction Agency

The best way to win a war is to avoid it in the first place. President Ronald Reagan used to drive both Mikhail Gorbachev and his domestic opponents crazy with his favorite pet phrase, "Trust … but verify." DTRA, the Defense Threat Reduction Agency, is how America verifies what's going on in the world of arms reduction.

Since the end of the Cold War, one of the major thrusts of military policy has been to deter, reduce, and counter weapons of mass destruction in order to maintain our national security. DTRA is where the Department of Defense gathers its resources, expertise, and capabilities in order to reduce any present or future weapons of mass destruction (or WMD) threat.

DTRA performs four essential functions:

◆ Combat support

◆ Technology development

◆ Threat control

◆ Threat reduction

Basic Training _____

You've already seen that the Pentagon is a world of acronyms. An agency's acronym is treated as if it were the actual name, so while you would say "the Defense Threat Reduction Agency," or "the Defense Logistics Agency," you drop the "the" and just say "DTRA" or "DLA." By the way, if you want to sound like one of the Pentagon peeps, pronounce those "DITT-ra" and "dee-el-ay." Why are some pronounced as words and others as letters? It's a military secret.

These four facets of DTRA efforts, in their words, "enable us to reduce the physical and psychological terror of weapons of mass destruction, thereby enhancing the security of the world's citizens. At the dawn of the twenty-first century, no other task is as challenging or demanding." Obviously, they have never tried to diaper a two-year-old.

We Want Your Bombs

One of DTRA's fascinating and handy tasks is what's called Cooperative Threat Reduction, or CTR. This may not sound fascinating until you know what it is, and since this is a book about the Pentagon, we'd like to share that information with you right now.

When the Soviet Union broke up, there were a lot of missiles, bombs, and nuclear warheads pointed at the major cities of the United States, not to mention your very own hometown. Suddenly, plenty of former Soviet nuclear scientists and labs were looking for work. One of the things that kept policymakers and military analysts in the United States up at night (and still does) is the thought that one or more of those weapons would fall into the wrong hands, or that some of those experts would follow a paycheck to a hostile nation. CTR, and its *Nuclear Cities* Initiative, are ways to help to reduce that threat by taking these weapons and these people off the market.

The CTR program was created by Congress in 1991 to help the countries of the former Soviet Union destroy nuclear, chemical, and biological weapons of mass destruction and associated infrastructure, and establish verifiable safeguards against the proliferation of these weapons. This program has substantially reduced the number of weapons of mass destruction and the threat they pose by helping to better account for weapons previously aimed at the United States.

Unfortunately, the knowledge about how to build these weapons, and a lot of the weapons themselves, is very portable. What happens if weapons of mass destruction, heaven forbid, should find their way to enemies of American interests?

Fighting Words

Nuclear Cities   The USSR. maintained towns closed to the public where top researchers lived, worked, and built bombs together. When the need (and cash) to produce great numbers of nuclear weapons disappeared, so did the economies of these "nuclear cities." One subset of CTR helps nuclear cities move toward more pastoral, yet lucrative pursuits, not entirely unlike paying farmers to not grow crops.

Once again, DoD calls on DTRA, which helps the Department create systems to counter the use or proliferation of weapons of mass destruction. So DTRA studies what the other guys have and tries to figure out what could happen if an enemy were to use conventional, biological, chemical, or other advanced weapons against us, either in war or as acts of terrorism. This is one way our military commanders figure out how best to counter such weapons.

DTRA is also in charge of on-site inspection activities in order to make sure that countries with whom we have arms control treaties are actually living up to their word. The flip side of that is that DTRA is the U.S. government's focal point for implementing U.S. arms control inspection and monitoring activities, showing the other team that *we* are living up to *our* word. When foreign personnel come to the United States to inspect and monitor our facilities here (and overseas as well), DTRA personnel escort them through the inspection process.

Remember those wonderful 1950s science-fiction/horror films where someone would always say, "We have to make sure this technology doesn't fall into enemy hands"? Well, that's all in a day's work for DTRA. Part of their job is to make sure that technologies supporting nuclear, biological, and chemical weapons and their means of delivery—weapons of mass destruction, in short—don't fall into the wrong hands. "Technology security" is the overall name for this aspect of DTRA's special responsibility. DTRA monitors the export of technologies and arms to friends and allies, and makes sure that this knowledge doesn't end up in the hands of people who don't have our best interests at heart. Unfortunately, in today's world, that's a whole lot of people. This kind of export control is why software boxes say things like "May not be exported without a letter from three Congressmen and the Secretary of Defense."

Much of the export control job is shared with the State and Commerce Departments, although some rejiggering of responsibilities was underway as we went to press.

> **Basic Training**
>
> Because arms control is a full-time job, and nuclear facilities and bases tend not to be located in the great cosmopolitan centers of the world, DTRA people get to live in some rather rough, cold, and unappealing places. A month in a trailer in Siberia can make a Washington assignment look pretty good.

> **Pentagon Parables**
>
> The government maintains a list of countries to which the export of arms or weapons technology are prohibited or severely restricted, not unlike the little list Mr. Iannucci used to keep of who was coming to detention hall after school. While countries move on and off the list, some are hardy perennials. As of this writing, the list includes Afghanistan, Angola, Armenia, Azerbaijan, Burma, Belarus, China (PR), Cuba, Cyprus, Haiti, India, Indonesia, Iran, Iraq, Liberia, Libya, North Korea, Pakistan, Rwanda, Somalia, Sudan, Syria, Vietnam, Yemen, Zaire, and Zimbabwe. (Don't be too surprised if post-Taliban Afghanistan moves off the list sometime soon.)

DTRA also directs and manages "chem-bio" defense efforts in the Department of Defense, drawing upon chemical and biological weapons defense expertise throughout the department. Chemical and biological weapons are sometimes referred to as "the poor man's nuclear weapons." They are relatively inexpensive and simple in terms of design and technology in comparison to nuclear weapons, but in some cases can cause widespread damage.

Building nuclear weapons takes massive, highly technical and expensive facilities, but anybody who can make fertilizer can make a chemical weapon. (And as we all know, even babies and politicians can make fertilizer.) So chemical and biological weapons are the mass destruction weapons of choice for rogue states, terrorists, and other bad guys. We've seen the use of a lethal chemical agent in a Tokyo subway, put there not by a government but a cult group, and allegations continue to occur about the possible development in Iraq of chemical and biological weapons—and the willingness of that country to use such weapons in combat.

The idea is to centralize and focus Defense Department efforts in chem-bio defense, so that the United States can be prepared and respond adequately in the event of chemical or biological weapons attacks against U.S. forces, territory, or our allies. If you think that's a lot more complicated than it sounds, you're right.

National Imagery and Mapping Agency

Like maps? We do. And so does the Defense Department. That's why they created NIMA, the National Imagery and Mapping Agency of the Federal government. NIMA's job is to provide "timely, relevant, and accurate geospatial intelligence in support of national security." In other words, they take pictures and make maps of what's going on out there in the world.

NIMA provides that geospatial intelligence "in all its forms and from whatever source." That includes imagery, which means satellite and other high-flying things taking pictures from above; imagery intelligence, which means analyzing those pictures; and geospatial data and information, so that the government and military have the knowledge foundation they need in order to plan, make decisions, and take action.

NIMA was established in 1996 to address the expanding requirements in the areas of imagery, imagery intelligence, and geospatial intelligence. Although it is a DoD combat support agency, NIMA also has the responsibility of providing information to Congress, the President, and appropriate government agencies.

Although some of its products involve intelligence, NIMA is a *white-world* agency, unlike some of its colleagues.

NIMA defines imagery as "a photograph or similar representation of any natural or man-made feature or object or activity on the earth and its precise position at the exact

Fighting Words

White/black Some Pentagon agencies and activities are "in the black world," which means secret. Black agencies have classified or partially classified budgets, and their specific activities aren't listed in the Secretary's annual report. There are, of course, varying degrees of blackness; some "white," or public, agencies have black compartments, while some agencies could be so black that the agency itself doesn't officially exist.

time the representation is acquired." That's just a long way of saying that they take pictures from satellites, airborne platforms, unmanned aerial vehicles, and the like. When you take those pictures, what you can figure out from them is Imagery Intelligence, which sounds like a very New Age herbal treatment, but it's actually a vital part of military defense. NIMA sells a great many of its pictures of the world. For more information, and to see the world from a very different angle, visit 164.214.2.59/geospatial.html.

Homeland Security Shopping Network

After all this heavy talk about weapons of mass destruction, biological warfare, and nuclear weapons sitting around the former Soviet Union ready to be sold to the highest bidder, what a relief it is to visit www.commissaries.com, the home page of the Defense Commissary Agency, where we found, "Click here to enter SHOPPING SPREES!"

Basic Training

Commissaries are a major political issue in Washington. Supermarkets near bases don't like government-subsidized competition. Commissaries say that they aren't subsidized, but live off their revenues. That's debatable. What isn't debatable is that the commissary benefit is a major factor in keeping military families happy. They don't make much money, so discount food is a serious part of the compensation package.

No, this isn't a place where you can purchase a tank or an antimissile weaponry system. The Defense Commissary Agency, headquartered at Fort Lee, Virginia, operates a worldwide chain of 281 commissaries providing groceries to military personnel, retirees, and their families. These individuals can purchase items at cost plus a 5 percent surcharge covering the construction of new commissaries and the modernization of existing stores. The prices are approximately 30 percent below commercial prices.

You'll find these 281 commissaries across the globe. If you happen to be in Iceland, be sure to visit the location in Keflavik. If you are going to Saudi Arabia, make sure you check out the commissary at Riyadh. Truly, the sun never sets on the commissary system, and that's because American military forces and their dependents are spread across the globe.

PX, I Love You

PX, or post exchange, is the military's way of saying on-base store. If the commissary is Safeway, PXs (or base exchanges, BXs) are like Target, with a selection of clothing, books, jewelry, and household goods. The term PX was first used in 1919, although the War Department first ordered the establishment of exchanges at every post back in 1895. Today, the PXs are run by AAFES ("AY-fees"), the Army and Air Force Exchange Service. (The Navy has its own exchange service, the Naval Exchange Command, or NEXCOM.)

Commissaries and exchanges are, in budgeteer-speak, "nonappropriated fund instrumentalities," which would *not* be a good name for a rock band. It means they don't get money every year from Congress, but have to live on what they take in. Of course, because they are on bases, their utilities and some employee benefits are covered by tax dollars, which reduces costs somewhat.

PXs travel with the troops. According to AAFES, the first supply ships that landed in Northern Ireland in early 1942 brought Army Exchange Services to the European troops. In 1950, when the Korean conflict began, the Japan Central Exchange began supplying PX items to troops deployed in Korea. In 1958, during the Middle East Crisis, when the U.S. Marines went into Lebanon, mobile PXs were en route within 48 hours. In Vietnam, in Panama in 1989, in Desert Shield, in Desert Storm in 1990, and in all military engagements in which the United States has taken part since, AAFES or its predecessors have been there, selling the candy, distributing the movies, and giving soldiers a taste of life back home.

Basic Training

AAFES' PXs and shopettes can't bring quite all the comforts of home. A perennial political issue in Washington is whether they should be allowed to sell the kind of magazines that Uncle Bud used to keep in his sock drawer. The arguments go between whether it's inappropriate for the government to sell such stuff, especially when trying to integrate women into the military, and the fact that a number of the customers seem to want it. Right now, the answer is no.

At their website, www.aafes.com, soldiers, sailors, airmen, and Marines can find frozen foods, health and beauty items, groceries, meat, and whatever else they need—and they can order it online. Is this a great country or what?

Tanks for Shopping with Us

But let's say you don't want to buy from the military, you want to sell to them. Look up the number for the Defense *Logistics* Agency, DLA. They buy major items for the military. This includes weapons systems, spare parts, fuel, food, clothing, textiles, medicines; literally everything you need to equip the modern military force.

DLA also handles putting together U.S. humanitarian and disaster relief efforts. It provides worldwide logistic support for the missions of the military departments during both peace and war. In other words, if you have a tank, a bazooka, or a Meal Ready to Eat, DLA is the agency to whom you should hawk your wares.

Fighting Words

Logistics   The science of supply. Every service has logisticians whose whole job is to figure out how to get the forces what they need, where they need it, when they need it there. An old military bromide says that "Amateurs study tactics; professionals study logistics."

Materiel   Stuff.

How many people does it take to procure goods and services for the American military? If you said more than 28,000 civilian and military employees working in all 50 states (and, presumably, all 435 congressional districts) and 27 foreign countries, you'd be right. They buy supplies, weapons, and other *materiel*. When you do the shopping for 1.2 million troops, that's a lot of Hungry-Man dinners. From T-shirts to jet fuel, DLA writes the check. As they like to say, "If America's forces can eat it, wear it, drive it, shoot it, or burn it, chances are DLA helps provide it." DLA also helps dispose of materiel and equipment that's no longer needed.

DLA disposes of some less-exotic items through public auctions in major cities. (Sometimes, exotic items do sneak in, but most of the classified stuff goes on eBay.) So if you need 3,600 mattress pads, or 2,880 poncho covers, you might be a DLA shopper, too.

DLA bills itself as the "war fighter's logistics combat support agency." In other words, DLA buys stuff. Its origins date back to World War II, when America's huge military buildup required the rapid purchase of vast amounts of munitions and supplies. DLA buys food, fuel, clothing, medicine, and spare parts for the military. If you have something you want to sell to the military, a new-fangled nuclear weapon, perhaps, why not visit their website, www.dla.mil.

Founded in 1961, DLA has supported every major war and contingency operation since, from Vietnam to Bosnia and Kosovo. Remember the Gulf War? DLA does. They spent more than $3 billion purchasing food, clothing, medical supplies, and weapons system repair parts for military services of the United States and several of our allies. DLA also provided more than $69 million worth of food, clothing, and medical supplies to the humanitarian relief efforts.

DLA's mission is all about streamlining the supply system to reduce costs and improve delivery times to its "customers" in the field. Its customers, of course, are your fighting boys and girls in blue, green, or whatever color happens to be the top-secret color of the day.

As an OSD operation, DLA is essentially joint, able to buy jet fuel for all services at once. And they pass the savings on to you.

Nice Green Eyeshades, Soldier

As you can imagine, the military has a lot to keep track of. In 1991, the Defense Department activated the Defense Finance and Accounting Service (DFAS) to reduce costs and improve the overall quality of Department of Defense financial management. They don't use guns or tanks to accomplish their mission. Instead, this arm of the Defense Department uses consolidation, standardization, and integration of finance and accounting operations, procedures, and systems. In short, they are accountants with attitude.

DFAS is a giant combined payroll and accounts payable department. Military payroll checks come from DFAS. Retiree benefit checks come from DFAS. Payments to vendors come from DFAS. For example, in 1998, in any given month, DFAS processed almost 10 million payments to Defense Department personnel, 1.2 million commercial invoices, 450,000 travel vouchers or settlements, 500,000 savings bond issuances, and 122,000 transportation bills of lading. Each month, DFAS disburses approximately $24 billion. That's billion. With a "b." A month.

DFAS moves all that money through a network of regional centers. You may ask why, if all they're doing is keeping books and writing checks, they need to be all over the country. (Congress wonders that from time to time, too.) But as electronic payments and automated systems make bookkeeping easier, DFAS is shrinking its workforce and consolidating operations.

At the same time, competitive pressure drives DFAS even harder to streamline. Yes, competition. Unlike some agencies that are monopolies, military customers don't have to use DFAS. The world is full of accounting firms that can do—or think they can do—what DFAS does, and DoD lets customers choose among them. So DFAS is a very dynamic agency, continually reinventing itself to compete.

The Tip of the Five-Sided Iceberg

These are but a few of the agencies and field activities that serve all of America's military. There's the Defense Manpower Data Center—combat actuaries—which keeps the statistics on the forces; The Uniformed Services University of the Health Sciences, USUHS ("YOU-shis"), or "Useless U," depending on whether you think the military needs its own medical school; The Defense Contract Audit Agency, which keeps tabs on whether your tax dollar is being properly spent; and many, many more. Together, these agencies are the Pentagon's world.

The Least You Need to Know

- ◆ DTRA tries to eliminate threats to ease the burden on the military.
- ◆ Without NIMA, pilots would have to ask directions at gas stations, and they hate that.
- ◆ Commissaries and PXs are supposed to live off their revenue.
- ◆ DLA is the largest agency in the Department of Defense.

Chapter 8

Playing with Others: The National Security Game

In This Chapter

◆ How the Pentagon fits into the national security structure

◆ NSC—the administration's referee

◆ Making budgets and making sausage aren't spectator sports

◆ Can you hold, Congressman? The Senator's on line 2

For all its power, the Department of Defense is one part of a much larger enterprise—the U.S. government. That means it has to work alongside agencies with very different orientations and missions.

That's not always easy. One side effect of the Goldwater-Nichols reorganization (from Chapter 6) was to increase the natural tension between DoD and the State Department. State is in charge of America's relations with other countries, which is why it maintains embassies and ambassadors throughout the world. But the CINC structure established by Goldwater-Nichols creates powerful military positions with omniscient views and plenipotentiary powers over whole regions. Officially, the CINCs act to support the ambassadors in every country. But an ambassador has power in one nation. A CINC is responsible for dozens, not to mention that he has bombers, troops, and ships at his disposal, while the ambassador has people at word processors. Who's more powerful?

NSC and the Interagency Process

Part of the answer is determined by the National Security Council. Created by the same 1947 law that established DoD, the NSC is where defense and foreign policy issues are hashed out before going to the President. The national security advisor to the President directs the NSC staff and advises the President, and based on the last few we've had, there is absolutely no way of describing a typical national security advisor other than "smart" and "able to function without family or sleep."

Now, because you read Chapter 6, you're probably standing on the ottoman hollering, "Wait a minute! Goldwater-Nichols established the chairman of the Joint Chiefs as the principal military advisor to the President!" You'd be right about that, and by the way, your dachshund is looking at you with a very worried expression.

The difference is that the national security advisor is more than a military advisor. National security includes not just military but diplomatic, economic, intelligence, and many other issues. NSC is above all a coordinating body, putting the pieces together and making sure all the departments are reading from the same TelePrompTer.

The NSC has its own small staff, organized by topics and areas of the world. They tend not to be very high profile people in public, but inside the defense community, they are significant personages. The NSC staffer for arms control, for example, is likely to have at least as much impact on the President's positions as the top arms control person at State. (Remember the idea that the person who manages the paper flow rules.) The NSC staffer is the one with the most direct access to the decision maker, and since he or she is in position to synthesize the views of different departments, the national security advisor and President will probably get their information from the staffer. That's why those who really want to get things done in the national security structure get to know and work very closely with their NSC counterpart.

Pentagon Parables

The NSC is supposed to be a coordinating body, reconciling the views of cabinet departments and distilling policy. During the 1980s, some NSC staffers took on more of an operational role, creating a deal that involved selling arms to Iran and using the proceeds to fund irregular operations against the government of Nicaragua. Those NSC operations led to a series of Congressional hearings, and the forcible return of the NSC staff to its previous policy role.

By law, the National Security Council itself is made up of the President, Vice President, and the Secretaries of State and Defense. Others, like the national security advisor, the Director of Central Intelligence, the Attorney General, and selected department secretaries, sit in as required.

When the President wants to make a major national security policy decision, NSC circulates a "Presidential Review Directive," basically a draft, for comment and concurrence. Once everybody's chopped on it, the draft becomes policy; if it's a big enough deal, it's issued as a Presidential Decision Directive (PDD). PDDs are infrequent enough that when the President signs one, it'll be in the front section of your newspaper.

Coordinate Yourself

Not every action needs to go through NSC. The Pentagon and State Department coordinate directly on a number of issues, most prominently export and trade controls. The relationship between State and Defense is not always an easy one, but no worse than you'd expect between any bunch of stripey-pants wimps and a passel of no-neck thugs. (And the stereotyping on both ends gets just about that bad.)

Given that they operate throughout the world, are a mammoth employer and landlord, and have interests in every part of life, it's not surprising that DoD coordinates with every department and agency imaginable, and a few that you're not allowed to imagine, thank you very much. You probably won't be surprised to learn that the CIA, for example, maintains a full-time liaison shop at the Pentagon.

Coordination works in different ways depending on the project at hand. Sometimes, an interagency team, with representatives from all the interested departments, will work on something together. Other times, phone calls and paper will pass back and forth between the departments. Which is to say, they work pretty much like your average gypsum corporation.

But the national security landscape got more complicated after September 11, 2001. In the aftermath, President George W. Bush created an Office of Homeland Security, a separate office from NSC dedicated to bringing together the various domestic security and response agencies. This obviously created a puzzlement for DoD, which had some parts that obviously fell under the homeland security rubric, while others didn't. Also, the nature of the Office of Homeland Security was unclear, as it had control of no funds (the ultimate measure of influence in Washington) and no staff. The great concern of DoD and other agencies was whether the new office could make unfunded mandates, ordering agencies to take actions that they would have to pay for out of their own budgets.

On June 7, 2002, some of that confusion was alleviated. President Bush announced that the Office of Homeland Security would be promoted to a cabinet-level Department of Homeland Security. With that announcement, the President reconfigured the homeland security office's responsibilities from coordination to line responsibility for a number of domestic functions cobbled together from other agencies.

At first blush, creation of such a department could be seen as a direct challenge to the Pentagon. After all, defending the United States is the Defense Department's most fundamental job. Yet here it is being hived off to another department that will become a rival in the annual budget creation process.

But there's a clear message in how the Homeland Security Department is to be constructed. Interestingly, while parts of the Treasury, Commerce, Transportation, and Energy Departments were broken off and reassigned to Homeland Security, the Department of Defense remained intact. In the bureaucratic world, that's a way of saying you didn't screw up.

Later, the Department found out that it had just dodged the bullet. The architects of the Department of Homeland Security had discussed putting the National Guard under the new department, but dropped the idea.

The Crystal Ball

The discussion of budgeting leads naturally to the question: How can we have a defense budget when we don't know what's going to happen next year?

The answer, of course, is carefully and systematically.

Since everything in the Pentagon has to have a name, budgeting is done using the Programming, Planning, and Budgeting System, or PPBS. (Some people add an E, for "execution," before the S. We're old school.) This isn't a computer system, but a procedure detailing how the hundreds of military and civilian offices that have to coordinate on a budget play in the process. PPBS is another legacy of the McNamara era, when systems ruled.

Fighting Words

Fiscal year It's an accounting term for the year-long period over which you budget. The Federal government's fiscal year runs from October to the following September; fiscal year 2003 (or FY03, as it's abbreviated) starts on October 1, 2002.

At any given moment, the Pentagon is working on three budgets. In December of 2002, for example, while the calendar will say 2002, the military will be running off of the fiscal 2003 budget. The fiscal 2004 budget will be essentially complete and ready for its rollout in February. And the planning process for fiscal 2005 will already be underway.

At the same time, budgeters are looking far into the future. Each fiscal year's budget includes a Future Years Defense Plan, or a projection of what the Department expects to spend over the next five years. So while executing FY03, introducing FY04, and planning FY05, they have already estimated FY06, FY07, FY08, and FY09, all of which will accompany the detailed budget for FY04.

Pentagon Parables

There may be no greater mystery in the Pentagon than that of the FYDP, the Future Years Defense Plan. Or is that the Five Year Defense Plan? That's the mystery. It started out as Five Year, and indeed the FYDP projects out five years. Then the official title got changed to Future Years. Yet official Pentagon documents still use both phrases, and apparently interchangeably. We're calling Columbo.

How Do They Do It?

The short version is that the civilians set the strategy, the services say how much it'll cost to carry that out, and OSD decides how much of that estimate they're really willing to pay. But the whole process starts, like everything, in the Pentagon, with *guidance*.

The guidance in this case is a large document, the Secretary's Defense Planning Guidance (DPG). Derived from the National Security Strategy (NSS) and the defense strategy, the DPG is a big deal in the building. While the strategy statements are broader documents for public release, the DPG is like a football team's playbook, showing what we're going to do and how we're going to do it. It is the basic document used for preparing the next year's budget. And the nastiest internal fights are over what gets into the DPG, because this is where it says we will have eleventeen aircraft carriers and forty-twelve fighter squadrons. (Please note that these numbers are unclassified.) The decisions are in the DPG.

Fighting Words

Guidance   An order, phrased nicely. "Are you going to clean that latrine, or am I going to have to give you some guidance?"

Basic Training

From time to time, you may hear of programs that have gone over budget. (It can make a bit of news.) That's when the actual outyear cost exceeds the cost projected when the budget was put together. Sometimes, the factors that cause cost growth can't reasonably be foreseen, like contractor strikes or materials shortages. Sometimes, the factors can be, "Oh, you wanted it to *float?*"

The DPG results from a marriage between the civilian-produced National Security Strategy and the Joint Chiefs' ongoing strategic reviews that also informed the Joint Strategic Capabilities Plan (see Chapter 10). This is where strategy and money intersect. The DPG lays down the requirements for each service—what capabilities they will be required to have.

From that come the POMs, the Program Objective Memoranda. This is each service's take on how it will follow the DPG, and how much it will cost. A POM is "built" over the course of several months of discussions about what programs the service can support and which programs it believes can make way for higher priorities.

Every program—every procurement, every construction plan, every line item in the budget—has a program manager to oversee it. And that program manager has to figure the cost of the *outyear tail* as part of putting the program together.

Fighting Words

Outyear Budgeteers' term for any year in the future. This year is the *current year*. The money that a new program will cost in the outyears is its **tail**. Yes, that's the second time we've defined tail, but the two are similar; one refers to the people required to support the current fighting force, the other refers to the money required to support the current program.

Leaky Budgets

At the same time, "POM builds"—service draft budgets—are being leaked to the defense press and Congress. Those leaks are a Machiavellian tool.

Leaks are used in some cases to reassure contractors and Congressional supporters that, indeed, the service put a particular program in its budget. At the same time, the leak shows that if the item isn't in the final budget, it was OSD's fault and not the service's.

At other times, someone may leak a POM build to show that a particular item is missing, in order to *spin up* Congressional and contractor pressure on OSD to put it in. And services are believed to deliberately leave things out of the POM that they really want, spend the money on something else, then leak the build in order to get political pressure on OSD to add money for the missing project, too.

Fighting Words

Spin up To generate or excite. The phrase comes from aviation, where you have to wait for the gyroscopes in a navigation unit to get to operating speed, literally to spin up, before using the navigational device. "Somebody got the Secretary all spun up about TRICARE."

Anyway, to put together those future budgets, OSD takes the stack of POMs, totals them up, then adds its own secret blend of herbs and spices. When OSD has a significant disagreement with the service POM, or vice-versa, those issues get written up into issue books, including commentary from the services and listing possible alternatives to the POM proposal.

Those issues are presented to the Defense Resources Board, made up of Assistant Secretaries of Defense, service secretaries, and the JCS Chairman and Vice Chairman. This is the real steel-cage match of the budgeting process, and can take several weeks (although they let the Chairman out from time to time to fetch Twinkies).

The Big Picture

Once the DRB has evaluated the POMs, the JCS gets its turn at bat. This is the "oh, yeah?" report. Using the OSD numbers and DRB outcomes, the Joint Chiefs evaluate the force that results. After all, when deciding on individual programs and line items, it's easy to lose the big picture. JCS puts it all together and submits to OSD a report on just what the force they propose to buy can do—and what it can't.

That's when only one desk matters. SecDef, albeit with a lot of help, makes the final decisions in what are called Program Decision Memoranda. That's the point of no appeal—until, of course, the whole mess gets presented to Congress, and the fun really begins.

Once that's done—and really, throughout the process—OSD works with the President's Office of Management and Budget (OMB) to make sure that OMB agrees on the major figures. OMB also sets the DoD *topline*, as, after all, the President submits the budget for the entire government, not SecDef. Issues between OSD and OMB are resolved by the President.

Fighting Words

Topline   Another budgeteer word. The total amount of a budget, with everything added up.

535 Secretaries of Defense–Dealing with Congress

People sometimes say that Washington is out of touch, that lawmakers don't care. Nothing could be further from the truth. Congress cares about absolutely *everything*. And that is never more clear than when trying to get a defense budget through.

After the budget goes up to the Hill, usually in February, the SecDef, Chairman, and service secretaries and chiefs testify before the four major defense committees in what are called "posture hearings," explaining the "posture" of the Department's budget. Congress is never shy about offering its advice, and they are particularly forward when the cameras are on.

At least six Congressional committees have to approve the defense budget: The House and Senate each have a Budget Committee that decides the defense topline, an Armed Services Committee that authorizes spending item by item, and an Appropriations Committee that, yes, appropriates the money.

If you find the difference between authorization and appropriation confusing, congratulations; you are qualified to be a member of Congress. Try thinking of it this way: Dad sends you a check and says it's for tuition and books. He just *authorized* the use of the money for those purposes. You give the money to your roommate, who's going by the administration building, and ask him to pay for your books and tuition. He uses it to buy pizza and beer. He's just *appropriated* the money. You didn't decide what it would be used for; he did. But who gets in trouble with Dad?

Substitute the House and Senate Armed Services Committees for Dad, DoD for yourself, and the Congressional appropriations committees for your friend, and you can begin to see why some of those budget hearings can get a bit testy.

During and after the posture hearing season, the services and OSD hold multiday briefing sessions for committee staffers, explaining the details and nuances of the proposed budget in the hope that the more they explain, the more likely it is that the proposed budget will survive intact.

> **Pentagon Parables**
>
> In 2001, SecDef Donald Rumsfeld, perhaps looking to emphasize OSD's primacy in budgeting, told the services not to follow their annual practice of submitting unfunded requirements lists. Hearing of that, some Congressmen wrote to the service chiefs requesting the lists anyway. Caught between the SecDef and Congress, the chiefs ... sent Congress the lists.

Congress Taketh ...

Congress takes away money from programs for several reasons. One is to punish programs that aren't performing as well as expected. (Some might say that when a program is behind schedule, taking away money sure isn't going to help it catch up.) Sometimes, it's just because they found a better use for the money. And sometimes, it's because program A was cut last year, which means that program B won't be needed until a year later than originally scheduled. So the money is cut from this year's budget, but should be there next year. (Ha ha ha. Try getting a cut program reinstated. Just try.)

... and Congress Giveth

On the other hand, Congress adds money to the budget, too, and for a variety of reasons. Yes, sometimes it's to buy items built in a member's district. But every year, Congress asks the services for a list of items they need, that didn't make the cut as the POM was built, or especially as the budget worked through OSD. Those "unfunded requirements lists" often form the basis of congressional additions. And if an item on the unfunded list happens to be built in the district of the Defense Appropriations chairman, everybody winds up happy.

Fighting Words

Plus-up A redundant name for the amount added by Congress to a budget. "They gave the F-22 a 2 million plus-up."

The Lecture That Comes with the Allowance

But money isn't the only thing Congress adds. They also can revise, impose, or eliminate laws governing the conduct of the military. Some of the most controversial items in the defense bill each year have to do with these nonfunding items, whether it's policy regarding whether women can serve in combat roles, rules defining what work can be done in government depots, or authorizing another round of base closure, the words in the bill are no less interesting to Congress than the numbers of dollars going to the home district.

Congress loves to add language to the defense bill. And they have a positive fetish for requiring the Department to write reports. If a Congressman (or, indeed, a staffer) believes that DoD is overlooking a previous provision, they may require the Department to write a report showing how well they have complied. Mandated reports can also be used to get a view on the record that some part of the Department would rather not become public, or bring to light something the Department really would rather people not know about.

And sometimes, Congress can add quite a bit of work. Every four years, the Department goes through a top-to-bottom study of the military's missions, how they'll go about meeting them, and whether the planned forces are up to the task. It's called the Quadrennial Defense Review (QDR). While such studies had been done a number of times before,

Pentagon Parables

Sometimes, Congressionally-required reports are a relief for the Pentagon. If the House bill includes a provision the Pentagon doesn't like, and it's not in the Senate bill, in the House-Senate conference, the Senate may offer to require a report on the issue as a compromise instead of including the House language the Pentagon didn't want. That makes the report easier to write.

they happened only at the whim of a SecDef. Congress decided it would be a good idea for each new administration to undertake such a review. The QDR is a major exercise for the department, coming as it does on top of the budgeting and planning processes. Yet, it's a useful exercise.

After the posture hearings, each committee "marks up" its bill, making the changes the members want. While the markup process is weeks in preparation, it culminates in a single, all-day session wherein the committee chairman proposes his version of the bill, and members offer amendments.

Basic Training

Along with their annual bill in each house, each authorization and appropriations committee in Congress issues a report. The report explains the bill's provisions, but often adds some additional restrictions or directives. The bill becomes law, while the report doesn't—but woe betide the program manager who disregards Congressional report language.

The Department is intimately involved with the markup process, answering questions and working to keep changes to a minimum.

After the bills are marked up and pass out of committee, they go to the full House or Senate for a vote. At that point, the Department's attention shifts … to the White House.

Before the bills go to the floor, the White House issues a Statement of Administration Policy, called a "SAP," defending their budget and pointing out disagreements with committee changes or proposed amendments. On occasion, the SAP will include the threat that the President will veto the bill if a certain change isn't rectified, or if a particular amendment gets attached.

And for Our Next Trick …

For all its complications, passing the defense bills is only a part of the Department's work on Capitol Hill each year. Almost every day of the year, SecDef, a service chief, or a CINC is visiting senior members of the defense committees to propose a new idea or explain a complication. And with DoD involved to some extent in the economy of every state and congressional district, program managers, base commanders, and OSD officials are always on the Hill talking to somebody.

Congressmen aren't shy about making work for the Department, either. Whether asking for comments on constituent letters, sending over casework on military pensions, or the Congressman himself calling the DepSecDef on a matter of particular interest, every Congressional office will communicate with the Pentagon daily.

But it's the activists who make most of the work. While every member of Congress has some interest in defense, a comparative few (maybe 20 in the House and 8 or 10 in the Senate) account for a large portion of the contacts with high-level officials in the Department. That's not necessarily a bad thing; some members of Congress have been involved with defense issues for many years and have been friends with people in high Pentagon places since they were in very low places—the local base commander, or even a Congressional staffer.

> **Pentagon Parables**
>
> A clear trend over the last decade has been the decrease in congresspeople with military experience. (That's one side effect of a volunteer military.) The result is that the handful of defense specialists in each house receive even more deference from colleagues. That's another good reason for the Pentagon to cultivate close relations with them.

The Least You Need to Know

 ◆ The National Security Council coordinates policy among Cabinet departments.

 ◆ Interdepartmental coordination is no fun, but necessary.

 ◆ Building the defense budget is a lengthy and painstaking process.

 ◆ Congress is somewhere between a close partner and a nosy aunt on most defense issues.

Chapter 9

Military Intelligence—Not Always an Oxymoron

In This Chapter

- Intelligence—a community without a community center
- Types of intelligence for intelligent types
- Look into the Big Ear
- Buenos DIA

Know your enemy—it's an idea as old as Cain and Abel. When the military fights someone, or even more when trying to deter someone from fighting, they need to know the enemy's strengths, weaknesses, and what they're most afraid of.

Each of the military services has its own intelligence arm, specializing in matters of specific interest. Usually, though, those service intelligence agencies are interpreting information provided by one of three agencies that work with or for the Pentagon. The CIA, the National Security Agency, and the Defense Intelligence Agency all carry on intelligence tasks, sometimes in a cooperative manner, sometimes not.

Ssh!

We'll begin the intelligence *tour d'horizon* with the Central Intelligence Agency, the CIA. The CIA was created in 1947 in the same National Security Act that created the Department of Defense. CIA is independent of DoD, although the defense community is a prime customer for CIA's work.

That legislation made CIA the top dog in the intelligence community, giving the Director of Central Intelligence (the DCI) the responsibility to coordinate the nation's intelligence activities in correlating, evaluating, and disseminating intelligence that affects national security.

In layman's terms, the CIA is responsible for knowing everything that happens outside the U.S. borders, while the Federal Bureau of Investigation (FBI) is responsible for knowing everything that happens within our 50 states. These obviously are no small responsibilities.

Fighting Words

Oversight When you and we leave something out, it's called oversight. When Congress keeps an eye on the CIA or other organizations, that's oversight of another kind. There's often a narrow line between overseeing and overlooking.

The Director of Central Intelligence is appointed by the President, and accountable to the American people through the intelligence *oversight* committees of the U.S. Congress.

The CIA essentially provides information to three audiences: the President, the Congress, and the military. Policymakers in Washington, whether in the White House, Pentagon, or Congress, need to know what's happening in the world before anyone else does. Information is critical; old information is like the leftover pizza that you kept in its box on the counter for three days: useless.

In time of war or threat of war, it's essential that the military have up-to-the-second information about troop movements, leadership intentions, and all the other ingredients that go into conducting or preventing war. The CIA today is responsible for such high-priority issues as nonproliferation of nuclear weapons, counterterrorism, counterintelligence (making sure that people aren't spying on us), international organized crime, narcotics trafficking, and arms control intelligence. After all, just because two nations sign an arms control treaty doesn't mean they're both living up to its principles. Somebody has to be the watchdog, and that role falls in large part to the CIA.

Coordination among agencies is very important. If the CIA knows from foreign sources about something that's going to happen inside the United States, they need to get that information to the FBI for action.

Similarly, the FBI needs to pass on areas of interest that the CIA may be able to help illuminate. One of the problems that September 11 highlighted was the difficulty intelligence agencies across the government have in coordinating the analysis and dissemination of critical information. One of the CIA's responsibilities is to forge stronger partnerships among the various intelligence collection agencies so as to make sure that sort of situation doesn't happen again.

Basic Training

Wait. Didn't we say in Chapter 7 that arms control is the Defense Threat Reduction Agency's job? Well, yes. The CIA is responsible for gathering intelligence from some sources, DTRA from others, and when they put it all together, it's DTRA's job to take action.

Who Runs the CIA?

CIA headquarters is a few miles from the Pentagon, on a hilltop in Langley, Virginia. The DCI serves as the head of the U.S. *intelligence community*, described in that little box coming along just about now …

Fighting Words

Intelligence community   The 14 organizations that gather or analyze intelligence information. Knowing the list from memory will impress your friends almost as much as knowing the Fellowship of the Ring: Central Intelligence Agency; Defense Intelligence Agency; National Security Agency; the intelligence operations of each of the branches of the military—the Army, Navy, Air Force, and Marines; the National Imagery and Mapping Agency; the National Reconnaissance Office, and then five other intelligence-gathering organizations under the direction of the President of the United States—the Federal Bureau of Investigation, and the Departments of Treasury, Energy, Justice, and State. We will look at some of these organizations later in this chapter.

The DCI ("dee-see-eye") by the way, is also the principal advisor to the President for intelligence matters related to national security.

Under the DCI, the Deputy Director of Central Intelligence assists the Director in running the CIA and the intelligence community. If the Director is absent or disabled,

Changes Since 9/11

Created in response to the September 11, 2001 attacks, a new position, the Associate Director of Central Intelligence for Homeland Security, is responsible for the flow of intelligence in support of homeland defense.

or if the Director's position is vacant, the DDCI runs the show. (If there are gum wrappers anywhere on the CIA premises, he is also responsible for picking them up.)

The Executive Director manages the Central Intelligence Agency on a day-to-day basis. He is assisted by an executive board comprising a Chief Financial Officer, Chief Information Officer, Security, Human Resources, and Global Support.

Spies and Analysts

The CIA has three main parts: the Directorate of Intelligence (DI), the Directorate of Operations (DO), and the Directorate of Science and Technology (DS&T).

The Directorate of Intelligence is the analytical branch of the CIA. It produces and disseminates all the intelligence the CIA develops on key foreign issues. The primary purpose of the Directorate of Intelligence is to minimize the uncertainties that U.S. officials face in making decisions about national security and foreign policies. Sometimes policymakers need analysis so they can comprehend complex issues. At other times, analysts within the Directorate of Intelligence will alert policymakers to an issue that they need to understand.

How do you "produce intelligence"? By taking facts and discovering the connections between them. Most of the time, analysts are looking at conflicting or incomplete information. Directorate of Intelligence analysts ask: What are the facts? What are the sources? How do we know these facts? Given fact A and fact B and fact C, what conclusions can we draw about enemy capabilities or intent? What is the impact if assumptions change? And finally, the all-important question: What remains unknown?

Pentagon Parables
Movies purporting to take place in the CIA usually show workers walking across the Agency's seal in the entryway. That's accurate. What you don't usually see, though, is the white wall etched with black stars, just to the left as you enter. Each of those stars stands for a CIA operative who died in the service of his or her country. Below that, a glass-encased book—the "Book of Honor"—lists the names of those whose names can be told. Some remain classified even in death; as of this writing, there are 79 stars and 44 names.

Directorate of Intelligence analysts get their information from a wide variety of sources. They are all called "all-source" analysts. They review everything from foreign newspapers to U.S. diplomatic reports to sensitive technical collection. Their mission is to figure out what's going on so the policymaker or military official they are seeking to educate doesn't have to sift through all the information that's out there. Intriguingly, the reports are not just written documents. Directorate of Intelligence analysts will use cartographers, graphic artists, statisticians, and computer technical specialists to provide the information necessary to the policymaker.

The Directorate of Operations gathers some of the information that DI analysts put together. They are in charge of "clandestine collection," which used to mean spying but nowadays involves getting information from a number of sources. DO is in charge of the field agents around the world who recruit and work with (or "run") sources.

Other information comes from the Directorate of Science and Technology. DS&T people collect information in newfangled ways that don't involve the Second Deputy Commissar passing you an envelope in a newspaper. They also gather it through "open sources," like *reading* that newspaper. If you put together enough open-source facts, you can sometimes discover an interesting truth behind them. (Put together half that many, and you can write a book like this!)

Intelligence comes in kinds, based on where the information comes from or how it's gathered. The classic form is HUMINT, or human intelligence—things people tell you. That's DO's specialty. The more interesting the person telling you something, the more interesting the HUMINT.

We'll talk about SIGINT, or signals intelligence, more when we get to the National Security Agency in just a few pages. Broadly, though, SIGINT consists of COMINT, or communications intelligence, what you can learn by listening in on somebody else's conversation; and ELINT, electronic intelligence, which tells you where a signal is coming from and what its characteristics are (if it's a radio, a radar, etc.). ELINT is the medium; COMINT is the message. ELINT can tell you a lot. Suppose you were to fly an airplane near a hostile country. With ELINT, you could see what radars were used to track it and what radios got busy—in short, it could tell you a lot about how the other guy responds. (If you hear him say, "Ah, it's just the Americans yanking our chain again. Turn on the usual radars," that's COMINT.)

IMINT is imagery intelligence, which means figuring out things by looking at pictures. That can be a lot more than just where targets are. Show a DS&T type a picture of a rocket, and they can tell you its size, its probable range, its—well, everything but the launch code, unless that's painted on the side of the rocket.

MASINT is also a DS&T thing. It's "measurement and signatures intelligence," or telling what a thing is by the way it reflects light, the gases it emits, or other technical characteristics.

The Other Puzzle Palace

If the CIA is the "Big Eye" overlooking the world, the National Security Agency is the "Big Ear." NSA defines itself as the "Nation's cryptologic organization," which means essentially that it studies coded information. NSA is responsible for gathering, analyzing, and producing for policymakers and the military all information that is derived through technical means or code breaking.

Changes Since 9/11

Two of NSA's biggest challenges were highlighted in the wake of September 11, when it was reported that the agency had intercepted communications that indicated some attack might be coming, but weren't translated until September 13. That speaks to the difficulty of getting through the sheer volume of communications NSA receives, and to the government-wide lack of linguists trained in certain languages.

Pentagon Parables

Although intelligence is as old as mankind, the development of COMINT is a relatively recent phenomenon—and not just for technical reasons. As recently as 1929, Secretary of War Henry Stimson disdained intercepting foreign communications, sniffing, "Gentlemen do not read each others' mail."

If you were to sum up the role of the National Security Agency, you could describe it the way they do: Information superiority for America and its allies, which NSA kindly explains is "the capability to collect, process, and disseminate an uninterrupted flow of information while exploiting or denying an adversary's ability to do the same."

The NSA provides intelligence information to the White House, the CIA and State Department, the chairman of Joint Chiefs of Staff and military Commanders in Chief, and other military commands including multinational forces and our allies. Occasionally, the NSA provides information to government contractors when it is appropriate.

The military expression for NSA's specialty is signals intelligence, or SIGINT. SIGINT has a fascinating past, and the modern era of SIGINT dates to World War II, when the United States broke the Japanese military code and learned of plans to invade Midway Island. This intelligence allowed the United States to defeat Japan's superior fleet. Military historians believe that SIGINT used in this manner shortened the war in the Pacific by at least a year.

NSA vacuums in signals—radios, cell phones, Gameboys, whatever—from around the world and runs them through (let's be really careful here) what is reputed to be the world's largest concentration of supercomputers. They're looking for words, phrases, particular phone numbers—well, you can imagine what they're looking for. And when it's encrypted, it's NSA's job to break the code.

Another responsibility of the National Security Agency is to protect all classified and sensitive information that is stored or sent to and through U.S. government equipment. In other words, if the President of the United States is speaking on the phone to a general somewhere in the Middle East, it's up to the NSA to make sure that bad guys cannot listen in. (The President gets a really good STU on his desk. And his own key.)

NSA guards communication two ways: By creating codes and encryption schemes, and by establishing and monitoring *TEMPEST* standards.

Basic Training

It's a little odd to be writing about the NSA. Until not too long ago, the existence and purpose of the agency were officially classified (like the National Reconnaissance Office, which has something to do with satellites, we think). In fact, the saying for a long time was that NSA stood for "No Such Agency."

That sentence needs a lot of explaining. *Codes* are ways of jumbling up what you say so that the subject isn't readily apparent. *Encryption schemes* can go beyond that, into affecting the medium, whether it's using radios that hop together from frequency to frequency to frustrate eavesdroppers, or hashing all the voice talk into ones and zeroes in some way that's evident only to the two phones. And *TEMPEST* is a set of rules that control how much radiation a piece of equipment puts out. It wouldn't be much good to have a computer that translated your note into an unbreakable code if someone outside could detect the keystrokes as you were typing in the message. One of the aspects of the Secure Compartmented Information Facilities that we talked about in Chapter 5 is their control of electromagnetic radiation.

The world is becoming more complex, more technology-oriented, and more dangerous. And encryption technology is getting easier and easier to buy or download. For all these reasons, the National Security Agency will only get busier in protecting the secret communications and secret information of the U.S. government, and breaking the secrets of others. If you're a math or computer type, they could use a hand.

Beyond Tang

Sometimes the work of the National Security Agency results in technological breakthroughs that become available in different forms to the average citizen. Some of the agency's research and development projects have significantly advanced state-of-the-art breakthroughs in the scientific and business worlds. The NSA obviously needs fantastic computers to perform high-level cryptanalytic (code-breaking) research. That need led to the first large-scale computer and the first solid-state computer, which are predecessors to the modern computers into which we now stare, every minute of every working day, no matter what we do for a living (well, almost). So maybe we thank them and maybe we don't.

The NSA also pioneered efforts in flexible storage capabilities, which led to the development of the tape cassette. (They swear they had nothing to do with the 8-track.) NSA also made ground-breaking developments in semiconductor technology and remains a world leader in many technological fields. In other words, your government dollars really are at work.

If you are a top code maker or code breaker, you probably work for NSA. The NSA will neither confirm nor deny this, but it is believed to be the largest employer of mathematicians in the United States … and perhaps the world. The mathematicians have two jobs: one is to make our codes unbreakable, and the second is to break everybody else's codes. The NSA is located at Fort Meade, Maryland, halfway between Baltimore and Washington, D.C. But don't expect to take a tour. They don't give them.

The NSA was established by President Truman in 1952 to provide signals intelligence and communications security activities for the government. The head of the NSA works with the Director of Central Intelligence as part of the intelligence community. The NSA is not a military organization, but it is "administered" by the Department of Defense.

We'd like to tell you how many people work at NSA, but that would be a secret. The budget … a secret, too. The NSA will say this about itself: If the NSA were a corporation in terms of dollars spent, floor space occupied, and personnel employed, it would rank among the top 10 percent of *Fortune* 500 companies. In short, it's big.

In the Black?

Spy novelists, conspiracy theorists, and others like to say that the NSA has an unlimited budget for cryptology purposes—the "black" budget—which is unknown even by other government agencies. The NSA rigorously denies that it has such a "black," or secret, budget. The actual budget and size of the NSA are indeed classified, but there is one piece of information that we can share with you. In 1997, the total figure for all U.S. government intelligence activities was released. It was $26.6 billion for fiscal year 1997 and $26.7 billion for fiscal year 1998. (Presumably the extra $100 million was for upgrades of Windows, although we cannot be sure of that.)

The NSA draws its employees from both the civilian and the military, about half and half. At the NSA you will find (actually *you* won't find them because you can't get in, but they're there): analysts, engineers, physicists, mathematicians, linguists, computer scientists, researchers, security officers, data flow experts, managers, administrative and clerical specialists, a movie star, the skipper, and Gilligan.

Although they won't let you into the NSA buildings proper, you can visit the National Cryptologic Museum, located on Colony Seven Road, just off Route 32 and Route 295 in Maryland. Here you'll find thousands of artifacts that illustrate the history of the cryptologic profession. You'll see how SIGINT—Signals Intelligence, or code breaking—shortened World War II. You'll see the role of the NSA and Signals Intelligence during the Cuban Missile Crisis. There is a replica of the NSA memorial wall, which honors over 150 cryptologists who have been killed in the line of duty since 1945. The hours of the museum are classified. No they aren't. Got carried away. You can visit from 9 A.M. to 4 P.M. Monday through Friday and 10 A.M. to 2 P.M. on Saturday.

> ### Basic Training
>
> A Mr. Reader writes, "Does the NSA know what website I download?" They could find out if they wanted to, but they say they don't. The NSA does not "spy on" or target Americans. The NSA's responsibility is to perform SIGINT operations against foreign powers or agents of foreign powers. Your privacy as an American is protected by the Fourth Amendment to the U.S. Constitution, protecting you from unreasonable searches and seizures by the U.S. government or any person or agency acting on behalf of the U.S. government. That's true whether you are living in the United States or working or traveling abroad.

Big Brother Is Watching Big Brother

A lot of people oversee the work of the National Security Agency. The executive, legislative, and judicial branches of the government combine to form an oversight process to make sure that the NSA complies with its regulations. The President's Intelligence Oversight Board and the Congressional oversight committees both in the Senate and the House are kept fully informed of the activities of the NSA, not that the Senators and Congressmen necessarily believe that. In addition to these entities, the National Security Council, the Department of Defense, and the Department of Justice also watch the watchers.

Pentagon Parables

Since 1978, the NSA has been forbidden by law to ask allies to spy on Americans to gather information that the NSA legally could not gather. This means that anything you have done since 1978 that the NSA is not supposed to know about is your little secret. To be sure, you can always file a request under the Freedom of Information Act, which will allow you to examine the records on you maintained by the National Security Agency, the FBI, and other governmental information-gathering agencies. The only problem with filing a Freedom of Information Act request is that once you file one, even if there was no file on you before, there is one now.

Does the National Security Agency assassinate people?

No.

Defense Intelligence Agency

Okay, we've already talked about the CIA and the NSA. You might think that's enough intelligence for one superpower. Well, you would be wrong.

Now let's meet the Defense Intelligence Agency, the Department of Defense's main contribution to the intelligence community. DIA employs over 7,000 military and civilian individuals worldwide, and provides military intelligence to warfighters, defense policymakers and force planners in the Department of Defense and the intelligence community. DIA describes its customer base as "the President of the United States to the soldier in the field."

Its stated mission is to support U.S. military planning and operations and weapons systems acquisition. Basically, these are the guys whose job it is to know what the other team has and what it can do.

DIA is headquartered at the Pentagon, although much of its operation is in the Defense Intelligence Analysis Center (DIAC, or "DYE-ack") a shiny silver building at Bolling Air Force Base in Washington. We wish we could tell you about the keen things that go on inside the DIAC. But at least we're allowed to say it's silver.

DIA covers all kinds of military intelligence needs—from highly complex missile trajectory data to biographical information on foreign military leaders. DIA employees travel the world and meet and work closely with their peers in other countries. It's an extremely secure organization; some DIA employees aren't allowed to travel overseas, and if your spouse was born in a foreign country, you won't be considered for employment there.

We're not saying that the Defense Department doesn't trust the intelligence produced by the CIA and the NSA (note that we're also not saying that it does trust the intelligence). The fact is that DoD has its own special needs, and those needs relate to the information the military requires in order to carry out its various missions. So it makes sense that the Department of Defense would maintain its own intelligence-gathering apparatus. Its information is pooled with the other agencies, although that arrangement has its good days and bad.

The DIA manages two basic kinds of information—HUMINT and MASINT. We were a little flip about MASINT before, but if, heaven forbid, another nation were to launch something at us, we would want to know what it is, how fast it's coming in, where it's headed, and what we can do about it. We can even explain that without resorting to strained peas.

When a weapon is fired, it leaves what is called a "signature." A jet engine burns at a certain temperature, emits certain gases, and leaves a plume of a particular length and width. Bombs throw shrapnel in a certain pattern. Signatures of weapons that are observed by MASINT means are converted into threat recognition and identification profiles that improve our smart weapons. In other words, through the use of MASINT, the DIA is able to look at the trail of a speeding weapon and determine how best to take countermeasures.

> **Basic Training**
>
> Modern conveniences aren't too compatible with communications security, which is why, if you go to a facility where classified work is done, the guards will be only too happy to watch your cell phone until you come out of the meeting. And your two-way pager. And your BlackBerry. And your Palm VII, thank you.

Congress and the President need the same information in order to understand foreign weapons technologies and to monitor treaties and arms control agreements. You and I benefit from MASINT through timely warning of forest fires and volcanic ash clouds, detection of pollution sources, and provision of data on natural phenomenon to support environmental studies. (Remember, though, that the DIA cannot prevent forest fires. Only you can.)

In addition to its intelligence mission, DIA runs the Joint Military Intelligence Training Center, which provides strategic and joint intelligence training both at the Pentagon and online. Students include Department of Defense military and civilian employees, other government and Federal employees and international officers. JMITC courses are also offered online, in order to train intelligence officers wherever they may be so that they can master the intelligence challenges of the twenty-first century. Also, this lets them play Minesweeper during class.

The Least You Need to Know

- The CIA gathers and analyzes information from every type of source imaginable, and some that aren't.

- The Director of Central Intelligence is responsible for coordinating the work of the entire intelligence community.

- NSA specializes in SIGINT and cryptology. They aren't allowed to assassinate people. Honest.

- You have no need to know anything about DIA.

Part  Marshalling Plans (or "I Think, Therefore I Blam")

America's military can't go getting all Iwo Jima on somebody without a lot of forethought. The plans they use—the ships, tanks, and aircraft they operate; the decisions on where to spend money—are made years and even decades before the first Marine hits the beach.

The Pentagon is where that thinking happens. That is its mission. You're about to discover what they think about.

WELL, AFTER THIS SEVEN HOURS PLANNING SESSION, WE'RE AGREED -- IT'S *PIZZA* FOR LUNCH.

NOTHING IN THE PENTAGON IS DONE WITHOUT A PLAN.

"3 P.M.: Blow Up Iraq. 4 P.M.: Pick Up Dry Cleaning." How Wars Are Planned

In This Chapter

◆ Planning 24/7/365 (366 in leap year)

◆ Slides, Charlie Brown, slides

◆ Fighting in America first

◆ How to tell if your hat is real

Planning a war is like planning a very big wedding. You need to know where it is, who's coming, how much food you need, and what kind of surprise you want to give your guests. Long before you get to planning a specific war, there are general studies and plans that get the Department in position for whatever comes next. Some use scenarios; others are more general looks at the shape of the world ahead and where likely challenges to the United States will come from.

You've Got to Write for Your Fights

Sometimes you know a war is coming. Usually you don't. You can't plan for every war in advance.

What you can do is know how you're going to do the planning when that war comes. In the Pentagon, that system is called JOPES, the Joint Operations Planning and Execution System.

Planning starts with a document, issued by the President, called the National Security Strategy of the United States. Each year, the National Security Strategy lays out the nation's overall goals and the means—including economic and diplomatic as well as military—by which we intend to meet them.

> **Fighting Words**
>
> **Classified annex** is a part of many Pentagon reports. Reports, especially congressionally mandated ones, will have an unclassified version releasable to the public, and a classified annex that includes the more interesting parts.

With the National Security Strategy in hand, the SecDef issues a Defense Strategy, laying out the military role in carrying out the National Security Strategy, and how the Pentagon can best support the President's goals. He also issues the Defense Planning Guidance, based in part on the results of the Quadrennial Defense Review, which tells the services what capabilities are expected of them, so they know what forces to buy.

> **Basic Training**
>
> The military likes to think of three levels of warfare: *strategic*, *operational*, and *tactical*.
>
> The *strategic* level includes the broad guidance: the aims of the war, what resources will be allocated to it, the alliance structure under which it will be fought, and other global political considerations. The Pentagon is very much involved in formulating the strategic objectives, and right from the top. The President and SecDef and the CINC in charge of the region, working with the advice of the Chairman of the Joint Chiefs, set the strategic objectives.
>
> The CINC is in charge of the *operational* level, deciding which units to use, coordinating how the war is to be fought, and managing the coalitions in his theater.
>
> *Tactical* is what they make war movies about. That's where you get the actual movement of forces on the ground, at sea, and in the air, and how they deal with the enemy moment to moment.
>
> For shorthand, think of strategic as national goals, operational as the joint force commander's goals, and tactical as your unit's goals.

That CINCing Feeling

Once the Defense Strategy is in hand, it's up to the CINCs to put together plans. At any moment, CINCs have a set of *CONPLANs*, contingency plans for how the United States might respond to different situations in their *AOR*. The CONPLAN includes the CINC's operational concept for the scenario, just a very broad idea of how he'd proceed. From that, they develop an OPLAN, an operational plan, which is the CONPLAN with details filled in. Ready for another word? If a CINC is serious about his OPLAN, it will include a TPFDD (say "tip-fid"). That's Time-Phased Force Deployment Data, a list of what forces the CINC needs to carry out the plan and when they need them.

Commanders are taught that their plans must follow the "principles of war," to the extent that's not an oxymoron. You can remember the principles of war by the simple Bullwinklian holiday of MOOSEMUSS:

Fighting Words

AOR Area of responsibility. That realm in which the CINC is king.

Basic Training

Having read about how the Goldwater-Nichols reorganization changed the building in Chapter 6, you won't be surprised to learn that it changed the way wars are planned, too. Whereas the Pentagon once hosted a war-planning staff, today it's the responsibility of the regional CINCs to know their regions and what contingencies may arise there.

- ♦ **Mass** Concentrate your forces where and when they can do the most good.

- ♦ **Objective** Focus your efforts on the desired result.

- ♦ **Offensive** You don't win by retreating.

- ♦ **Simplicity** Keep the plans clear and only as complicated as they need to be.

- ♦ **Economy of Force** Use only as many people and things as you need for each task, especially those that aren't your main thrust.

- ♦ **Maneuver** Keep the enemy off balance by being where they ain't.

- ♦ **Unity of Command** War is not the time for a committee.

- ♦ **Security** Guard against what the other guy will try to do.

- ♦ **Surprise** Do to him what and where he doesn't expect.

Most of these make sense just off the top, right? And some help the others. Simplicity helps maneuver, unity of command helps simplicity, and so on. Of course, some need to be reconciled. Mass makes maneuver harder, and surprise may contradict simplicity. But that's why commanders get the big tent and extra cookies.

Once the OPLAN is done, the action goes back to the Pentagon. The CINC's guidance for preparing his plans comes in part from the JSCP ("jay-scap"), the Joint Strategic Capabilities Plan, issued by the Joint Chiefs of Staff. The JSCP assigns tasks to the CINCs and apportions major forces.

The Joint Chiefs of Staff also decide which CINC will be *supported*, and which will be *supporting*. The supported CINC is the man who is in charge of the conflict, while the supporting CINCs help out with forces and other services. (Afterward, the supported CINC will buy pizza and a six-pack for everybody.)

The structure the supported CINC assembles in wartime is a Joint Task Force, or JTF. He will meld fighter squadrons from the Air Force, special operators from SOCOM, and whatever else the Joint Chiefs will let him have into a single organization that is the pinnacle of jointness.

While the CINC can organize anyway he wants, a typical JTF has commanders for each component, or type of force. That's important, because the components are not divided by service. The JFACC, or Joint Forces Air Component Commander, controls all of the aircraft, whether Air Force, Navy, Marine, or coalition. (Army helicopters are generally considered part of their ground units, and are operated by the ground component commander.) The component commander issues tasking orders detailing the duties of each unit in his component.

Briefly Speaking

At every stage of the process, the war plan will be translated into briefing slides. Cavemen used drawings to communicate; ships use flags and semaphore. Pentagonites communicate with each other via the briefing. No job is done until it has been briefed to somebody.

The results of a study? Presented as a briefing. A proposal to buy more fighters? Briefing. Lunch menu in the SecDef's mess? Not usually. But the PowerPoint brief has become a source of competition, as briefers from various services vie to push the envelope of the art form. The rivalry has become so intense that periodic memos remind presenters that slides chockablock with animations are neither very informative nor looked on favorably.

Here's a quick vocabulary hint: Briefings are also called "briefs," except maybe in the POAC locker room. And you don't attend a brief, you "take" or "give" a brief.

So pervasive is briefing culture that a brief doesn't have to be given to a roomful of people. Even when communicating one-on-one, like with your boss, it's common to give a "desktop brief," flipping through paper versions of your slides. Or, if you brief regularly, there's the spiffy three-ring notebook that folds into a little easel, so you can give the desktop brief the illusion of projection.

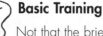

Basic Training

Not that the briefing needs to be created by that particular Microsoft program, but any electronic slideshow in the building is referred to as "PowerPoint," and Microsoft Office is the standard package used in the Pentagon. PowerPoint is such a big deal that it has its own *Complete Idiot's Guide!*

Briefs even get a life of their own in the building, held in the same breathless esteem as baseball cards.

"Have you seen Hansen's force protection brief?"

"No."

"It's even better than the Roberts computer security brief from '86."

"Wow. I have Roberts on the original acetates."

"No way!"

Briefings are also a way to get noticed by superiors, although that's not always a good thing. For every story of a briefer being "discovered" and gaining the boss's favor, there's a corresponding tale of a briefer who challenged the boss's ideas or, heck, just gave a bad brief, fleeing the office in a cloud of hurled pages. So be careful. In the building, good software is no substitute for a bit of content and a lot of political smarts.

The problem is, once they work up their TPFDDs, every CINC winds up needing more forces than they have available. So the Joint Chiefs have to decide who gets what, which can lead to a revised JSCP, which means the CINCs have to look at their plans all over again, which means they need more forces … and the cycle begins anew. This is known as auction pinochle.

(Okay, this isn't really known as auction pinochle. But Groucho Marx wrote that line, and it was just too good to pass up. It is actually known as Reverend Diego Bernstein.)

How's It All Gonna End?

So Robert Redford turns to Allen Garfield in *The Candidate*, just after he's beaten all the odds and won the election he's been fighting for, and says, "What do we do now?"

Every OPLAN has to deal with that moment, the point at which the war is won. You may have captured thousands of enemy prisoners. You may control somebody else's country. At the very least, you have a mess of troops and tanks and *MREs* to ship home.

Fighting Words

MREs   Meals, Ready to Eat. The standard combat ration, which typically includes an entrée, side dish, crackers, fruit cup, and utensils, all individually sealed and encased in a waterproof plastic pouch. Soldiers will tell you that the phrase "Meals, Ready to Eat" is inaccurate on at least three counts.

Tank crews used to heat their MREs in the exhaust stack (they may still, but it's no longer approved procedure, thanks to the less than salubrious effects of carbon monoxide sauce). In early 2002, the same folks responsible for creating the MRE announced they'd invented a carefully engineered sandwich that could last six months without refrigeration. Yum.

The first challenge is to determine when you've won. "Conflict termination" can be defined in a number of ways, but it's up to the national leadership—the strategic level—to tell you what that point is. The operational commander can recommend a stop, but he's involved in the operational level of war and may not have a view of all the political interests involved in deciding when to terminate a war.

Compare the termination of war in Vietnam with that in the Gulf. In Vietnam, U.S. forces were withdrawn from the country over an extended period following long and onerous peace talks. American national objectives, to the extent they were ever understood, were not achieved. By contrast, the Gulf War ended as if cut off by a knife, at a specified time, following a rout on the battlefield and an abbreviated, no-negotiation surrender process. While debate continues over whether all national objectives were reached, it is reasonable to say that all *established* national objectives—principally restoration of the *status quo ante* in Kuwait—had indeed come to pass.

Fighting Words

Status quo ante   Latin for "the way it was before." Most statements of goals of a war include at least returning the situation to where it was before the bad guys attacked, like Iraq staying on its side of the bed and not taking all the covers.

Similarly, while the operational commander may be involved in negotiations and the signing of surrender documents, the terms are dictated in Washington. The defeated army isn't surrendering to the guy at the table; it is surrendering to the United States of America.

(Note that all of this is very good theory, and bound to get *SNAFUed* in practice. For examples, take a look at the Persian Gulf books in the reading list, Appendix B. They make it clear that in that case, different people may have had different ideas about who was in charge of what. And don't get us started on MacArthur.)

The CINC is also responsible for planning for military operations other than war, or MOOTW ("moot-wah"). MOOTW can be a controversial subject.

Fighting Words

SNAFU Such a common term in American vernacular that it's usually not capitalized anymore, SNAFU originally stood for Situation Normal, All (Fouled) Up. Which seems a bit cynical.

Side Jobs

There's no question that the military exists to fight and win wars. But what should its role be in other kinds of operations?

Most people would agree that peace is good. Certainly, for all their warlike image, professional soldiers believe more fervently in peace than most people; after all, they're the ones whose lives will be at risk if peace fails.

If peace is good, you might think peacekeeping a good thing. Some nations, like Canada, specialize in keeping the lid on former enemies as they work out their differences. If the United States is to participate in peacekeeping missions, though, we have to send the military. There's no other national force except the Scouts, and they're not available during cookie season.

But is that what our military should do? With all the trouble in the world, and all the demands on a shrinking force, aren't there better ways for American forces to spend their time—like training, for example?

The debate over MOOTW is driven by some bad experiences. American Marines went to Beirut in 1982 to help enforce peace after an extended civil war. A suicide bomber destroyed their barracks in October of 1983, killing 216. Ten years later, U.S. forces supported a UN humanitarian operation trying to relieve a civil war-induced famine in Somalia, but 18 Rangers were killed and 77 injured in a firefight.

Basic Training _____

Want to impress people with your knowledge of the guiding principles of MOOTW? Just remember the word SLURPO:

- ◆ **Security**   Protect your forces.
- ◆ **Legitimacy**   Don't go without a reason.
- ◆ **Unity of effort**   Make sure your forces and allies are all working together.
- ◆ **Restraint**   Don't use more force than necessary.
- ◆ **Perseverance**   Stay until the goal is accomplished (and let your adversaries know you will).
- ◆ **Objective**   Keep your eye on the ball; don't forget why you're there.

Not that it will get you any dates.

Part of the problem is that putting U.S. troops into a peacekeeping situation changes the dynamic of the situation. Few countries or groups have animosity toward Canadian or Norwegian peacekeepers. Americans can be another matter. Also, a lesson adversaries around the world took from Vietnam (and perhaps Beirut) is that the American public won't tolerate casualties. If someone wants American peacekeepers out, they believe all they have to do is kill a few troops and the Americans will go home.

It's also fair to say that there's a significant difference of opinion about how American power should be used in the world. Some think that it's a noble and appropriate task for the last superpower to use its might to help keep peace. Others believe U.S. troops should only be used where American interests are directly affected.

Fighting Words _____

What's the difference between **peacekeeping** and **peace enforcement?** Peacekeeping is when the combatants agree to have a force separating them. Peace enforcement can be more aggressive, involving inserting yourself between the fighters to create peace where none exists. The situation in Beirut and U.S.-supported UN actions in Bosnia, Haiti, and Somalia fall more in the category of peace enforcement.

Peacekeeping isn't the only operation other than war for which our troops are used. They evacuate Americans from countries at war, provide humanitarian relief to people in need, fight forest fires, help interdict drug smugglers, and even airdrop hay to stranded cattle herds in wintertime. But *peacekeeping* and *peace enforcement* are the main tasks other than deterrence and, occasionally, actual warfare for which American forces have been used in the last 20 years.

You'll notice that we haven't mentioned where in this continuum you actually declare war. As you saw if you read the sidebar in Chapter 5, you probably don't declare war, for reasons of domestic politics and international law. (Go back and read. You'll enjoy.)

Terms of Engagement

Before putting the first soldier or airman into battle, it's critical to establish rules of engagement, or ROEs. ROEs are critical, because without clear rules about who can shoot, at what, and when, Private Blotznik can unilaterally start World War III.

International law decides with whom we can go to war. For more on that, let's take a look at Afghanistan. In the recent U.S. action there, our forces captured a number of fighters affiliated with the al-Qaeda terror organization. You may have heard them referred to on the news as "illegal combatants." That doesn't mean they're underage or that they fought dirty, not that we'd put either past them. But it means that they were not a legitimate army.

If someone shoots at a U.S. soldier on the street in Germany, it's not war, it's a common crime. If an Iraqi soldier shoots at a U.S. soldier in the desert of Kuwait in February of 1991, it's not a crime, it's war. What's the difference?

When armies fight, it's war. Under international law, a legitimate army has organization and uniforms. When a Taliban fighter shot at a U.S. soldier, it was war, because the Taliban Army in Afghanistan was an organized national force and thus "legal combatants." The al-Qaeda, by contrast, were not a legally recognized army, so even when operating in a ragged unit, an al-Qaeda fighter shooting at a U.S. soldier was committing a crime.

As you can see, these rules go back to the days when uniformed national armies met on a battlefield, colors flying, while civilians watched from the sidelines. It may seem odd to distinguish among people shooting at you in this way, but in these distinctions lies the legal order required to prevent the atrocities against civilians that have characterized many modern wars. (For more on the evolution of warfare from the feudal to the future, see Chapter 21.)

It's also important to note that rules of engagement and a plan of action aren't chicken-and-egg. ROEs are formulated only after a commander decides on his or her OPLAN. The question is "given what we want to do, what are the rules of engagement?" not "given the rules of engagement, what can I do?"

Coalitions Large and Small

If all the joint force commander had to do was fight the war, life might be easier. But at the same time, he is managing relations among the nations of the *coalition*, dealing with backseat drivers from Washington ("Thank you, Senator, we'll take your idea into consideration."), and after the war, coordinating the work of a number of non-military entities like humanitarian and relief organizations.

Fighting Words

Coalition A set of countries acting together in wartime. Operation Desert Storm was fought by a 38-country coalition led by the United States. It's different from an **alliance**, which is more permanent and usually involves signed documents.

Those interagency operations provide an unusual challenge to the CINC. They bring into the AOR entities with different agendas, command arrangements, and even syntaxes, as many independent agencies are emphatically nonmilitary in nature. Such operations may add considerably to the tasks of a CINC and his staff, while at the same time these nonmilitary organizations don't operate in support of (nor are supported by) the commander. In short, interagency operations are even today a difficult beast to manage.

They have become so common that the 1997 Quadrennial Defense Review found that existing peacetime operations were tying up almost as much of the U.S. force as a war or its equivalent, called a *major contingency*. In response, the administration issued guidance to assist the CINCs in their work. Presidential Decision Directive 56 (called PDD-56), issued in 1997, recognized that "complex contingency operations" involving a number of agencies were becoming a standard mission, and attempted to bring some order and discipline to their operation.

Before PDD-56, the CINC was the focal point for planning and implementing regional military strategies requiring interagency coordination. But this responsibility came without the necessary authority to enforce decisions. Further, CINC command staffs, as warfighters, had little training or experience in planning for operations involving nonmilitary agencies, and so weren't familiar with what, if any, useful tools those organizations could provide.

And as a JCS publication delicately put it, "[Because] the divergent agency cultures typically challenge the military ethos of results orientation … concentrating the powers of different agencies toward national security objectives is difficult."

The NSC Steps In

PDD-56 was designed to streamline interagency planning and help U.S. government agencies and international organizations engaged in peace operations work together.

Fighting Words

Out of hide Paying from the existing budget. From the old fatherly adage, "I'm going to take this out of your hide."

It fundamentally recognized these interagency operations as a legitimate mission, and ordered that they be planned and budgeted for. That was important, relieving commanders from doing these missions *out of hide*, and managing them on an ad-hoc basis.

Of at least equal importance to the CINC, though, is that PDD-56 brought interagency operations the same structure, standards, and processes found in military-only operations, so at least everybody could talk to each other and knew who was boss.

Testing Your METL

While all this planning is going on, the forces are getting ready, too, through training, doctrine development, and experimentation.

These preparatory tasks are the duty of Joint Forces Command. JFCOM oversees the services' training, and is in charge of the UJTL, the Universal Joint Task List. The UJTL is a list of everything a joint force should ever be able to do.

From that list come METLs, Mission-Essential Task Lists, which are those parts of the UJTL that are your unit's jobs. (When METLs are joint, they are of course JMETLs.) So when you go to train, the commander asks, "What is my METL?" meaning "What do you want us to do, and how well do you want us to be able to do it?" The METL sets the standard.

The METL also allows you, as the commander, to tell your superiors just how the unit is doing. SORTS, the Status of Resources and Training System, communicates your unit's readiness, along with the factors that may be causing shortfalls, through your chain of command to the Pentagon, where it's reviewed by the JROC, who you met in Chapter 3. That's how the Pentagon knows, day to day, which units are ready to go and which should stay home and practice shining their shoes. So if your broken-down *six-bys* are keeping the unit from training to standard, or everybody got food poisoning from the SOS and can't get out of their bunks, SORTS will tell the bosses—if, that is, you decide to put that info into SORTS in the first place.

JFCOM is also the citadel of operational experimentation and joint doctrine.

Experimentation is just what it sounds like: coming up with and trying out new strategies and systems.

Doctrine sounds like it would describe every detail of how to do what you do. In fact, doctrine provides just the general principles of operation, and commanders can bend doctrine if need be—and if they can justify it later.

> **Fighting Words**
>
> **Six-by**   Usually written 6x6, the standard medium military truck for years and years. The Army is now procuring a new "family of medium tactical vehicles" (read: mess o' trucks) but they'll still be big and green, and the soldiers will still call them six-bys.

As in weapons research, plan and doctrine developers use red teams and white teams to check their work, especially during war games. (Doctrine war games are played in conference rooms, not on battlefields. The services and JFCOM have elaborate facilities for just this purpose.)

A red team, sometimes called "red cell," is the part of your planning group that pretends to be the bad guys and beat your plan, so its flaws can be identified early. (It's also a verb: "Did you red team this?")

The white team is the referee, deciding whether your tactics or assumptions have any basis in the real world. Think of them as the Dungeon Master, ruling whether your +4 cloak of invisibility bested the red team's +6 sword of fire.

Getting Something Strange

Experimentation isn't limited to our own forces. One of the Pentagon's more interesting jobs is "Foreign Materiel Exploitation." This means getting ahold of the other guy's stuff and driving, shooting, or flying it until we understand what it does and how it does it. This isn't new; there are pictures of German Messerschmitt and Japanese Zero fighters with the U.S. stars and bars on them that we captured during the Second World War. Today, foreign equipment can be come by in a number of ways; let it suffice to say that it's an easier job since the end of the Cold War. Capitalism really did win. Cha-ching.

On the odd occasion when we have some foreign equipment to exploit, it's done at ▮▮▮▮▮▮ and ▮▮▮▮▮▮▮▮▮▮ and ▮▮▮▮▮▮▮▮▮, facts that have never before appeared in print!

At the same time that strategic studies are trying to project where and with whom American forces might fight, others are working on how that war might work tactically. That effort takes place on two levels. One is in the services' think tanks, where they look at new ideas for tactics and how to incorporate new technologies. Then those ideas are tried out in the field against the best opposition America can find—America.

The services maintain units whose sole job is to beat our own people, using capabilities and tactics similar to those we expect to face in a real conflict. The Air Force and Navy maintain Aggressor squadrons that fly against other units, using smaller, more nimble aircraft and their best guess at opponents' tactics. This was another lesson of Vietnam. Previously, we had trained our pilots against each other, using our own aircraft, but soon learned that an enemy with different tactics and equipment could prove formidable by attacking in ways we didn't expect. So the services switched to DACT—Dissimilar Air Combat Training—recognizing that our enemies were, inconveniently, not like us.

The Navy flies its Aggressors out of Fallon Naval Air Station in California; the Air Force from Nellis Air Force Base, Nevada. Both take advantage of relatively unpopulated areas to fly real missions and dogfight in the spacious skies of the West. Nellis is also home to Red Flag, a regular event where fighters, bombers, and tankers join to fly real missions as they would be flown in combat against realistic opposition. The Navy and Air Force ranges are fully instrumented, allowing crews to examine the results repeatedly in full detail, like a football team studying game films.

The Army maintains similar programs at the National Training Center at Fort Irwin, California and the Joint Readiness Training Center at Fort Polk, Louisiana. There, units from around the country come to practice against the permanent opposing force, or OPFOR, which uses foreign tactics.

The same lessons that led to dissimilar training also inspired the creation of the Navy Combat Weapons School, a program designed to make the top pilots better, both so they can perform better in combat and so they can pass their knowledge along to squadronmates. This school, better known as TOPGUN, uses the Fallon ranges as well.

> **Basic Training**
>
> After a 1986 movie starring Tom Cruise purported to tell the story of trainees at TOP-GUN, a lot of memorabilia appeared bearing the school's name. A quick check to see whether your ball cap is the real thing: The school's name doesn't have a space between "TOP" and "GUN."

The Least You Need to Know

◆ Contingency planning is the responsibility of the geographic CINCs.

◆ Military operations other than war, like peacekeeping, can be controversial.

◆ JTF component commanders can give orders to forces of every service.

◆ MOOSEMUSS and SLURPO are not comic characters, but important in military planning.

How to Buy a Jet Fighter

In This Chapter

- ◆ Buy what you need, but need what you buy
- ◆ Old is better than new (or at least easier)
- ◆ Milestones and millstones
- ◆ How you get paid, and how much

Procurement starts with requirements. (It's not that some general gets up in the morning and decides he likes the new 2003 tanks better than his 1997 model.) And requirements come from a lot of places.

We talked in the last chapter about how the CINCs and Joint Chiefs constantly update their plans, and that the Joint Chiefs dole out the available forces. But they also maintain the Joint Strategic Capabilities Plan, listing all the things the military needs to be able to do. Based on that, they figure out what the force structure should be—how many units of different types we need, which eventually translates into a requirement for a certain number of planes, submarines, and other hardware.

That sets the necessary quantities and basic characteristics. Obviously, if you have more capable weapons, you might not need as many of them.

Even if other countries didn't improve their militaries, and American research discovered no new technologies, systems age and need replacement. The continuing development of technology here and elsewhere adds to the list of requirements for a system, by helping define what it should be able to do, and establishing key performance parameters (KPPs). This is essentially a list of how well the new system is required to do different tasks. After all, if you're going to buy a new piece of equipment, you might want it to be better than the old one, and definitely better than what the other guy has. This is also the way men buy lawnmowers.

You Can't Beat the System

These days, the Pentagon doesn't buy an airplane or a ship. It buys a "weapon system." The difference is that a weapon system is more than just the plane. You buy the airplane and the technical manuals and the service equipment and the logistics support. Systems even include the simulators used to train pilots. It's like getting the Quarter-Pounder Extra Value Meal instead of just the sandwich. Look at the brochures and ads and you'll see that Boeing doesn't sell the T-45 trainer jet, it sells the "T-45 Training System."

Pentagon Parables

One of the odd things about living in Washington (and there are many) is the advertising. Listen to the radio, and where in another city there'd be an ad for a carpet store, you hear about the virtues of one company's integrated information technology solutions for Department of Defense needs. Walk through any of the Washington area airports and you'll see billboard ads for fighter jets. The number of people targeted by these ads is very small, but apparently the companies find it worthwhile. We're waiting for them to offer cents-off coupons.

The distinction between a weapon and a system hides a difference that's important inside the Washington Beltway. The defense budget is divided into sections according to what the money's used for. Procurement funds buy the tanks and planes; "operations and maintenance" (O&M) funds pay the costs of using and supporting them day-to-day. If you include the simulators, support equipment, and so forth as part of an integrated system, more of the money can come from the procurement account, which is Congress's favorite place to add extra money. That makes funding the program easier. The Pentagon will spend about $72 billion in procurement in FY03.

Whoops, we just used a word that needs some clarification. There's a difference between a *system*, which is hardware, and the *program* used to buy it, which is the funding. They're often used interchangeably; depending on what newspaper or website you read, the Secretary wants to cancel the Crusader program, the Crusader system, or the Crusader. They all have the same functional effect, because if you cancel the system you have nothing for the program to fund, and if you cancel the program, you have no funding for the system. But now you can correct people at parties.

Assuming you don't have a Boeing showroom in your neighborhood, where do you go to get T-45 brochures? Well, to the air show, of course. But not just any air show.

Parlez-Vous Fighter Plane?

Each year, the world's military aviation community comes together to kick tires and see what's new at one of two major air shows. In even numbered years, it's Farnborough, England; in odd years, Paris. (Not the Paris in Texas.)

Like any industry trade show, the vendors show off their wares. Unlike, say, a flange convention, manufacturers also rent mammoth suites, called chalets, to wine and dine the government buyers and their multibillion dollar checkbooks. In the suites you'll find good food, multimedia displays, models of the products, and, yes, brochures.

The most impressive display is outside the chalet windows. Dozens of aircrafts of all kinds are parked all over the airfield. And the days are full of aerial demonstrations. (We're sure they have something like this for tanks, but it just doesn't seem as exciting, somehow.)

Pentagon Parables

Aerial demonstrations of your product can help or hurt. In 1976, a big European fighter contract was up for grabs among several companies. General Dynamics test pilot Neil Anderson brought the then-new F-16 low over the field, did two gut-wrenching 360-degree turns right in front of the chalets, and exited stage left. It was such a display that pilots of competing fighters decided to wait a good long while before flying. On the other hand, in 1999, a prototype of the Russian Sukhoi-30 fighter crashed in front of the world's aviation elite, echoing the crash of a MiG-29 10 years earlier. (The pilots ejected in each case, which may have helped Russia sell ejection seats, if not fighters.)

Old Weapons Never Die

Manufacturers spend oodles of cash on air shows, trade shows, and the like in hopes of getting government sponsorship for new projects.

See, you, the taxpayer, pay for most of the development of new weapons. General Motors doesn't ask its customers to pay it for designing a new car. They do some market research, put the car in the showroom, and hope you'll buy it. But the cost of developing a new weapon system is now so high that even the major aerospace companies can't afford to build one just on spec, in the hope that the Pentagon might want a few. So today, the government picks up most of the tab, then sends you, Mr. and Ms. Taxpayer, the bill.

Fighting Words

Lessons learned

Although it sounds like a casual phrase, digesting lessons learned is a formal and significant process in the military. After each major conflict—and, in some cases, any major engagement—a "lessons learned" team goes over the action to prepare a formal report on what happened, what didn't, and how the results could be improved upon. The findings are incorporated into service training and planning.

But the cost is also so high that the company has to ensure it recoups its part of the money somehow, whether *IR&D* or preparation for production. Take the case of the F-18 fighter.

One of the *lessons learned* from Vietnam was that American fighters needed to be able to dogfight better.

In response, the Air Force created the Lightweight Fighter program, a competition for a small, cheap, agile fighter. General Dynamics proposed its F-16; Northrop offered the F-17. The Air Force ended the competition with a side-by-side fly-off, which the F-16 won. (They would use the same kind of competition for the Advanced Tactical Fighter, won by the F-22, and the Joint Strike Fighter, won by the F-35.)

Pentagon Parables

A graphic of the history of the defense business would look like one of those drawings of a little fish about to be eaten by a bigger fish, which is about to be eaten by a bigger fish, and so on. The two companies involved in the 1974 lightweight fighter fly-off are poster children for that ongoing consolidation. Northrop merged with Grumman and is now Northrop Grumman. McDonnell Douglas was formed by the merger of the McDonnell and Douglas companies; McDonnell had a specialization in fighters, while Douglas made civilian transports as well as military aircraft. McDoug, as it came to be known colloquially, has since been absorbed into Boeing. General Dynamics' aircraft business combined the North American and Convair companies (Convair being itself an amalgam of Consolidated and Vultee). It is now part of Lockheed Martin, but check back next week.

Losing the Lightweight Fighter contract left Northrop with the F-17 design and no customer. While they looked at selling it overseas, no customer was in prospect.

Then the Navy decided it wanted a twin-engine fighter to replace its aging F-4s, A-4s, and A-7s. While other contractors had to start their designs from scratch, Northrop joined with McDonnell Douglas to alter the F-17, adding features the Navy needed, like a strengthened landing gear and a tail hook to let it land on carriers. Rechristened the F-18, the design became the Navy's next strike fighter, and still serves.

That's one way to recoup your costs. McDonnell Douglas is pursuing yet another method of getting back its investment dollars. The company designed the A-12 Avenger stealth bomber for the Navy. When SecDef Dick Cheney canceled the A-12 while it was still in development, citing cost and weight overruns, McDonnell Douglas and its partner, General Dynamics, sued DoD to get back a portion of what they had spent and the profit they expected to make from building the plane. As we write this book, nearly 10 years later, a final settlement is still making its way through the government. (But we don't recommend suing your biggest customer for billions of dollars as a general business strategy.)

Once a system is in production, it's hard to replace. Even if technology moves ahead, the existing system has advocates in the service, the Pentagon, and Congress. The company that makes it knows that they might not win the contract to build the replacement, so it's in many folks' interest to keep the old widget in place as long as possible. No small amount of the resistance to transformation of the various services comes from those who know that changes to the current way of doing things might render their favored systems irrelevant.

Sharing the Load

Teaming arrangements like the McDonnell Douglas–General Dynamics partnership on A-12 are common in the industry, and for several good reasons. Perhaps one partner is particularly good at one aspect of design, like stealth, while the other has more efficient production plants, and teaming is cheaper than adding that capability to your company. Maybe one company doesn't want too much government business in its portfolio, and the other needs steady work to keep from laying off people they expect to need in a few years. When was the last time you saw Ford and GM designing a car together? In the defense business, that sort of thing happens all the time.

Teaming also has a political advantage. If one shipyard has two Senators and a Congressman to help keep its program funded, two yards will have twice the clout.

Sometimes, teaming arrangements are deliberately arranged to keep competition in an industry. For years, attack submarines were built by two yards, General Dynamics' Electric Boat Company and Newport News Shipbuilding. As the annual number of new submarines dropped, it was hard for both yards to keep their workers busy, especially in specialized disciplines like welding exotic metals. But the yards found that they couldn't just lay off workers until the next sub came along, because—get this!— a lot of them would leave town if they didn't have a job. So the government approved a plan where each company makes some of every sub. That way, they both have a pretty good idea how many workers they need and when the next job is coming. And should we start to buy more subs every year, there are still two yards to compete for the work, which should help keep prices down.

Arrangements like these are often referred to as "maintaining the industrial base," doling out enough work to each company in a critical industry to make sure they'll still be there when needs increase.

The Wild Green Yonder

In the 1950s, the Navy and Air Force maintained the industrial base by just buying everything they saw. Fighter bases looked like used-car lots, with a few F-94s over here, and some F-84s over there, and how about a deal on this spanking new F-86?

But as the price of systems grew, so did the debate they engendered. Every generation has its controversial airplane procurement. In the 1960s, it was the TFX, which became the F-111 fighter-bomber. The F-111's cost was one source of controversy; another was a high rate of losses until pilots learned to trust the breakthrough radar that let the plane fly at almost treetop level. (Pilots would see hills coming up, decide that the radar wouldn't react in time, and override it. It turned out that the radar's judgment was often superior to the pilots'.)

> **Basic Training**
>
> While it's PA&E's job to watch over program cost growth, some there take the job zealously. One analyst, Chuck Spinney, has been renowned for decades, inside the building and out, as a curmudgeon on acquisition programs, often quoted publicly criticizing programs of which the Department is quite fond. If the Department of Defense is the *Muppet Show*, Chuck Spinney is both Statler and Waldorf.

In the 1970s, the hotly debated B-1 bomber was canceled, then reinstated by the next administration. The B-2 "stealth bomber" shocked critics in the 1980s with its half-billion-dollar price tag. And we already talked about the 1990s' most controversial program, the A-12.

But those controversial programs are the high-visibility exceptions to most of what the Pentagon buys.

What Was and What Is

Once a service develops a requirement, it goes before the JROC, the Joint Requirements Oversight Council, which you'll recall is basically the service vices, or vice chiefs, presided over by the Vice Chairman of the JCS. The point of the JROC again comes from the drive for jointness; it is to make sure that new systems meet joint needs, and that services aren't all trying to build the same thing at the same time. The JROC approves the KPPs that will, of course, go into your ORD (pronounced "ord," an Operational Requirements Document that sets out what your system has to do).

If the JROC says okey-dokey to the ORD, your program goes into a three-step program:

> ◆ **Milestone A,** where you define not only what you propose to build, but also the schedule and development strategy you plan to use.

Fighting Words

Defense Acquisition Board (DAB) The senior review panel for all DoD acquisitions. The DAB (pronounced "dab") includes the USD for Acquisition, the Vice-chairman of the Joint Chiefs, the service acquisition chiefs, and more. A program manager briefing the DAB on a milestone review has the pulse rate of a marimba band. Reviews are called DABs, as in "How was your DAB?"

This is the introduction to the Component Advanced Development (CAD) phase, combining technology development with demonstration of how the system works. Sometimes more than one contractor or team will make it this far, each with its own idea about how to meet the requirement. In CAD, you're figuring out what the plane or ship or tank should look like and how to make one that meets all the requirements.

Each program has a program manager, one individual whose job it is to see that the system is developed on time and on budget, while meeting those pesky KPPs. The program manager is military, although he or she will work with a civilian counterpart representing the contractor or team.

How do you know whether your program has successfully made it through CAD? Two ways. Typically, if there is a competition, the winner is chosen at the end of CAD. If you win, you were good enough. At the end of CAD, you go to:

> ◆ **Milestone B,** where a formal review decides whether the system is ready to continue. Who decides? Why, the decision authority, of course. That's whoever is designated to make the call, but for major programs, it's usually USD (AT&L).

After successfully making it through Milestone B, you're in System Design and Development, or SDD. This is where you make your technologies and prototype into a producible system. Then, step three;

◆ **A formal DAB,** when the Defense Acquisition Board decides whether you're ready for production.

At each milestone review, there's an opportunity to insert technology from DoD's Foreign Comparative Test program, run by AT&L. Each year, a number of projects proposed by allied countries are evaluated for their suitability to U.S. military requirements. Sometimes, they will be bought on their own. In milestone reviews, the foreign technologies are looked at to see whether they could help the system work better. As you might imagine, it takes a strong advantage in value or performance for a foreign system to bump a U.S.-made one.

That's less true for international programs. Consider the F-35 Joint Strike Fighter, now under development. Other countries can pay their way into participation, the amount depending on how involved they want to be. Pay enough, like Britain did, and your country's specific requirements get incorporated into the system. Pay less, like Norway or Turkey, and you might help with the design, or get to produce some of the system in your country. The United States encourages international programs because the chances are pretty good that a country participating in the program will wind up buying the system. That means we're more *interoperable* and our contractors are happier. Besides, we're friends with these folks. Accepting large amounts of money to let them work on your project is what friends do, and goes back to Tom Sawyer whitewashing that fence.

All that's fine if you need to buy a fancy weapons system. But a lot more government contracting is comparatively mundane. Hiring somebody to mow the grass at your base or supply some sort of ground "meat" to make SOS isn't that sexy, but do it for 1.2 million troops and their families and support personnel, and you run into some big money.

That's why the Defense Logistics Agency, which you met in Chapter 7, has offices all over the country.

Of course, if you need a stapler or a copier for the office, you don't have to run through a bunch of milestone reviews. Smaller stuff can be bought with government purchase cards, essentially credit cards with a $72 billion line of credit issued to select officials. Many more Pentagonites carry government travel cards, regular credit cards that can be used for official travel expenses, which rarely includes that TAG-Heuer Monza watch you've been ogling.

Depot a Go-Go

Okay, how do you fix a fighter? That depends. Increasingly, maintenance and logistics support are included as part of a system purchase, which means that the manufacturer provides the support. Airline makers already do that for their commercial customers, with repair teams around the world and warehouses of parts ready to go by overnight express where they're needed. In the last few years, they've applied that same approach to supporting military aircraft. At many bases, part of the maintenance crew is now contractors. It's a new world for the Pentagon, but contracting out maintenance and support again means more uniformed people can be assigned to military-unique missions.

Basic Training

Repairs usually fall into one of three categories, although the names vary by service. **Unit level** repairs can be carried out on the spot by the unit's own maintainers. **Intermediate level** repairs require that the part, airplane, or vehicle be sent to a facility in the forward area. **Depot level** maintenance requires that the subassembly or the entire platform go to a central facility in the United States to be completely rebuilt. Modern systems try to make more and more repairs possible at the unit level, or combine functions in modules that can be replaced while the old or bad one is sent back to the depot.

The depots have different competencies. Tinker Air Force Base in Oklahoma fixes jet engines. Anniston Army Depot in Alabama overhauls (and in some cases helps build) armored vehicles. Electronics go to Tobyhanna Army Depot in Pennsylvania. And there are many more.

One of the most controversial systems in the Pentagon is the A-76. It's not an airplane, it's the process used to decide whether a particular job will be done in the public or private sector. A-76 (named for the DoD publication that contains the rules) tries to do what may be impossible—even out the bidding between government employees and private contractors. (Neither side likes the rules very much, which is often taken in Washington as a sign that they're pretty good.)

The biggest fight on A-76 (and one going on as we write this book) is what the deciding factor in an A-76 contract should be. If you go to buy a ladder or a book, you're probably looking for the *best price*, because the product is the same no matter where you buy it. If you're looking to buy a car, you might want to take the *best value*, the one with the most extras for a given price. It's easy to judge who wins a best price competition. But best value is more subjective. Is it worth paying more to get the car with a sunroof but an AM radio, or the one with a fancy radio but cloth seats? That's a value question. Add a couple of zeroes and some heated lobbying on both sides, and you see why acquisition is so fun.

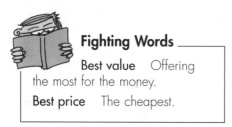

Fighting Words

Best value Offering the most for the money.

Best price The cheapest.

Sometimes, you don't have a lot of choice. Federal law, zealously enforced by Congress, requires that 50 percent of all depot work be done in publicly-owned depots. The idea is to make sure that in time of need, the government isn't subject to a company's whims or competing priorities. At a government-owned depot, government work comes first. (Of course, the contractors would say that the taxpayer shells out a lot of money to keep those depots open.)

One compromise is that some government facilities aren't all government. They are GOCOs, Government-Owned, Contractor Operated. In a GOCO, the buildings and the workers belong to the government, but a private company manages the place. They are most common where the government has some unique capability that it would cost a private company considerable money to duplicate, like the ammunition production facilities at the Radford Army Ammunition Plant in Virginia. With a GOCO, the contractor pays the government for use of the facilities, but the capacity remains in Federal hands, so it's there if needs arise.

Congratulations. You Won. Now What?

If you win a contract, part of your negotiation will include the type of contract. They come in two basic colors, although a variety of stripes and options are available within each.

- **Cost-plus** contracts start with what the system costs you to build and adds something on top for your trouble. It could be a fixed fee, so your profit is a certain fixed amount, but the total cost to the government can vary as the actual cost of the system—the labor, parts, and other components—changes over time. It can be an incentive fee, or an award fee, where you make more profit by hitting certain cost or performance (but usually cost) targets, like a designated hitter who earns more if he gets so many hits. The bummer of cost-plus contracts is that government auditors are in your operation every day, scrutinizing your processes and books so they know that what you say something costs really costs that much before the taxpayers shell out for it.

◆ A **fixed-price** contract is the government's favorite, because you, the contractor, take all the risk. You guarantee a price regardless of what the item costs you to produce. That may sound like a really bad idea, but it has a couple of advantages. First, you're more likely to win a contract if you offer a fixed price. Second, it gives you a lever with your workers and suppliers to keep costs down; they know that you can only afford to pay them a certain amount, because if their price goes up, you aren't getting any more money from the government. Some fixed-price contracts include automatic price escalation to keep pace with inflation. Third, the level of scrutiny, at least on the finances, is different.

Unlike a car salesman, you don't have to wait for your profit until the end of the deal, because the government makes "progress payments" as you are able to demonstrate increasing system maturity or actual deliveries.

The ultimate contractor jackpot is a multiyear contract, one where you know in advance what you're going to build for up to five years. Multiyears are rare, in part because Congress doesn't like them very much. But they let you lock in supply contracts and predict your workload, which makes your production more efficient and cheaper. It also protects you from the uncertainties of the annual authorization and appropriation process, which is why Congress isn't so keen on multiyears.

The Dark Side

But what happens if you don't win, or if somebody else isn't happy that you won? Many contract awards are protested, where the loser or losers claim that the selection authority violated one or some of the criteria in making the award.

As soon as a contract protest is received, work on the project stops. The protest is adjudicated by the General Accounting Office, which is Congress's version of PA&E, in a process that can take months. So a protest can be a tool for a losing contractor to get a winner to share some of the work; the sooner the winner settles the protest, the sooner they can start getting progress payments. (We're certainly not suggesting that anyone in the defense business would actually be so base as to file a protest just to spite a competitor. Nobody would do that, would they?)

And even if you win and there's no protest, or you win the protest, life is still uncertain. Congress could cut funding for your program. Technical glitches could slow you down and raise costs. Or, out of the blue, you could get a stop-work order, and even a *T for C*, or Termination for convenience of the government—A phrase that strikes terror into the hearts of contractors. All procurements, no matter how well planned or seemingly important, can be shut down if Uncle Sam feels like it. Perhaps there's something better to do with the money. Maybe the SecDef doesn't like the shade of gray you painted the ship. A "termination for cause" means you didn't live up to the contract, and that can be fought on its merits. A termination for convenience is much harder to defend against, because who are you to say what's convenient for the government?

Look at all these steps and complications, add in the factors of evolving technology and the uncertain Congressional funding cycle, and you can begin to understand why, while a new fighter could go from sketch to sky in 18 months 60 years ago, it takes more than a decade today.

The Least You Need to Know

- A tank, ship, or airplane is almost always bought as part of a system.
- The Pentagon will spend about $72 billion in procurement in FY03.
- Clothing, food, and other day-to-day items are bought with O&M money.

Chapter 12

Living in the Nuclear Age

In This Chapter

- ◆ Nuclear strategy ... is it an oxymoron?
- ◆ Deter the Petersons, if you can
- ◆ Shoot now or forever hold your missiles
- ◆ START to SORT the SALT

When the Pentagon was put together early in the Second World War, some airplanes were still built with wood and fabric. By the end of the war, the atomic bomb had been devised, constructed, and employed. The world had moved firmly and ineluctably into a new era, and that meant the Pentagon had to change the way it thought about war.

At first, when the United States already had a monopoly on the atomic bomb, there wasn't much to think about. After all, the United States had the world's dominant conventional military. Being the sole nuclear power was just icing on the cake.

But in 1949, the Soviet Union detonated its first nuclear bomb, and the calculus changed radically. The new goal was to make sure that they didn't use the bomb on us, and the easiest way was to threaten to use the bomb on them. The result was that everybody got MAD.

Do You Get MAD?

MAD stood for Mutual Assured Destruction, which sounds like a bad insurance company. MAD is often misunderstood as implying that if a nuclear war started, the United States and Soviet Union would automatically fire everything they had and wipe each other out. Each certainly had the capability to do that. But MAD meant that *because* each side had the capability to destroy the other, neither would dare start the war. MAD wasn't a war plan, but a deterrent philosophy. More importantly, it was a reality. Because it was impossible to defend against a determined nuclear attack, the best we could do was to ensure that the Soviets would recognize that launching one would mean suicide.

MAD drove the structure of U.S. forces, particularly in the 1950s. In fact, it drove the controversial (and later abandoned) decision to build bombers rather than carriers; long-range bombers could carry the big war to the Soviets in a way carriers couldn't.

> **Pentagon Parables**
>
> After the Second World War, the world believed the United States to be the only nuclear super-power. The truth is that after Hiroshima and Nagasaki, the United States had no nuclear weapons left and needed over a year to build another. Of course, we didn't let the world know that.

And nuclear deterrence was defense on the cheap. It cost a lot less to have a bomber and missile force with nuclear weapons than to pay enough troops to provide the same deterrence, if that were even possible. (Remember back in Chapter 3, where we discussed the SIOP, the Single Integrated Operations Plan? This was when it was, for all intents and purposes, truly *single*.) So in a very real sense, the United States sacrificed conventional combat power in favor of a nuclear force.

Let's Get Flexible

But that decision heightened the growing problem with using the threat of nuclear war to restrain the other side. What if the other guy started a little war somewhere, or overthrew a government friendly to you? Would you start a global thermonuclear war in response?

Fortunately, it's not just authors who ask those kinds of questions. As early as 1950, with the Korean War beginning, the National Security Council came up with the notion of "flexible response." MAD said that nuclear forces would deter nuclear aggression, while flexible response declared that any attack would be met proportionally. We wouldn't automatically shoot nukes in response to a conventional attack, but would use conventional forces, at least at first. In a paper called NSC-68, NSC pointed out that flexible response didn't replace MAD, but augmented it.

The problem is that nuclear deterrence is comparatively inexpensive defense. Having drawn down forces dramatically after the Second World War, it wasn't clear at first that the public was ready for a major increase in military spending. Flexible response didn't really become policy until President Kennedy explicitly endorsed it.

Flexible response was a mixed blessing. It breathed new life into the conventional military, and may have helped move the world away from nuclear war. On the other hand, the buildup in conventional forces and policy of meeting Soviet aggression proportionally around the world may have helped ease the United States' way into Vietnam.

The idea of flexible response also led into an unexpected area. In order to get the flexibility to respond in ways that were not all-out nuclear war, both sides developed a range of smaller nuclear weapons. At one point, the United States had nuclear warheads ranging from 20-*megaton* city destroyers to small devices that could be carried by one soldier. Later, the search for usable nuclear weapons gave rise to the neutron bomb, a weapon that emitted a lot of radiation with comparatively little blast, so buildings would be left standing but unpopulated. That idea was so sufficiently horrific (particularly to our European allies, in whose neighborhood it might be used) that President Carter canceled the program.

Nuclear weapons were controlled within a strict regime in which no nuclear weapon could be detonated without orders from the highest national authority. A generation of Cold War movies introduced us to the missile silos in which two separate individuals had to verify orders and simultaneously turn keys separated at more than arms length in order to launch an intercontinental ballistic missile. But even with the man-portable nukes (dare we call them handheld?), a system of "permissive action links," the details of which are still highly classified, made sure control of the devices remained with national leadership.

> **Fighting Words**
>
> **Megaton**   The equivalent of a million tons of TNT. The bomb dropped on Hiroshima was about 12.5 kilotons, or 12,500 tons of TNT. That flattened everything in a 1.5 mile radius. At one point, when Khruschev was still in charge, the Soviets tested a hydrogen bomb with a yield of over 50 megatons, or 50,000,000 tons of TNT. That's a lot.

Part of the impulse for building all these nuclear weapons came from the fact that precision guidance systems weren't nearly as advanced as today. (Remember, the transistor wasn't invented until 1957, and integrated circuits didn't follow until the mid-60s.) Today, precision guidance allows targeters to choose what window of a building to hit. Then, though, the way to make up for a lack of precision was to have a big bang, and that's what nukes gave you. Which is why Navy ships and subs carried nuclear-tipped torpedoes and the Air Force even had air-to-air rockets with nuclear warheads.

Lack of precision also explains why Soviet nuclear weapons of the Cold War era were huge, because the Soviets didn't make very good guidance systems. If you're playing marbles and you don't have very good aim, use a beach ball. That was their philosophy with nukes: We don't know if we'll hit close to the target, so we'll make a big enough bang that it doesn't matter.

The problem was, those big warheads looked to us like city busters, which was particularly frightening. Here's why.

Hostility on the Block

Let's assume that you're going to fight a nuclear war. First, you'll need an enemy. Let's pick the Petersons, down the block. (After all, did he ever return your leaf blower?)

You have one nuclear weapon. So do they. So you have a choice: Aim at the Petersons' house, or at their nuclear weapon, in the silo in the backyard. (For purposes of this exercise, we'd best assume that the *radius of effects* of your nuclear weapons are about 40 yards.)

Fighting Words _____

Radius of effects   The area affected by the detonation. Nuclear weapons have two primary kinds of effects: blast and prompt radiation. The blast radius, where things get knocked down or vaporized, is much smaller than the area subjected to intense radiation and heat. Then later, there's fallout, which is why you want to nuke the Petersons on a day when the wind is blowing away from your house.

For a calculator of the effects of a nuclear detonation in your neighborhood, go to www.pbs.org/wgbh/amex/bomb/. It's in the "Special Features" section. For extra fun, put in your ex-husband's zip code.

What you really want is for the Petersons to not launch their weapon at you. How would you deter them from doing that? Aim at their house? Or do you aim at their weapon, so if you decide to go to war, you can disarm them but not cause massive Petersonian casualties?

And if you decide to aim at their weapon, do you think the Petersons believe that's what you're doing? If they think you're aiming at their house, they have a reason to launch first and save themselves.

Add to that the fact that your weapon is much more accurate than the Petersons', which means you can probably hit their silo, while their big old blunderbuss of a missile (which they got at the garage sale when the Sullivans moved) is only accurate enough to hit some part of your house if they aimed it at your TV antenna.

So you have a pretty good idea that they aren't aiming at your weapon, because they can't be sure of hitting it. They are probably aiming at you. At the same time, they know that you can hit their silo and disarm them. So they again have a strong reason to shoot first; if they don't use their weapon, they'll lose it. But you also have a good reason to shoot first, because if things get hot, their missile is likely coming for your house.

When both sides have a reason to shoot first, you have an unstable situation. But that's not unlike the situation that the United States and Soviet Union faced during much of the Cold War. The United States had more accurate missiles, capable of a *counterforce* strike that would largely disarm the Soviet Union. The Soviets' lack of accuracy meant that they needed huge warheads to take out our silos. But those same warheads would devastate cities (what strategists call *countervalue* targeting), and we didn't know which they were pointed at.

> **Pentagon Parables**
>
> From the 1950s through the early '90s, many Pentagonites involved in strategic matters kept models of the U.S. and Soviet missile lineup on their desks. Because Soviet miniaturization technology was behind ours, their warheads were heavier than ours and their rockets were much bigger. All one needed in order to convince a visitor of the Soviet threat was to pull out one of those models showing their missiles towering over ours. (The Freudian implications of all this are best left unexplored here.)

The wonder of Cold War stability is that it was all based on managing these kinds of perceptions. If your enemy believed you had a warehouse full of snowballs, he'd be a fool to start a snowball fight, even if he could only see two in your hands. Unless he thought he had a bigger warehouse than you did. The nuclear standoff depended on each side keeping the other somewhat uncertain about just what they were up to, but in no doubt as to the consequences of an attempted first strike.

Each side tried to make sure that the other could not achieve a disarming first strike, and equally importantly that the other side would never *believe* it could accomplish one. That led to the structure known as the triad, basing nuclear weapons in three different ways. By deploying nukes on land-based missiles, bombers, and hard-to-find submarines, the Americans and Soviets denied each other the notion of a disarming first strike. Each side would always have enough retaliatory power left after a first strike to make the attacker pay dearly.

Each leg of the triad had its own reason for being:

- **Land-based intercontinental ballistic missiles (ICBMs)** carried the biggest wallop, and were the most sure to arrive on target once launched. But they were launched from silos in the ground, which meant the other side knew exactly where they were and almost certainly had its own missiles pointed at them. So ICBMs were use or lose.

- **Bombers** could carry more warheads than missiles, especially before *MIRVs* were invented. And in times of tension, you could put them in the air, or even on patrol near your enemy's borders, as a sign of your seriousness. Best of all, bombers could be recalled after being sent on their mission, while missiles could only be brought back with big bungee cords, and we didn't know how to make them that big then. But bomber bases were also large, easy to hit targets. So you had to get your bombers in the air as soon as you thought war might be imminent.

> **Fighting Words**
>
> **MIRVs** Multiple Independently-Targeted Re-entry Vehicles. Instead of one warhead, a MIRVed missile had several, each of which could go to a different place. Not to be confused with MaRVs, maneuvering re-entry vehicles that steered in odd paths to confound defenses, or MERVs, a coven of smooth talk-show hosts.

> **Pentagon Parables**
>
> You've probably seen film crews running to their bombers while klaxons blare. Through much of the '50s and '60s, a significant percentage of the strategic bomber force sat on high alert, ready to get off the ground in five minutes. An ICBM would take about 20 minutes to arrive from the Soviet Union; we might have 15 minutes warning or so once it was picked up on radar. So a five-minute alert gave the bombers enough time to get away from the base, often in a rather random pattern so the Soviets couldn't just target the likely fly-out paths.
>
> This requirement led to a design innovation on the B-1 bomber: A start button on the nose gear strut that the pilot hit on the way into the plane, so the bomber would actually check itself out and fire up while the crew buckled in.

- **Submarine-launched ballistic missiles (SLBMs)** usually didn't carry as much punch as ICBMs, but their stealth made them much more likely to survive a first strike. Until some inventions that were once quite classified but now appear in Tom Clancy books, ballistic missile submarines were almost undetectable except by other submarines that happened to be close by.

When to Strike ...

The "use or lose" nature of ICBMs, and to a lesser degree of bombers, meant planners had a tough decision to make. If it looked like there would be a war, could we afford to wait for an attack to come in before launching our missiles? Or should we *launch on warning*, when we had indication that an attack was about to take place or, indeed, that missiles had been launched?

It may seem sensible to launch as soon as we detect a Soviet launch. To get that warning, in the 1950s and '60s, the United States built—with the help of its allies—the DEW and BMEWS radar systems. The DEW Line, for Distant Early Warning, was a series of radar stations in very cold places, aimed at detecting incoming bomber raids. BMEWS, the Ballistic Missile Early Warning System, was its counterpart for missiles. Together, these systems gave the United States at least a rudimentary ability to launch on warning.

Fighting Words

Indications and warning An entire specialty has grown up in the intelligence world trying to anticipate an attack. Indications are things like recalling certain units to duty or refueling of missiles that give you the idea something might be up. Warning is when you see unmistakable proof that an attack is about to begin, or just has begun.

But strategists found out early that wasn't always a good idea. One night, just after BMEWS went into service, the system picked up a significant target coming up from the direction of Russia. Operators watched, horrified, as the radar return continued to grow, looking to all the world like a massive Soviet attack. The wires were burning all the way to Washington when somebody noticed that the target speed wasn't quite right.

BMEWS had accurately given warning of a large object coming up over Russia—the moon. (This became known as "the night the moon hit the fan.") And, from time to time, flocks of birds would arrange themselves just so and fly in a way that scared the bejeezus out of a radar operator, until the "missiles" landed to feast on somebody's corn field.

These errors didn't happen often, but they were enough to raise serious doubts about the wisdom of launching on warning. Bombers, sure, you could always bring them back. But you had to be pretty sure that launching your ICBMs was the only way to keep them from becoming craters before firing them off.

I Dig Rock

The vulnerability of fixed sites led to another question: Missiles, heck; how do you protect your headquarters? A great concern was the "decapitation" attack, one focused on national leadership that would leave the United States powerless because nobody had the authority or the means to authorize retaliation.

That led to three major efforts and lots of minor ones. The major efforts were:

Developing Hideaways for National Leaders

A set of secure bunkers was scattered around Washington, far enough away that they would not be affected by a nuclear attack on the city, but close enough that officials could be taken there quickly. One such site has been declassified and opened to the public. It seems that much of Congress would have been relocated to a large warren of rooms buried beneath the Greenbrier resort hotel in West Virginia. (Not that all-out thermonuclear war would have made it any easier to get a tee time.)

Some of the other sites remain classified. For example, after the attack on the Pentagon on September 11, 2001, a number of Congressional leaders were spirited to an undisclosed location until the threat of further attacks had passed.

Keeping Command on the Move

Starting in February of 1961, and continuing until July of 1990, an EC-135 command aircraft was continually in the air over the central United States. Called Looking Glass, because it mirrored the command and control functions of a ground-based headquarters, it carried a flag officer and a full battle staff capable of controlling the full military forces of the United States. Even after the continuous Looking Glass patrols ended, the aircraft—now Navy E-6Bs—remain on high alert.

Protecting the Command Center

The net of DEW, BMEWS, and other sensors had to come together somewhere so that somebody could know what's going on out there. But where could you put such a valuable center without it automatically becoming a target?

The Pentagon decided to hide its control center under a big rock. In May of 1961, engineers began to hollow out Cheyenne Mountain, a 7,100-foot peak just south of Colorado Springs. In the giant hole inside, protected by hundreds of feet of rock and massive blast doors, 15 buildings, as tall as three stories, sit on springs to help them absorb the shock of an attack. This is the nerve center of the global aerospace sensor network.

Cheyenne Mountain is also home to the operational elements of NORAD, the North American Air Defense Command, so named because Canadians are allowed to push buttons once in a while.

Make It Go Away

The nuclear balance of terror was no fun for either side, and as they incurred increasing military expenses in the 1960s, the competition in strategic weapons threatened to bankrupt both. Nuclear arsenals grew and grew, to the point at which a new word was coined: *Overkill*. It's commonly used today, but then it was a term of art, referring to how the number of warheads on each side far exceeded the number of militarily useful targets on which to drop them.

The pointlessness of overkill, and the need to spend money in other parts of their societies, led the United States and the Soviet Union to begin a series of negotiations to restrict and then reduce nuclear arsenals.

The Strategic Arms Limitation Talks (SALT) began in earnest in 1969, even as U.S. soldiers and Soviet "advisors" fought each other in Vietnam. In May of 1972, President Richard Nixon and General Secretary Leonid Brezhnev signed the first SALT treaty, which froze the number of heavy bombers, silos, and submarine launch tubes at their existing number. That left the Soviets with about a 40 percent advantage, with 2,400 launchers to the United States' 1,700.

> **Fighting Words**
>
> **Strategic weapon**
> Notionally a weapon fired from one country's territory at the other country, although submarines counted, too. Strategic weapons were those aimed not at the other guy's army in the field, but at his homeland.

> **Pentagon Parables**
>
> SALT I limited the number of launchers, but it left a loophole you could fly a big missile through. It did not affect the number of warheads that could be launched from those tubes. The Soviets took advantage barely a year later, introducing larger, multiple-warhead missiles.

The Anti-Ballistic Missile Treaty

At the same summit, Nixon and Brezhnev signed a treaty limiting defenses against incoming missiles. Each side had been developing defensive systems; the United States won the naming battle, as ours was the Safeguard, and the Soviets' was the GALOSH.

Why prohibit defensive missiles? In the calculus of the Cold War, a nation with defenses might believe that it could launch a first strike on the other, while its ABM system would protect the launching nation from attack. Missile defenses were seen as *destabilizing*, because neither side really trusted the other to refrain from a first strike. And the other side would have incentive to build many more offensive missiles to overcome the new defenses.

Fighting Words _____

Destabilizing Making war more likely. In the Cold War, both the West and the Soviet Union had the goal of keeping their strategic relationship stable. Although lower-level conflicts might be tolerated or encouraged, neither side wanted those to escalate into nuclear war.

The ABM treaty limited each side to two sites with no more than 100 defensive missiles each, and that was amended in 1974 to one site—enough to defend a city or a field of silos, but not much else. And that's how they were used: The Soviets chose to defend Moscow, while the United States deployed Safeguard at Grand Forks, North Dakota, to protect an ICBM field. Due to the high cost of operating the system, though, Safeguard was shut down barely a year later.

Back to the SALT Mine

SALT I was merely the beginning to a long process. Six months after signing SALT I, negotiators were back at the table working on SALT II. SALT II went after the warheads, putting limits on bombers, launchers, and MIRVed launchers like those the Soviets had popped up with. It took nearly seven years to get those levels fixed to both sides' grudging satisfaction.

Then an important word changed. The L in SALT stood for Limitation. The next series of talks was called START, for Strategic Arms *Reduction* Talks. And talks they were, and talk they did. It took ten years this time, but in July of 1989, Presidents Bush and Gorbachev signed a treaty reducing U.S. and Soviet strategic nuclear forces by 40 percent each. And less than four years later, Presidents Bush and Yeltsin signed START II, which would reduce deployed U.S. and Russian strategic warheads to between 3,000 and 3,500 warheads per side. (It's still overkill, but not as much over—and the *trendline* is running in the right direction.)

Fighting Words _____

Trendline The general direction of a movement. It comes from the PowerPoint culture mentioned in Chapter 10; sometimes, if your data points are all over the place, you put a trendline on the chart to clarify the direction things are going.

While START II was negotiated faster than any of its predecessor treaties, the process stalled from there. Treaties have always had to be ratified by the United States Senate, and START II wasn't a popular treaty on Capitol Hill. It took nearly three years to get ratification. But then, a new complication arose.

The Soviet Union, upon dissolving, did not leave Russia with a tradition of legislative approval of treaties. The new Russian Duma—their version of the U.S. Congress—was even more leery of START II than the U.S. Senate, in part because compliance would be very expensive for a cash-strapped Russia. Finally, after assurances and American agreement to additional protocols (including a delay in the effective date, to put off having to spend that money) the Duma ratified START II in April of 2000, seven years after it was concluded.

The most recent chapter in arms negotiations introduced a new acronym: SORT, or Strategic Offense Reduction Treaty. Note that the T is Treaty, not Talks; SORT is a finished document rather than a process.

SORT, agreed to by Presidents G.W. Bush and Vladimir Putin in May of 2002, would cut deployed arsenals by two-thirds, a remarkable number considering the tortoise-like process of reductions previously. The catch is that SORT cuts the number of warheads that are *deployed* (out in the field), not the number that *exist*. SORT allows each side to put its extra warheads in storage; as long as they are not mounted on a missile or other delivery vehicle, they don't count.

The Senate and the Duma will have to ratify SORT.

In 2001, the second Bush administration announced its intention to withdraw from the ABM Treaty, under the clause that allowed withdrawal on six months notice. Deploying an anti-ballistic missile system had been a goal of administrations since 1983. But until this announcement, research had been constrained to live within the treaty's limits on what size and speed of interceptors could be tested. The announcement of withdrawal was less to enable deployment (which was, after all, still years away), than it was to get the United States out from under some of the testing strictures. (Missile defense will be discussed in more detail in the next chapter.) The withdrawal became effective June 13, 2002.

One Superpower, Many Nuclear Powers

The end of the Cold War wasn't an unalloyed boon for the Pentagon. To be sure, the specter of nuclear destruction and the use of smaller countries to fight proxy wars made the Cold War tense and unpredictable. But planners will tell you it was a much easier time to plan and strategize, because there was one big enemy, we kinda understood their thinking, and the strength of the two superpowers kept other nations in line.

Without the restraint of superpower competition, old ethnic and other enmities were free to come to the fore, often in areas that the Soviet Union had managed to keep a lid on while it was in business. The post-Cold War challenge to strategists was simple to understand: It's easier to try to balance two marbles on a board than ten. Strategists called the Cold War "bipolar," because the world politically turned around two centers of gravity, the West and the Soviets. That has since devolved into today's "multipolar" world. Pick your pole: The United States is still a superpower by any sense of the word, with enough allies that it could count as a pole. Russia might be one. China? Sure. But count in the uniting European countries and a plethora of other regional, economic, or religious alliances, and you see why it's a tough time for those who grew up with just one opposing power center to worry about.

That becomes of especial concern when so many states have, or are pursuing, *weapons of mass destruction*. India and Pakistan have tested nuclear weapons, and Israel is widely believed to have them. Despite setbacks in its program, Iraq is probably trying to build one. And who knows what the Dallas Cowboys would do if they got one, too.

Fighting Words

In its simplest form, a **weapon of mass destruction** is any weapon that you don't aim at one person, but which kills indiscriminately within the range of its effects. Usually used to refer to nuclear, biological, or chemical weapons. Nuclear weapons use energy released by fission and/or fusion to destroy property and kill people. Chemical weapons, like nerve gas, kill by causing some part of the body to not function. Biological weapons can include viruses and natural poisons like anthrax spores, concentrated into lethal doses. You don't want to take a brief on some of the world's biological weapons too soon after lunch.

Still, the sequence of talks that began in 1969 with SALT has brought some maturity and a bit more security to the nuclear age. Unfortunately, a lot more folks have come to the party.

The Least You Need to Know

◆ Nuclear deterrence is as much a matter of your adversary's perceptions as actual military might.

◆ The triad of bombers, missiles, and submarines was created to deny the opponent a chance at a successful first strike.

◆ The United States still has protected command and control sites to survive a first strike.

◆ Strategic arms control has made erratic but steady progress in reducing the major powers' arsenals.

Chapter 13

Spear It in the Sky: Missile Defense

In This Chapter

◆ Why missile defense is such a big deal

◆ A different way of thinking about stability

◆ Hitting a bullet with a bullet—or a laser

◆ How to defeat missile defenses

Each of the military services has received its own chapter in this book, because each contributes to defense in a very different way, each has a large independent budget, and each has its own ideas about how the military should fight (and the best color uniform to do it in).

Recently, though, another part of the Pentagon has become almost a separate service in its own right, with a distinct mission, approach, and sizable funding stream. While it's called the Missile Defense Agency (MDA), its size and scope go far beyond the other agencies we've already talked about. And the controversial nature of its mission means that MDA will continue to be more prominent than other defense agencies for a long time to come.

Ask the average American whether we have defenses against incoming missiles, and the answer will usually be either "yes" or "why are you calling me at this hour?" The correct answer is no. That's why, with the brief exception of the Safeguard system (see Chapter 12), the United States has relied on the threat of retaliation to keep enemies from launching missiles at our country.

In 1983, someone had a different idea.

President at the Creation

In March of 1983, President Ronald Reagan gave a speech outlining a world in which nuclear weapons would be largely rendered obsolete. (And he hadn't even read Chapter 12 at the time!) He envisioned a "Strategic Defense Initiative," or SDI, an attempt to render the strategic nuclear threat ineffective by building defenses that could stop incoming missiles.

The ostensible purpose of SDI was to get away from relying on an enemy's perceptions to deter attacks. After all, what if an irrational enemy possessed strategic missiles? Would they be deterred by the threat of U.S. retaliation? Or what about an enemy who had no fear of death, or some independent entity with no country to retaliate against? (We'll discuss these and more unconventional scenarios in Chapter 21, so stay tuned.)

SDI proposed to go beyond deterrence, to shield America regardless of the identity of her attacker, by defeating incoming missiles if deterrence failed. In such a "defense dominant" world, officials hoped, countries might compete to see which could build the best defenses, which would appear to yield a much more stable planet than one where nations competed to build the greatest offensive power.

To be sure, SDI also played in the perception game. If an enemy believed America's defenses were effective, he or she would have no reason to launch an attack, because all the missiles would be intercepted by the defense. (After three interceptions, he would have to punt.) So the hope was that missile defenses would both enhance deterrence and serve as insurance if deterrence failed.

It wasn't a new debate. The question of how to balance offense versus defense goes at least to the days when knights had to decide how much armor would protect them without adding so much that they couldn't move around. (And think of the poor horse!) When a knight got better armor, his foe would buy a better lance. That's the classic spiral: Better defenses beget better offenses, which require better defenses, and so on until recess ends and everyone has to go in for Social Studies.

But because the subject was nuclear war, and because President Reagan's idea was so much more readily understandable than the old calculus of stability summarized in Mutually Assured Destruction (MAD) policies, his proposal received more attention and support than defense debates traditionally have.

Building Constituencies

After President Reagan's speech, the Department put together a team specifically dedicated to making the vision of SDI come true. In the beginning, it was called SDIO, the Strategic Defense Initiative Organization, and it got stuck in some fairly dank quarters of the Pentagon basement. (In fact, until SDIO moved in, many Pentagonites were unaware the building *had* a basement.) SDIO spiffed the basement up nice, although they didn't put in a pool table or dartboard like you would if you spiffed up your basement.

Not everyone bought into the idea of defense dominance. Some argued that human nature being what it is, missile defenses would lead to an unstable and unrestrained arms race, as countries sought to build enough missiles that they could overwhelm any shield. SDI, they prophesied, would be an especial goad to countries like China, with a small nuclear arsenal. Why? While missile defenses might not be able to cope with a massive raid from a Soviet Union, it would probably be easily robust enough to shut out a smaller player. That, opponents argued, would give minor nuclear powers incentive to become bigger ones. And those countries weren't bound by SALT or START to restrain their arsenals.

At the same time, critics argued that declaring a long-term program like SDI gave existing nuclear powers (which really meant the Soviet Union, as neither Canada nor Alabama had long-range missiles at the time) motive to strike soon, lest their missile arsenals be made impotent. And there was a small matter of the cost. Development of a missile shield would push the cutting edge of technology for decades to come, and that's not cheap. Worst of all, opponents said, there were just too many ways to render that investment irrelevant. (We'll look at some of those later in this chapter.)

Ch-ch-chain of Kill

A missile intercept begins with warning. (We discussed indications and warning in Chapter 12. It's good, you should read it! Love, Mom.) In many cases, intelligence or other sources may indicate that someone is getting ready to fire a missile. (Unfortunately, it rarely takes the form of "Now, Mr. Bond, I will prepare to fire my missile.")

Obviously, we would dedicate a tremendous amount of sensor assets to that indication, unless it's a complete surprise. Most scenarios involving a missile attack on the United States presuppose that it arises out of some other international tension, during which we'd probably be watching the other guys anyway.

Whether you have warning or not, the next step is to *detect* the launch. Rocket launches are fairly cataclysmic events, as anyone who has been chased around the backyard by an Estes model WAC Corporal with a B motor can tell you. That should make them easy to detect. It isn't quite that simple.

> ### Fighting Words
>
> **Bolt from the blue**   An unexpected, unwarned attack. The phrase refers to a lightning strike. This is obviously the most challenging (in Pentagonese, *stressing*) scenario for an attack. Fear of a Soviet bolt from the blue is why, for much of the Cold War, bombers were on constant alert and Looking Glass was in the air 24/7.

Right now, a constellation of satellites called DSP is orbiting the earth. They were launched using the name Defense Support Program because at the time, nobody was supposed to know what they were, and the name "Rocket Launch Detection Satellite" was considered a tad unsubtle. Using infra-red sensors, DSP looks for unusual amounts of heat concentrated in a small area, like oh, I don't know, a rocket launch, maybe?

Because the DSP satellites look for heat, they pick up some interesting phenomena that aren't related to rockets, like oil well fires, gas-pipeline explosions, and other hot disasters. All of these are checked out just to make sure that the disaster in question isn't the one we're looking for.

Those other phenomena, plus weather and possible deliberate decoys or obscuration mean that launch detection isn't automatic. It's a *man-in-the-loop process*, with the individual in question sitting at a console inside Cheyenne Mountain.

> ### Fighting Words
>
> **Man-in-the-loop**   Not automatic, but requiring a real human to make a real decision. The loop in question is our old friend the OODA loop; while machines can observe, orient, and act, some decisions have to be left to people. Decisions to start wars are, so far, man-in-the-loop, which may disappoint fans of the movie *War Games*.

Once a launch is detected, the next step is cuing other sensors, literally saying, "Hey! Lookit what I found!" Systems that detect launches, like DSP, tend to use a single phenomenology—that is, they know how to do a job one way. In DSP's case, that's infrared. But that single sensor can't answer the most important questions: What just got launched, and where is it going? If it's just a weather rocket or a really big tiki torch, we don't want to shoot at it. Similarly, if it is an ICBM but headed out to a test range in the middle of the ocean, it's not worth knocking down.

Why do humans have two eyes? You and we know that it's because otherwise, sunglasses would look really dorky. But the reason scientists like to give (and who invited them?) is that it gives us depth perception. One eye can't measure how far away something is. By combining information from both eyes, especially the angle each eye has to turn to see the item, we can figure out distance and the direction of motion.

So it helps a lot to have a second sensor looking at whatever got launched, to determine where the object is headed. That's why the first sensor cues others.

Today, some of those other sensors are ground-based radars, like the BMEWS we talked about in Chapter 12. And MDA is hard at work on the next generation. Their sensor suite includes upgrades to existing early warning radars, new radars using a wavelength called "X-band," and two new satellite systems, SBIRS-Low and SBIRS-High.

SBIRS stands for the Space Based Infra Red System, and you pronounce it "sibbers." SBIRS-High will be like DSP, continuously staring at the world, never blinking, like a cop on stakeout but without the Krispy Kremes. SBIRS-Low is the alert sidekick, with a more agile sensor to accomplish the "Hey! Look over here!" functions.

Because of SBIRS' sensitivity and the characteristics of X-band radar, these systems will (it is hoped) be able to do much more *discrimination* and *characterization* of the incoming objects, the "what is it?" jobs. The goal is to pick out the warheads from a cloud of debris or decoys so the system doesn't waste shots on loose launcher parts or tuna cans tossed out of the space shuttle.

Detection, cuing, and discrimination are all part of the *kill chain*, the series of steps required before actually blowing something up. Break any link of the chain, and you don't get a kill. (Of course, with *redundant* systems, breaking the chain isn't that easy.) That brings us to the last and most pyrotechnically gratifying step: Something goes boom.

When the human in the loop decides it's time to shoot, MDA divides the missile defense system into three segments, boost, midcourse, and terminal.

Fighting Words

Redundant Duplicated, but in a good way. (Not like "Wilson, the company's decided you're redundant.") Redundant systems have more than one way to get a job done, so if one fails or is knocked out, the system should still work. Military aircraft have redundant control systems, for example, so if one fails, you can still land wheel-side down.

The last thing a missile interceptor sees when it does its job right.

(DoD photo)

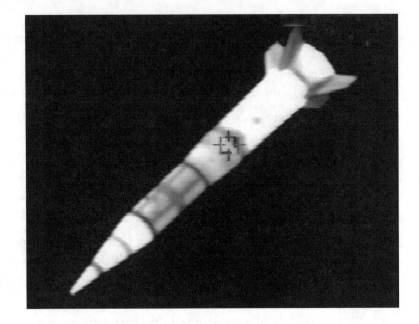

Hot Launch

Boost phase is oriented at hitting missiles during the first couple of minutes of flight. Remember the discussion of MIRVs from Chapter 12? You can have a number of warheads on a single missile. Hit the missile before they separate, and you have a much easier job.

During boost phase, the missile's engine is lit, which makes it easier to find. Also, the aerodynamic stress on the missile makes it easier to kill, as a relatively small hit will cause a catastrophic failure. (Remember, the destruction of the space shuttle *Challenger* came from one small leak in a gasket. Put a hole in an ICBM's fuel tank, or even elsewhere on its skin, and the missile isn't going to live long.)

Along the same lines, one of the perceived merits of boost-phase kill is that the weapons blow up over whoever's shooting them at you, which seems to fit any decent definition of justice.

What's in the Boost Phase Toolkit?

Missiles are under consideration as boost-phase weapons. They are most likely to be placed on ships, with the idea that the ship could linger off a potential enemy's coast, ready to respond if the enemy fires a ballistic missile.

The Need for Speed and Other Problems

Many missile defense systems envision shooting down an enemy missile with one of our missiles. In boost phase, that is a particularly tough problem.

We probably won't know when a missile is about to be launched at us (if we did, we might be able to do something about it), so the enemy missile is bound to have a head start. Whatever we shoot at it has to be fast enough that even after we detect the launch, pass the word to whomever has the authority to say "shoot!" get that authorization to the right ship or plane carrying our weapon, and actually fire, it can still catch up to the ballistic missile. That's not so easy.

Pentagon Parables
The need for speed in missile defense is part of why the G.W. Bush administration decided to withdraw from the ABM Treaty. The treaty was intended to prohibit strategic defenses but allow tactical ones. The United States and Soviet Union made the distinction by prohibiting testing defensive missiles that went above a certain speed. Once the United States decided to go ahead with a boost-phase missile defense, the speed limit had to go.

Of course, if only we could invent a weapon that travels at the speed of light, there might be a better chance for boost-phase systems to work. And no sooner do you read it than your wish comes true!

Welcome to the Future

That's a second boost-phase system, the *Airborne Laser* (ABL), a big ray gun. Whether you like missile defense or not, ABL is clearly a step into the future, in which *directed energy* weapons can take the place of bullets and bombs.

The ABL will be a giant laser inside a Boeing 747. A rotating mirror is mounted on the plane's nose to point the laser beam at the target.

If you think about that for a minute, you can see that if ABL works, it will be quite a feat. It's hard enough to keep your drink from sloshing on an airliner, and here MDA proposes to be able to keep a laser beam from an airplane fixed on a precise point many miles away (the number of miles is classified, but it's farther than you could throw your inflight meal, although not as far as you might want

Fighting Words

Directed energy Ray guns. Any weapon that hits the target with a beam of light or other energy rather than a solid object like a missile or bullet. They're finally here.

to throw it). At the same time, remember that the atmosphere is full of clouds and vapors and pollutants, but the beam has to remain focused and coherent. Just like a bright flashlight looks dim from far away, laser power diminishes as a square of the distance to the target. And there needs to be some mechanism to tell the laser controller where the laser's hitting and how much power is making it to the target.

Put all of that challenge together, and you can see why laser physicists whistle on their way to work; the day is full of interesting problems.

Perhaps the biggest challenge for ABL, though, is that in order to work, it has to be near the launch site, which is probably not a friendly area, especially when you're flying something as big and easy to target as a 747. Then again, would you want to be the fighter pilot told to go shoot down this plane with a giant laser in its nose?

That's another facet of ABL that makes it a weapon of the future. Who's to say that it will only be used to shoot at missiles? What points up can also point down, as the saying sort of goes.

The first test of a low-power ABL is scheduled for 2004.

A third system is even farther in the future. The *Space-Based Laser* (SBL) would be a bunch of lasers constantly in orbit around the earth, so we wouldn't have the problem of whether the ship or the ABL was in the right place at the right time.

Of course, SBL is a major technical challenge. And it isn't likely to be popular with other countries; how would we feel if the Chinese had powerful lasers orbiting over our country 24/7? But one of the SBL's greatest appeals is that it could shoot at incoming weapons both in the boost-phase and the midcourse. (Midcourse, which is discussed in more detail in the next section, is the middle portion of the missile's flight.)

A blast from the past, *Space-based Kinetic* defense could also serve as both boost-phase and midcourse phase defense. In the early days of SDI, the system architecture included "smart rocks," small interceptors in space that had enough intelligence to detect and get in the way of warheads. They didn't have explosives, but would destroy the warheads by running into them, using the kinetic energy of the collision to damage the warheads or throw them off course. (Think of a Honda running into a deer, and you have an idea of kinetic kill. Neither comes out very well, although you can't then dress the Honda and put it in your freezer.)

Fighting Words

Architecture The overall design of a system, including how the components work together and share tasks.

Smart rocks were supplanted by a smaller, smarter variety called "brilliant pebbles," and as technology advanced, scientists began to toy with "genius gravel." (We are not making this up. Scientists are just naturally zany people.) Those space-based concepts eventually gave way to a simpler, ground- and sea-based architecture. But in 2002, MDA revived the space-based kinetic program, although it is in the early stages of design.

The Middle of the Action

The *midcourse phase* is the easiest period for a defense system to act. That's the long period after the engine has shut off and the *bus* and warheads are floating through space. They have only a limited ability to maneuver, so their path is fairly predictable.

In addition to the space-based ideas we just talked about, two other systems take advantage of that long coast period of the midcourse phase of flight.

Ground-Based midcourse defense (GBMD) is the most familiar part of the BMD system. The tests you've seen on TV, whether successful or not, were probably of the ground-based system. A test site for ground-based midcourse, which will eventually turn into a 100-missile deployment, is expected to be built at Fort Greeley, Alaska, starting in the summer of 2002.

Fighting Words

Bus   The upper portion of a MIRVed missile that the warheads ride on while waiting to be released to go to their individual targets.

The decision to situate the ground-based midcourse at Fort Greeley was not a simple one. The missile defense system is tasked to defend all 50 U.S. states. While the Alaska location makes the most sense to defend against missiles coming from North Korea or China, it's a tougher job against shots from, say, the Middle East. DoD also considered putting GBMD near the old Safeguard site in North Dakota, but ultimately decided it would have an easier time defending the East from Alaska than the other way around.

Also, because much of the live BMD testing takes place over the Pacific (typically shooting a simulated threat from Vandenberg AFB in California and an interceptor from the Reagan Test Site on Kwajalein Atoll), the Alaska location meant that the GBMD site could be an integral part of testing.

There are also sea-based midcourse defense systems; as with Airborne Lasers, the trick is to have your ship in the place it needs to be when it needs to be there.

Getting It in the End

Anything that gets past the boost and midcourse phases moves into what MDA calls the terminal phase. This is what started out as tactical missile defense, the systems that defend small areas, or "point targets."

Neither the Navy nor the Air Force has terminal programs at this time (the Navy had one in the works, but it was cancelled). We suppose one could try to use the Airborne Laser in a terminal mode, but trying to lase a streaking warhead coming downhill is almost impossibly different from rupturing a lumbering rocket going up. So the bulk of terminal defense falls to the Army.

> **Basic Training**
>
> While missile defense programs are deployed and operated by the services, the bulk of their development is funded by MDA. So when we say "an Army missile defense program," it means one where the missiles are painted green and operated by soldiers, but the bulk of the R&D funding may not have been Army money. The dollars are still green, though.

The most common terminal phase program is the *Patriot PAC-3*. PAC stands for Patriot Advanced Capability. The Army's Patriot missile was originally designed to shoot down attacking aircraft. A modification called PAC-2 gave it some antimissile capability; that's what was used with middling success in the Gulf War to protect Allied bases and Israeli cities from Iraq's "SCUD" missiles. PAC-3 is optimized for the antimissile role.

> **Basic Training**
>
> Why do Russian missiles (of which the SCUD is one) have such silly names? Do they really think we'll be scared by FROGFOOT fighters or BACKFIRE bombers?
>
> The reason is that the Russians don't get to decide what their systems are called in the West. The names are assigned by NATO, with a simple code (names starting with F are fighters, B bombers, and so on). This began in the days when we didn't know what Russian systems were really called, or to hide the fact that we did.

THAAD, the Theater High Altitude Area Defense, operates at the edge of space. Like Patriot, it is made up of mobile launchers and radar. Unlike PAC-3, it intercepts high enough that if you miss, you still have time to fire another THAAD or a PAC-3 at the same target. (That gets us into firing doctrine, which we'll explain better a couple of pages from now.)

Arrow is an Israeli midcourse program that the United States puts a lot of money into. Its capability is similar to THAAD. The Arrow system is already operational in Israel, although there's no plan for the United States to buy any.

MEADS (say "me-adds," as in "me adds money to budget for missile"), the Medium Extended Air Defense System, is a U.S.-German cooperative development. Italy was in there for a while, may still be, maybe not, depending on what day of the week it is. However, every year the DoD says "MEADS is ready for deployment" and puts it in the Army budget, while Congress says "No it isn't" and puts it back in the MDA budget for further development.

Except for the lasers, all of these systems are "hit to kill." That means they don't just explode near the target, they run right into it. That's what you'll hear described as "hitting a bullet with a bullet."

> **Fighting Words**
>
> **Fire control** This can be a confusing phrase. On board ship, the fire control party are the guys with hoses who try to put out fires. In the missile world, fire control is the system that helps you target and launch a missile. Some Navy ships have both.

Having the speed that helps in boost phase makes terminal defenses work better, too. A faster defensive missile gets to its target sooner, meaning that the interception takes place higher in the sky. That way, the debris of the interception doesn't fall on the people you were trying to defend—and neither do any chemical or biological agents that may have been in the warheads.

The best part about all these terminal systems is that they're mobile. They can go with the troops to protect them, or be deployed to a threatened area to guard targets, as when Patriots were sent to defend Israeli cities during the Persian Gulf War.

That's the system. Now, let's break it.

How Do You Beat a Missile Shield?

There are at least five theoretical ways to defeat even a good missile defense.

1. Overwhelm it.

2. Underfly it.

3. Outfox it.

4. Incapacitate it.

5. Ignore it.

I. Overwhelm It

You're standing at one end of a tennis court with a racket. The ball machine is shooting balls at you, and you can hit them back pretty easily.

Then somebody puts a second ball machine out there. You start working a lot harder, but you can probably keep up—as long as the two machines take turns firing. But add a third ball machine and a fourth, or start them shooting balls simultaneously, and pretty soon a lot of balls are whanging off the fence behind you. Your capacity to respond is finite.

So, too, is the capacity of a missile defense (or really any) system. The most obvious way to beat a defensive system is to send it more targets than it can handle.

If you're designing a missile defense system, you always want to have more defensive missiles than incoming targets. That way, you can fire more than one at each target, increasing the Pk against each incoming warhead. To continue with our example, your chances of hitting the tennis ball back are greater with two players per ball machine than one.

Fighting Words

Pk The capital P stands for "probability"; the small k for "kill." The probability of kill for any weapon system—the chance that it will destroy the target with a single shot—is determined by repeated testing against the sorts of targets it would be used against in combat. Pks of weapon systems are among the more closely guarded secrets in the Pentagon.

As a tennis player can keep hitting balls back only until his Gatorade runs out, so a missile defense system only has a limited number of assets. For example, the initial deployment planned for the ground-based portion of the current missile defense program includes 100 interceptor missiles. What happens if there are 101 warheads coming in?

In fact, that's an even more complicated problem than it seems, because when someone shoots a missile at you, you don't really know how many more may be coming. So you have to make sure you don't fire all your defensive missiles at the first incoming warhead and leave none for the second.

If you have a limited number of interceptor missiles, you can increase your chances of a successful interception by changing your firing doctrine, the rules you use to decide how to shoot. For example, you could decide in advance to shoot two of your missiles at each target coming in. This is called a salvo, just as when a ship fires all its artillery at once.

If you have time—which is to say that the incoming missile is coming from a long distance away—you can use the "shoot-look-shoot" doctrine, which is just what it sounds like. You take a shot, see if you killed the target, and if not, shoot again. That way, instead of sending two interceptors against a particular target, you might be able to destroy it with one and save the second for a later target.

But no firing doctrine will help if someone shoots 101 missiles against 100 interceptors, which is a strong reason behind continuing to limit arms through negotiation. It's no coincidence that after President G.W. Bush declared his intention to withdraw from the ABM Treaty and build a missile shield, he negotiated a new arms reduction treaty with Russia. One way to make sure your missile defense can work is to reduce the number of targets it might face, and even though U.S.-Russian relations have changed radically for the better in the last ten years, Russia still has a formidable strategic arsenal.

Basic Training

It may not be surprising to learn that the word "kill" is used fairly freely in the Pentagon. It is interchangeable with "destroy," so you can "kill" buildings, bridges, trucks, and warheads even though their sentience remains indeterminate, except for the talking car in *Knight Rider*.

2. Underfly It

In order to shoot down an incoming warhead, you have to spot the incoming missile, identify it as such, pass the information to the right place, tell an interceptor where to fire, and actually hit it. This takes a long time, by which we mean a matter of minutes, which is a long time when a weapon of mass destruction is headed toward your country, and quite possibly your base. Fortunately, the world is a big enough place that we have that time; a typical ballistic missile would take more than 20 minutes to travel from Russia to the United States.

You can cut that time by not launching a missile from your homeland so far away. That was part of the idea behind SLBMs, the submarine-launched ballistic missiles you read about in Chapter 12. While they start out closer to the target, though, that doesn't cut the flight time as much as you think.

Fighting Words

The period required from detection of a target to firing on it, whether in missile defense, artillery, or torpedoes, is called the "sensor to shooter" time.

Consider Barry Bonds hitting a home run. Now imagine him hitting a pop fly. The home run goes a lot farther, but usually in a much flatter arc. He hits the ball just as hard for the pop fly, and the same amount of energy might go into the ball. To go a shorter distance while using roughly the same energy, the pop has to travel in a much higher arc. So it can be in the air just as long as that home run ball, and may go even higher.

That's how typical submarine-launched ballistic missiles travel. They start out closer to the target, but still follow a high ballistic arc. While that doesn't give the defensive system quite as much time to react as an ICBM coming from the other side of the world, it's still more time than needed.

But ballistic physics aren't a secret from anyone, especially if you had Professor Romer for PHYS 103. So an enterprising attacker could use a "depressed-trajectory" SLBM. By using less initial energy, and incorporating fancy guidance, it's possible for a missile to fly a much flatter arc. To use the baseball simile, the ball still gets to the shortstop, just more like a sharp liner than a pop fly. That *flight profile* would give a defensive system much less time to react—effectively, it gets inside the defense's OODA loop, which you'll remember from Chapter 3 (and will probably remember even if you forget everything else in this book, just because it's so much fun to say. OODA loop! OODA loop!).

Fighting Words

Flight profile The speed, direction, and altitude of a particular missile or aircraft. You can draw a line showing the missile's altitude throughout its flight and another its path over the ground. Add markings for time and speed, and you have your own personal flight profile, always an impressive resume item.

Depressed-trajectory SLBMs are harder to detect and react to than traditional SLBMs. But cruise missiles are harder yet.

Cruise missiles, like the American Tomahawk, resemble small airplanes. They can be as precise as any ballistic missile. Their name comes from the fact that they can "cruise" along for a long period, and don't have to follow a ballistic arc. Cruise missiles can be launched from ships, airplanes, submarines, or the ground, and can carry conventional warheads or weapons of mass destruction.

Because cruise missiles don't have the huge heat plumes that ballistic missiles do, and because they fly low and slow, they are harder for sensors to find. Also, ballistic missile defenses are designed to shoot down things that are coming down, high and fast, rather than coming across, low and slow. So cruise missiles are hard for a system designed against ballistic missiles to kill. They are the best way for an enemy to underfly a missile defense system.

3. Outfox It

The goal of a ballistic missile defense system is to destroy *missiles or warheads*. The enemy knows that. Even without buying this book, he knows about lasers and defensive missiles and sensors.

That's why a smart enemy (and that's not always an oxymoron) will take countermeasures. Want to beat a sensor system? Hide your warhead in a cloud of chaff, or a big balloon that doesn't look like a warhead. Not everything on the bus has to be a warhead; some can be decoys, that look and act like a warhead but don't have a weapon inside. Deploy enough of those, and you might get the defender to use up his 100 missiles on your decoys. Worried about lasers? Simoniz the rocket—literally, polish it so it will reflect laser light. Or make it spin so that the laser can't keeping shining on the same spot.

The best thing about these and other ruses is that they aren't mutually exclusive. Just as we can have a defense in all phases of the rocket's flight, they can have a polished missile that carries decoys, hides the warheads in balloons, spins, and plays "Jingle Bells."

Of course, we have counter-countermeasures. And they have counter-counter-cou … well, never mind, or this paragraph will never end.

Fighting Words

Missiles/warheads
The **missile** is the whole system, including the engines, fuel tanks, and everything. Most of that gets dropped off along the way, leaving only the **warhead,** the part that goes bang.

4. Incapacitate It

The kill chain for missile defense is vulnerable in many places. Break it and even if there's a redundant capability somewhere, you'll improve your chances of getting through.

Each of the major pieces of the BMD kill chain can be broken. Space sensors are in some ways the most vulnerable. They are in predictable places, which makes them comparatively easy targets for an anti-satellite weapon. Satellites can also be blinded. Communications can be jammed. Ground stations and big radars are subject to attack by conventional means or special forces. An enemy could detonate one of the warheads in space, overloading missile defense sensors with light, heat, and infrared energy, and creating an electromagnetic pulse to fry sensor electronics. The tremendous release of radio frequency emissions could also interfere with ground radars. And some scientists theorize that a nuclear explosion in space would create a condition, similar to aurora borealis, where the upper atmosphere would become electrically charged, forming a wall to radars.

Of course, these countermeasures aren't without risk on the attacker's side. Setting off a nuclear blast in space could do more harm to their warheads and missile guidance systems than to the defense. So it might not be a great idea, but it's one the attacker would have to weigh.

Here's a question for you: Suppose we detect a coordinated attack on American sensor satellites. If we let it ride, an enemy could blind us, letting him attack without even enough notice to try to defend against incoming missiles. We could lose part of our nuclear arsenal unless we launch it right now—it's a use or lose situation. But should we start a war, much less a nuclear one, over a few satellites being incapacitated? Aren't you glad you have a Pentagon and an Assistant Secretary for Policy to help figure these things out so you don't have to?

5. Ignore it

A common fallacy of debaters on both sides of the missile defense debate is to speak of the system as if it is a protection against nuclear weapons. It isn't. It's a protection against missiles. Who says a nuclear warhead has to arrive by missile?

In the '50s and '60s, the United States had strong air defenses against incoming bombers. Those defenses aren't what they once were, because the bomber threat isn't what it used to be, either. Why? Our defenses had gotten so good that it wasn't really worth an opponent's time trying to get through them when there were other ways to deliver the warhead.

Pentagon Parables

The Soviet Union didn't do badly at air defense, either. (We'll give them a mulligan on the German kid who flew a Cessna to Red Square.) But America switched up on them. In the early 1960s, the United States seemed ready to deploy the high-altitude B-70 bomber. The Soviets then spent a tremendous amount of money to optimize their air defenses against just that threat. In the meantime, the administration canceled the B-70, and the next bomber, the B-1, was designed to operate at very low altitudes.

Air and missile defenses are built to stop another military, someone who has bombers and missiles. Yet there are ways of delivering weapons of mass destruction other than a missile. After all, nuclear devices, while heavy for their size, aren't that big.

We already talked about cruise missiles. But you can put a nuclear device on a ship, and sail it into a port. Put it in a small airplane, and fly it almost anywhere in the country. Put it in a van, and drive it downtown. Anywhere you can take a keg of beer, you can take a nuke.

From the defensive perspective, that's a nightmare. But looking at it as someone who wants to beat a missile defense system, it's ideal.

Quick Quiz

Which of the following is not a good way to beat a missile defense system?

❑ Overwhelm it.

❑ Underfly it.

❑ Outfox it.

❑ Incapacitate it.

❑ Ignore it.

❑ Pants it and give it a Dutch rub.

The Least You Need to Know

◆ President Reagan proposed a national missile defense system in 1983.

◆ "Defense dominance" was an entirely different way of thinking about the strategic balance.

◆ Missile defense is not the same as defense against weapons of mass destruction.

◆ There are many ways to try to evade missile defenses.

Part 4

The Forces: Zoomies, Jarheads, Swabbies, and Grunts

The Pentagon may be a hive of thinkers, of planners, and budgeteers, but all that cogitation isn't going to deter an enemy. It has to be turned into action or at least the threat of action.

The people who turn plans into action are the men and women, volunteers all, who wear the uniforms of the United States. They are the tip of the spear. Come see how the history, traditions, and way of thinking of each military service affects how it operates, and how they sharpen that spear.

Chapter 14

An Army of 1.3 Million

In This Chapter

- ◆ Playing with transformers
- ◆ The division of divisions
- ◆ This was the Army
- ◆ The future is green

The oldest of America's military services, the U.S. Army is trying to think young.

For decades, American military planning focused on one scenario: how to defend against a massive Soviet invasion of Europe. The specter of thousands of tanks coming west through the Fulda Gap in Germany drove many major hardware decisions.

Those decisions had the greatest effect on the Army. They bought the most advanced tanks in the world. Their helicopters were designed to kill other tanks. And they structured their units for a short-notice war on friendly territory in an environment with robust logistics chains back to the United States. And that all worked, to the extent that the Soviet tanks never rolled.

Today's Army is simultaneously trying to figure out how to keep that strength and move to a force more relevant in a world where the location of the next conflict is harder to forecast (who knew before September 11 that we'd be fighting in Afghanistan?) and the prospect of a mass tank battle is much less likely. In a very real sense, the Army was unprepared for victory in the Cold War.

Fortunately, the Army has a plan for how to migrate from today's force—which they call the "legacy" force—through an "interim" force to their goal, the "objective" force. This is "Army Transformation." We'll keep you hanging until later in the chapter for a description.

Commanders and Commands

The Army is run by a Chief of Staff. Below him, imagine the same structure as the Joint Chiefs (which, after all, got it from the Army), with sections for personnel, intelligence, operations, and so on. The three-stars in charge of those functions for the Army are called Deputy Chiefs of Staff. The abbreviation DCS gets pronounced "dess," though, so the DCSOPS is the "dessops," DCSPER "dessper," and so on.

Outside the Pentagon, the Army is organized into major commands. Like the CINC structure, some are functional and some are geographic. Forces Command (FORSCOM), at Fort McPherson, Georgia, is in charge of the units and soldiers. Army Materiel Command, near the Pentagon, handles buying stuff. U.S. Army Europe (USAREUR, or "USE-ar-your"), in Germany, runs the forward forces; 8th U.S. Army does the same for Korea.

TRADOC, Training and Doctrine Command, develops tactics and measures readiness from its home at Fort Monroe, near Norfolk, Virginia. And while you've probably heard of the Army Corps of Engineers, you should know that they don't just build dams and water projects. Sometimes they do work for the Army, too, as we'll see in just a little bit.

On the fighting end, FORSCOM's part of the Army is structured into 12 combat *divisions*, each made up of *brigades*. By varying the composition of those brigades, divisions are tailored to a specific function.

> **Basic Training**
>
> The 12 combat divisions are numbered 1, 1, 1, 2, 3, 4, 7, 10, 24, 25, 82, and 101. The odd numbering system can in part be explained by the Army's interest in heraldry and history. When changes in force structure mean *standing down, or closing,* a unit, they give the unit's number and its history to a less-storied one. So one day, you could be in the 6th, and the next day, without changing beds, you could be in the 234th.

For example, There are seven *infantry divisions*, or IDs, the 1st, 2nd, 3rd, 4th, 7th, 24th, and 25th. While most infantry divisions are similar in size—around 14,000 soldiers—they are by no means alike.

The 1st and 2nd IDs are straightforward infantry divisions, with four brigades of infantry and armor and one aviation brigade, which is to say helicopters. 1st ID is known as The Big Red One for its insignia (a big red 1). It's headquartered in Wurzburg, Germany; the 2nd, at Camp Red Cloud, South Korea.

3rd ID, called the "Rock of the Marne" for their achievements in the First World War, is a *mechanized* infantry division, meaning that the troops bring more tanks and helicopters along. They live and play at Fort Stewart, Georgia.

4th Infantry is armor-heavy, and has an aviation brigade. It also has the first *digitized brigade* in the Army. Digitization means that the entire unit is wired up electronically, with displays inside the tanks and headquarters for the Army Battle Command System and FBCB2 ("eff-bee-see-bee-squared"). Those systems show a tank commander where his friends and foes are, along with topographical and other information continuously, in real time. That helps cut down on *fratricide* and helps the tank commander make better decisions. It also means the brigade commander knows where all his units are, giving an eagle's-eye view of the battlefield not possible before.

7th ID, the "Bayonets" out of Fort Carson, Colorado, and 24th ID at Fort Riley, Kansas are *division minuses*, which means that one or more of their brigades has to come from the reserve component. Because of this, the total number of soldiers in the 12 divisions equal 10 fully-manned active duty divisions. 24th ID is also a mechanized brigade like 3rd ID.

> **Fighting Words**
>
> **HOO-ah!**   An all-purpose Army cheer, hoo-ah is also a common interjection in Army speech. It's formally "HUA," standing for Heard, Understood, Acting. So when a commander is discussing plans, subordinates will mutter "hoo-ah" when we might say "yup" or "okay." It also means spirited, as in "Specialist Jones has a lot of hoo-ah."

> **Fighting Words**
>
> **Fratricide**   Shooting at someone from your own team. This has been a problem since the beginning of war. As you can imagine, with longer-range weapons and fast-moving aircraft, identifying whether a target way out there or down there is yours becomes especially tricky. Also called *friendly fire* or *blue-on-blue*, from war games where the good guys are always blue and the bad guys are always red.

> ### Pentagon Parables
>
> Early in 2001, the Army held an exercise at the National Training Center pitting the 4th ID's digitized brigade against the nearly invincible OPFOR. With its view of the battlefield, the 4th kicked the OPFOR up one side of the engagement box and down the other.

25th ID, like 10th Mountain, is a light brigade. You might not mind being assigned to it, as the 25th operates from Schofield Barracks in Hawaii. One brigade, though, lives at Fort Lewis, Washington. So pack carefully.

You'll rarely hear anyone refer to "the 1st Cavalry Division." It's 1st Cav, and it's all about tanks. Well, there are 17,000 soldiers, but all units have soldiers. Not all have three brigades of armor (tanks and other heavy fighting vehicles), plus one aviation, as these do. You'll find them at Fort Hood, Texas, when they're not out driving around.

As you can see from the name of 1st Cav, the Army gave up horses hard. In a similar nod to history, attack helicopter units are "Air Cavalry."

Perhaps the units best known to the public are the *airborne divisions*, the 82nd at Fort Bragg, North Carolina, and 101st, the "Screaming Eagles," at Fort Campbell, Kentucky. Airborne means that the division's personnel—down to the last cook—are parachute-qualified, so they get on a plane in the United States, travel to a war zone, jump out, and start fighting as soon as their boots touch the ground. (Their luggage will go to Denver. *Everyone's* luggage goes to Denver.)

> ### Basic Training
>
> All of these divisions have engineer brigades, which build things like bridges and shelters or blow them up, as needed. They work for the Corps of engineers, with a castle patch on their sleeves and filled with the spirit of the engineer motto, *"Essayons!"* ("Let us try!"). Why they have a French motto, *nous ne savons pas.*

The 101st is designated as an air assault specialist, which means that the division is helicopter-heavy, with two aviation brigades to accompany its three brigades of infantry.

1st Armored, headquartered at Wiesbaden, Germany, is also about tanks. The difference is that it has fewer tanks and more troop carriers than 1st Cav.

The 10th *Mountain Division* started as Alpine troops in the Second World War. The 10th is a light division, both in terms of its equipment and the number of troops, with two brigades of infantry instead of three. That lightness means the 10th is often the first to be dispatched to contingencies. The 10th is headquartered at Fort Drum, in upstate New York.

Each Army officer belongs to a *branch*, which is like pledging a fraternity but the rooms aren't as good. The branches are organized by subject matter, and each has its own school. If you are an artillery officer, your mecca is Fort Sill, Oklahoma, home of the artillery school. Engineers and chemical officers look to Fort Leonard Wood, Missouri; the aviation branch to Fort Rucker, Alabama. MPs and signal officers are trained at Fort Gordon, Georgia. While you will be assigned to different units throughout your career, it's unusual for an officer to switch branches. Once an artilleryman, always an artilleryman.

Globally Engaged

The Army has a clear-cut mission: Fight and win the nation's wars. The Army has the responsibility of defending the United States and its territories, supporting national policies and objectives, and defeating nations responsible for aggression that endangers the peace and security of the United States.

The Army does all that with approximately 1.3 million people. This includes half a million active duty soldiers, another 350,000 in the Army National Guard, 200,000 in the Army Reserve, and approximately 225,000 Army civilians. On any given day, more than 140,000 Army personnel are "forward stationed," or deployed, which is to say ready to fight around the world.

"Nobody Ever Surrendered to an Airplane"

The Army believes that putting "boots on the ground" is the only way to win a war. While they acknowledge the contributions of those pesky other services, without soldiers, you can't take and hold territory, occupy buildings, enforce peace agreements, or rebuild a country.

It's also clear that committing soldiers on the ground is a different level of commitment for the United States than bombing or shelling. Having a carrier show up off the coast may worry an adversary, but having soldiers knocking on his boudoir door is rather more likely to get him to see your way of thinking.

The Army's tasks don't end with fighting and winning wars. It's also responsible for keeping war fighting organizations and tools ready for worldwide employment, which is military-speak for making sure the planes can fly, the tanks can drive, and the meals ready to eat are, well, ready to eat. (Two out of three ain't bad.) In addition, the Army is now involved in a variety of missions other than war, which we'll discuss in detail.

> **Basic Training**
>
> The Major Theater War measurement evolved into the Major Regional Contingency, and most recently to nothing at all. In the 2001 Quadrennial Defense Review, the Department decided to move away from basing requirements on scenarios like wars or contingencies in favor of "capabilities-based" planning, where what matters is how good our forces are regardless of where or how they are to be used.

I Want My MTW

MTW stands for *major theater war*. This doesn't mean that they're showing the same Tom Clancy flick at two 24-plexes within a 10-mile radius. Rather, a major theater is the big one, an all-out war involving a substantial commitment of forces, money, and time. Like the other services, the Army today is structured to fight and win two, nearly simultaneous, major theater wars at the same time.

The Army explains this as follows: the first MTW? No problem. The second one will require a little more effort, a little more money, and perhaps a little more time, but we can get that one done, too. Memo to international scalawags who think that they can pull a fast one while we're busy fighting an MTW somewhere else in the world: Think again. Signed, U.S. Army.

History of the U.S. Army

The U.S. Army came into existence on June 14, 1775, over a year before the Declaration of Independence was signed. The U.S. Army needed eight years to defeat the British in the War of Independence, and four years to defeat the South in the Civil War. The U.S. Army has defended the United States against external threats for two centuries, from the War of 1812 with Great Britain through World War II to the present day. The Army also serves the nation in natural disaster relief, economic assistance, providing domestic order, and many other missions.

Where's G.I. Joe ... and Jane?

Terrorism notwithstanding, the Army has an immense amount of business around the globe. They are busy all the time, and the sun never sets on the U.S. Army. Let's travel the world and see where the Army can be found.

First stop, the Balkans. The U.S. Army is part of two NATO forces, one helping keep peace as Bosnia recovers from civil war, the other helping Kosovo rebuild. These forces rotate in from different units, alleviating stress on any one division. For a time, the Bosnian part of the operation was handled by the Texas National Guard, the first time a Guard unit has taken command of a deployment, and showing the Army's *Total Force* policy in full effect. The candle still burns elsewhere in Europe, where the Army takes part in NATO training exercises involving forces from as many as 28 nations.

Fighting Words

Total Force   The Army likes to think of its reserves and Guard as part of the main force; in fact, active Army units are designed to include *reserve component* elements whenever they fight. They call this one-big-family approach the "total force," or Total Army.

Moving on to the Middle East, we find a continuous presence in the Persian Gulf region of an Army headquarters and a mechanized task force comprising of both ground assets and attack helicopters, Patriot missile units, and other supporting forces. This presence helps to keep the peace in this area and offers enhanced rapid response capability in the Middle East, while demonstrating U.S. commitment there. At the same time, these assets could be involved at a moment's notice in military operations, should there (Iraq) be any country in that area (Iraq) wanting to cause trouble (Iraq). Slightly further to the northwest, we find approximately 900 U.S. soldiers helping to monitor the peace treaty between Egypt and Israel.

On to the Korean peninsula, where you'll find 25,000 soldiers stationed in South Korea, a major force for regional stability in Asia. There is nothing like sending in the troops to show that you're serious, and our soldiers strengthen our position and the position of the Republic of Korea (South Korea) as it negotiates an end to the half-century-old standoff with its neighbor to the north.

On to Africa. Here you will find Army Special Operations Forces deployed in support of humanitarian de-mining operations. This includes training locals in mine awareness, which is to say helping them to recognize what a landmine looks like and where they are likely to be found. Special Operations Forces are also involved in clearing mines and providing emergency medical care.

Basic Training

You'll also find the U.S. Army in Japan, where the United States has maintained bases at Yokohama. Because unfortunate incidents involving American personnel (mostly not Army) and civilian Japanese young women have caused a rupture in U.S.-Japanese military relations, the presence of American soldiers in Japan is somewhat limited.

Crossing the southern Atlantic Ocean, we find the Army at work supporting the war on drugs in Latin America, the Caribbean, and the heroin trafficking region for southeast and southwest Asia. The Army is involved in Latin American countries such as Colombia through training of counter-drug battalions.

And let's not forget Haiti. Although the mission in Haiti in large part ended in 1996, the American military presence continues. Approximately 200 soldiers were performing security missions and providing medical and civil assistance projects in that beleaguered nation. In short, when a military presence is necessary—when it is time to show the U.S. flag, provide support for our allies, or be in a state of preparedness for whatever may come—the U.S. Army is on scene, around the world, around the clock.

The relationship of the U.S. Army with Latin American armies was enhanced for more than a half century by the presence of the U.S. Army School of the Americas, located at Fort Benning, Georgia. More than 60,000 military personnel and civilian leaders have experienced high quality professional military education ... in Spanish at Fort Benning. *¿Como están, y'all?*

The school closed to revise its curriculum after criticism that it trained repressive forces in numerous countries. A successor, the Western Hemisphere Institute for Security and Cooperation, opened in 2001.

Pentagon Parables

The Army, any general will tell you, is about soldiers. For decades, the Army wooed recruits with the idea that they could "Be All That You Can Be." In 2000, that approach changed, with ads inviting prospects to become "An Army of One." This went over very poorly with veterans and many already serving, since the Army thrives on teamwork, not individualism. However, the ads weren't trying to attract veterans or people already in the service. On the other hand, they did quite well with the target audience.

(Even the "Be All That You Can Be" approach changed over time. For a while, the head of Army Recruiting Command was a former artillery officer, who dictated that Army TV ads had to show somebody firing artillery.)

Coming Soon

Everything we told you in this chapter may be wrong. That is, because of the transformation effort mentioned earlier, the structure of the Army may change radically. We started off this chapter talking about transformation; let's end with how the Army intends to get there from here.

Transformation isn't just about changing hardware. It's about digitizing—as the 4th ID is demonstrating, that makes big changes in the way you fight. Transformation is about changing training, to better prepare soldiers for the missions they're actually likely to carry out in the twenty-first century. And transformation may—and we emphasize *may*—be about changing the division structures that have formed the Army for so long.

The Army is already changing the hardware. While the big M1 Abrams tank is still the star of the armor show, plans are underway for what's called the Future Combat System. As you can tell by the name, it's not just a new tank, but includes changes to training and operations. Part of FCS will require figuring out how the Army best gets its jobs done given today's technology. Can unmanned vehicles, on the ground or in the air, do things better than ones with soldiers inside? Should tanks fire lasers instead of shells? The answers will be part of FCS.

Between now and then, the Army is bringing forward some new ideas. One is the Interim Brigade Combat Team, or IBCT, something between an infantry brigade and an armored one, that's quickly mobile, but brings along armored troop carriers to give the soldiers some protection in the field. That required a new armored vehicle capable of being deployed anywhere in the world soldiers are, which meant it had to fit aboard a C-130 transport plane. The first IBCTs are being stood up as this book goes to press.

> **Pentagon Parables**
>
> In choosing a new armored vehicle, the Army found itself in a great debate between those who believe that real Army vehicles have tracks like tanks, and those who believed that tires mounted on regular round wheels offer better speed and adequate survivability. While the army chose a wheeled vehicle for its "interim force," the debate is far from over.

We started to write a whole section on the Crusader program. Then Secretary Rumsfeld announced that he wanted to cancel Crusader.

Well, he didn't at first. At first, he said he was *thinking* about canceling Crusader. Which isn't really canceling, right? So the Army went on fighting for it. Which, it turned out, was a mistake, because what the SecDef really meant was that he was canceling it after all. The Army is figuring out how to carry out the missions planned for Crusader with something else. (The Army is doing a lot of figuring out these days.)

Oh, what is a Crusader, you want to know? It's a 40-plus-ton mobile howitzer—a big gun—designed to pump out four rounds a minute instead of the current one or so, which is a lot to your artillery types.

Quick Quiz

Which of these is the nickname of a real Army division?

❏ The Little Beige Two

❏ The Rock of the Marne

❏ The Orange Howler Monkeys

❏ Dr. Leipzig's Merry Contraption

❏ Bob

That takes care of the infantry and artillery branches. What's next for aviation? The Comanche helicopter started as a program called LHX, or Light Helicopter Experimental. It was intended to be a fast, stealthy scout. Now it's a fast scout and attack helicopter, which is a very different bird. And it's extremely stealthy—in fact, as of this writing, only two exist after 15 years of development. This is what might be called a "troubled" program. More figuring.

As you can see, the Army is very busy—and for once, the soldiers in the field may have it a lot easier than the leadership in Washington. Lots of changes are coming. But in the end, the Army's mission remains the same: Fight and win.

The Least You Need to Know

◆ The Army has 12 combat divisions, along with independent regiments and other units.

◆ The Army integrates reserves and National Guard into one total force.

◆ Right now, the Army is figuring out how to shape itself for the new kinds of conflicts and challenges following the Cold War.

Chapter 15

It's Not Just a Job ...
the Navy

In This Chapter

- ◆ Water, water everywhere
- ◆ Five fleets, no waiting
- ◆ No time for naval contemplation

Here's the first thing the Navy wants you to know: Two thirds of the earth is covered with water.

Here's the second thing the Navy wants you to know: Eighty percent of the world's population lives within 200 miles of the coast.

Here's the third thing the Navy wants you to know: The amount of water isn't shrinking, and neither is the number of people near the sea. But the Navy is. Same amount of water, fewer ships. That makes life challenging for the Navy.

The people most concerned about that are the Secretary of the Navy and two individuals who report directly to him: the Chief of Naval Operations and the Commandant of the Marine Corps.

Under these individuals serve the operating forces—sailors, aviators, and Marines.

Meet the Fleets

The Navy consists of five separate fleets, each responsible for a different area of the globe.

Second Fleet, *homeported* in Norfolk, Virginia, provides combat ready forces to support U.S. and NATO activities from the Adriatic Sea to the Arabian Gulf. It reports to the Commander in Chief, Atlantic, or CINCLANT in Navy-speak. Being a Navy CINC is a big job; CINCLANT commands 183 ships, 1,202 aircraft, and 127,000 people.

CINCPAC—can you guess what that means—oversees 3rd Fleet, homeported in San Diego, and 7th Fleet, out of Yokosuka, Japan. Third Fleet operates in the eastern Pacific, while 7th covers the west, or WESTPAC. Together, the Pacific Fleet covers more than 50 percent of the earth's surface, just over 100 million square miles. The Pacific Fleet counts 200 ships, 2,000 aircraft, and a quarter of a million sailors and Marines at sea in the Pacific, Indian, and Arctic Oceans, from the U.S. West Coast to the Arabian Gulf.

Sixth Fleet, homeported in Gaeta, Italy, is tasked with protecting U.S. interests and aiding U.S. allies in Western Europe from Portugal to Russia and in North Africa and the Middle East. Sixth Fleet has maintained a naval presence in the Mediterranean for almost 200 years, dating back to the Barbary pirates.

> **Fighting Words**
>
> **Homeport** Where a ship lives when it isn't deployed, like a base for the Army. The crew's families usually live at the homeport.

> **Basic Training**
>
> Navy uniformed leadership in the Pentagon broadly follows the functional structure of other services. Unlike the Army, Navy leaders are called by their numerical designators, albeit with an N in front (the Deputy Chief for Operations is the N3, for example). Their Marine counterparts are, quaintly, referred to by their titles.

Sixth Fleet generally includes a *carrier battle group* and an *amphibious ready group*. Most recently, 6th Fleet has been active providing military logistical and humanitarian assistance during the Balkan crisis in Kosovo.

And the Indian Ocean and Persian Gulf regions fall to 5th Fleet, which is commanded out of Bahrain, although the ships homeport in various locations. Fifth Fleet involves 15,000 sailors and Marines operating over a 7.5 million-square-mile region. It's responsible for keeping open the Strait of Hormuz, a vital waterway linking the Arabian Gulf with the Gulf of Oman and the world, which is of passing interest because 70 percent of the world's proven oil reserves pass through the strait. Fifth Fleet also contributes to Operation Southern Watch, the mission that enforces the "no-fly zone" over southern Iraq.

Navy surface ships generally sail as part of a group. Carrier Battle Groups, or CVBGs, include about 20 ships, with a full range of capabilities from air defense to antisubmarine warfare.

While carrier battle groups center on, well, carriers, Amphibious Ready Groups, or ARGs, are structured around Marine Corps amphibious ships. Those ships look like small carriers, but carry Marine helicopters and landing craft. ARGs are receiving a lot more attention since the end of the Cold War because of the renewed emphasis on *brown water* operations.

A DESRON, or destroyer squadron, can include cruisers. It often deploys as part of a CVBG or ARG, but can also operate independently.

> **Fighting Words**
>
> **Blue water/brown water**   Blue water refers to the high seas, the areas between continents. Brown water is what Navy people call the areas close to shore. Carriers and other major ships are part of the blue water Navy. Add the land areas near the brown water, and you have the littoral area, which is the domain of the Marine Corps, discussed in Chapter 17.

Battle group rotation is the key to naval operations. A carrier group will spend six months in homeport, followed by six months "workup," or practicing skills expected to be needed in the deployment. Then they'll deploy for six months, or "haze gray and underway," as sailors call it. That rotation means commanders know what forces they'll have available at any given time, and sailors know when they'll be home or away from home. Military personnel say that however busy they are, it's more bearable if they know the schedule in advance.

Of course, deployments can be extended should circumstances require, especially if a CINC wants two carriers in one place for a while. With 12 deployable carrier groups and five fleets, you can see that maintaining presence around the world requires keeping that schedule faithfully.

> **Basic Training**
>
> As you can see from CINCLANT and DESRON, the Navy has a really funky way of abbreviating its commands. It starts simply enough: The Commander in Chief of the Atlantic Fleet is CINC (okay) LANT (Atlantic, natch) FLT (Fleet, yuh-huh). Then they run it all together like a deranged German noun: CINCLANTFLT. As the responsibility decreases, the name gets longer: Commander of Naval Surface Forces, Pacific is COMNAVSURFPAC. He's the boss of the Commander of Cruiser-Destroyer Group Two, or COMCRUDESGRU TWO.

The Navy used to have Surface Action Groups, centered on battleships, but the last of those massive ships was retired in 1992.

Quick Quiz

Identify the naval commands from their abbreviations:

- CINCLANTFLT
- COMSUBPAC
- CINCUSNAVEUR
- NINCOMPAC
- COMMACOMMADOORONRON

In addition to the numbered fleets, geographical commanders oversee type commanders, the admirals in charge of air, surface, and submarine forces respectively, and task forces. Typically, they will have a task force for submarine operations and one for antisubmarine operations, which makes seating at command dinners tricky.

So Many Navies

The Navy operates on, above, and below the sea. Perhaps not surprisingly, each branch has tremendous pride in its own traditions and general studliness. That means more than a little competition.

The surface Navy has the most direct ties to the original Navy. For many years, surface officers had the edge in promotions and good assignments.

Naval aviators appeared just prior to the Second World War, and were considered something less than "real Navy." Since Vietnam, though, "airedales" have been ascendant, with more and more flight wings turning up in the Pentagon.

Pentagon Parables

The sailor versus aviator rivalry was very visible for quite some time. Aviators wore brown shoes, while surface officers wore black. That lasted until 1976, when the Navy said everybody could wear black shoes, thank you very much.

By the way, the people who fly airplanes in the Air Force are pilots. The people who fly airplanes in the Navy are Naval Aviators. This message is brought to you by the Naval Aviators.

Caught more or less in the middle are "dolphins," as submarine officers are known for the dolphins on a submariner's insignia. Because they have a smaller community, it tends to be more tightly knit, but that also makes it harder for submariners to advance en masse.

The Navy has a different approach to education from its ground-bound comrades. Once officers receive their commissions, the surest way to advance is to amass sea duty. That makes it hard for career-minded officers to attend the Naval War College in Newport, Rhode Island, or other professional schools. Recognizing that difficulty, the Navy requires less professional education than do other services.

Don't Feed the SEALS

If you want to get a real education, go to San Diego, California, and try to hang with the Navy SEALS. SEALS are the special forces group within the Navy. (We'll talk about Army and Air Force special forces in Chapter 18.) The term SEALS stands for Sea, Air, Land, because a SEAL has to be able to operate equally well in all of them. SEALS become adept at this during their arduous training in the waters off the Coronado beaches near San Diego.

SEALS trace their history to the World War II units responsible for reconnoitering and clearing beach obstacles for troops going ashore during amphibious landings. Today's SEAL teams conduct unconventional warfare, counter-guerilla warfare, and clandestine operations.

For a fascinating discourse on Navy SEALS, check out www.navyseals.com. (This is a seriously cool website. SEALS rule. You can even get an email address at this site—you@navyseals.com. Think of it.)

> **Basic Training**
>
> One of the key aspects to SEAL training is the ability to practice military orienteering—the ability to start at one location and move somehow to another location without being found. The SEALS disparagingly refer to civilians as people who follow "lines of drift"—things like bridges or roads that tend to channel people and animals in a certain way. SEALS make their own.

Intriguing Navy Traditions

The greatest honor the Navy can render is the 21-gun salute. For centuries, it was the practice of warriors to demonstrate their friendly intentions by firing their cannons to show that they were empty as they entered a new port. The odd number of firings in the 21-gun salute may come from the superstition that odd numbers were considered lucky. (In places of spiritual reflection like Las Vegas and Reno, odd numbers such as 7 and 11 are still considered to have lucky powers.)

Basic Training

And now, the critical question you've been dying to ask: Why are ships called she? Let's ask the Naval Historical Center:

It has always been customary to personify certain inanimate objects and attribute to them characteristics peculiar to living creatures. Thus, things without life are often spoken of as having a sex. Some objects are regarded as masculine. The sun, winter, and death are often personified in this way. Others are regarded as feminine, especially those things that are dear to us. The earth as Mother Earth is regarded as a common maternal parent of all life. In languages that use gender for common nouns, boats, ships, and other vehicles almost invariably use a feminine form. Likewise, early seafarers spoke of their ships in the feminine gender for the close dependence they had on their ships for life and sustenance.

In other words, they don't know either.

The first official salute by a foreign nation to the U.S. flag took place on February 14, 1778, when Captain John Paul Jones fired 13 guns from his Continental Navy ship *Ranger* and received nine in return from the French fleet anchored in Quibberon Bay, France. Captain Jones may have fired 13 guns in honor of the 13 U.S. colonies, or that may have been all the ammunition he had.

Ship names in the Navy provide fascinating clues to American history. For example, in pre-revolutionary times, the American colonists named their ships after important British figures. The *Alfred*, the first ship of the new Continental Navy, was named in honor of Alfred the Great, the King of Wessex, who built the first naval force in England. Another was the *Raleigh*, commemorating Sir Walter Raleigh.

After America began to seek independence, developing its own Constitution and forming its own Congress, you saw ships in the water with creative names like *Constitution*, *Independence*, and *Congress*. Thank heaven the Founding Fathers didn't designate a national poodle.

As time went on, the size of the ship being built dictated whether the name would be a person, a city, a state, or something nasty like a hornet or wasp. Navy ship classes are named for the first ship in the class, so for example, submarines using the hull design of SSN-699, the *Los Angeles*, are called "*Los Angeles*-class" subs.

A tradition also evolved that ships lost at sea would give their names to new ships, such as the *Lexington*, *Yorktown*, *Atlanta*, *Triton*, and *Shark*. (Don't get us started about *Enterprise*.) If you would like to have a ship named after you or a loved one, contact the Chief of Naval Operations, who is in charge of such matters. However, unless you or your relative are a famous American past president or military leader, you may be better off just going out and buying your own boat.

Pentagon Parables

The Navy's fundamental problem: Ships last for decades, but they cost a whole lot to build. In the 1980s, plans had the Navy going to a fleet of 600 ships. Then the Soviet Union folded its chips, and we realized that maybe we'd like to have some tax cuts, and now the fleet is 315. By 2012, at the current rates of construction and retirement, it'll be closer to 150.

Don't laugh, it can happen. Less than 100 years ago, the British Royal Navy ruled the seas of the world. As of this writing, the mighty British Navy is 27 ships. Britannia Rules the Tub.

Sailing Forth

The Navy's future is shocking. After powering ships by wind, coal, diesel, turbine, and more, the next generation of ships will be electric drive.

The Navy has three major ship concepts under development. A new submarine class, the *Virginia*, will appear first. Then the next aircraft carrier, CVN-77, will be an interim design, partway down the road to its successor, a new-generation carrier called CVN(X). And the biggest program, DD(X), will result in new destroyer, cruiser, and littoral ship designs, all from the same technology.

All of these ships are slated to eventually have electric drive. Right now, the ship's engine drives the screw, either directly or by making steam that turns the shaft. (Yes, that's why driving a ship is called "steaming.") With electric drive, the dangerous steam lines and boilers will be gone, replaced by generators and big electric motors. That lets ships run more quietly, which makes them harder to detect. It also means that there will be plenty of electricity for, umm, we don't know, weapons that use electricity rather than guns and missiles, maybe? Just guessing.

For carriers, abundant electricity will also make it possible to launch aircraft with electromagnetic slingshots rather than today's steam catapults. All these technologies are under development as you read this book, and many will appear before you finally sell it on eBay.

If you think about it, the Navy is the Pentagon in miniature. It has ships, airplanes, and a ground force (the Marines). Wherever, whatever, whenever, the Navy can do it all.

The Least You Need to Know

- The Navy has five fleets, each responsible for a different part of the globe.

- Battle groups operate on a regular rotation, keeping the pace of operations (usually) predictable.

- You do *not* want to mess with a SEAL.

Meet the Zoomies: The Air Force

In This Chapter

◆ Many shades of blue

◆ Your wishes are their commands

◆ What the Air Force is good at

Reaching to the sky, sun glinting off glistening silver, the futuristic shape breathes technology and power. It seems in motion even as it sits confidently on its concrete pad. There is no doubt to whom this belongs; it could only be the cutting-edge force of an awesomely powerful country.

And that's just one of their buildings.

The chapel at the United States Air Force Academy in Colorado Springs, Colorado, tells you most everything you need to know about the Air Force. It is modern, it is blatantly distinctive, and it is maybe just a little bit over the top.

Fighter Jocks, Trash Haulers, Rocket Men, and More

Think of the Air Force, and you probably think of fighter planes. The pilots—or "fighter jocks"—like it that way. But the Air Force is much more than that.

Bombers and fighters work for *Air Combat Command*, one of seven functional and two regional commands that make up the Air Force. ACC is headquartered at Langley Air Force Base (AFB) in Virginia. It oversees both the newest and oldest hardware in the Air Force arsenal; the B-2 stealth bomber and forthcoming F-22 and F-35 fighters on one hand, and the B-52 bomber on the other. Current Air Force plans call for the B-52s to serve until they are 80 years old, which is no reflection on the military's retirement plans.

Pentagon Parables

The Strategic Air Command (SAC) ran the bomber part of the Air Force until 1992, when SAC and the fighter guys, Tactical Air Command, were combined to form Air Combat Command.

Fighting Words

Two-letter Remember how the Air Force has its own distinct and funky series of office designators? The operations chief, what in the Army would be the DCSOPS and in the Joint Staff the J-3, is the AF/XO. Under the XO is the AF/XOI (recon), the XOC (command & control), and others. The next level down has four letters (AF/XOIW is info warfare) and so on. So the two-letter is the boss.

Air Mobility Command is in charge of getting things from place to place—not only the Air Force's things, but the other services' stuff, too, when tasked by U.S. TRANSCOM, which you met in Chapter 8. If the Army needs to move a brigade overseas, it's the Air Force's C-5s and C-17s and C-130s that will get them there. Cargo aircraft and their pilots are known to other portions of the Air Force as "trash haulers," no doubt affectionately.

Air Force Space Command includes an often-overlooked part of the service: the missileers. The Air Force operates the intercontinental ballistic missiles buried in silos through the Midwest. Like flying or logistics, missilery is its own career field in the Air Force, although service culture dictates that most of the guys who make it to the *two-letter* jobs are fighter pilots.

Air Force Materiel Command, headquartered at Wright-Patterson Air Force Base in Ohio ("Wright-Pat" to the cognoscenti) is like the Defense Logistics Agency in that it manages purchasing for the Air Force, but it oversees a lot of development and technology activities as well.

Air Force Reserve Command manages the part-time Air Force from Robins AFB in Georgia. That means they oversee 75,000 reservists and 110,000 Air National Guardsmen and women, complementing the work of 355,000 regulars.

Air Force Special Operations Command is at Hurlburt Field in Florida. When we see the words Special Operations, we get a little tingle in our spines. We walk a little taller. We're just feeling a little more jaunty as we go through our day. Why? Because Special Ops are the cool guys. They're the ones who fly specially modified aircraft, often below radar, often in low visibility, often in covert ways, in any kind of conflict. In other words, if it's dirty, if it's dangerous, if it's secret, if it's life-threatening, Special Ops is there, making it happen, and usually in enemy-controlled or politically sensitive territories. You can read more about Special Operations in Chapter 18.

Air Education and Training Command (AETC) is in charge of turning teenagers into airmen, keeping them smart, and helping them move ahead. Appropriately, headquarters is at Randolph AFB in Texas, the busiest flight-training base in the Air Force.

The other major Air Force commands are Pacific Air Forces (PACAF, or "PACK-aff"), at Hickam AFB, Hawaii; and U.S. Air Forces Europe (USAFE, pronounced "you-SAFE-ee"), at Ramstein AFB in Germany. USAFE and PACAF are operational commands that combine elements of the other Air Force commands. Each command is divided into numbered air forces, which cover certain geographical areas. Numbered air forces include "wings" of like capability: a bomber wing, a fighter wing, a missile wing, and so on. Wings are split into squadrons. Once the Air Force had 40 fighter wings; today, it has 10.

> **Basic Training**
>
> AETC also oversees the Air War College at Maxwell AFB, Alabama. Some courses can be taken by correspondence, a useful aid when Air Force personnel can be ordered to the other side of the world in 15 hours. Maxwell is also home of the Air Force Auxiliary, the Civil Air Patrol, which is best known for searching for lost aircraft.

Let's Fly Away

In 1997, the Air Force changed the way it deploys for air missions. In response to a need to control operational tempo and get the right blend of airpower for any job at hand, they developed the Aerospace Expeditionary Force (AEF). An AEF includes squadrons of different kinds of aircraft with different capabilities.

While Air Force folks won't like the comparison, the AEF is rather like a Navy aircraft carrier battle group. We don't mean that their power is the same, but like a carrier group, an AEF has a blend of capabilities. And like a carrier group, it deploys on a rotational schedule.

An AEF will typically spend 10 months in general training, followed by two months specific training for its upcoming deployment. The deployment will be for another three months; then the training cycle starts again. That way, at least one of the 10 AEFs (roughly the equivalent of two fighter wings) is always ready to go. Because the AEF has different kinds of aircraft, whatever aerospace capability a commander needs is just a phone call away.

For rapid response, smaller Air Expeditionary Wings, each with multiple squadrons and a command element, can get there even faster, and require less than the 135 C-17s and 36 rented 747s needed to deploy a whole Air Expeditionary Force.

In the most urgent cases, we'd send an Air Expeditionary Group. An AEG contains one or more squadrons and a command element.

Pentagon Parables

In Chapter 11, we discussed the Air Force of the 1950s, with many different, special-ized types of airplanes. Today, we can't afford that level of specialization, especially when the goal is to get many capabilities on the ground as fast as possible. So every airplane bought has to carry out a variety of missions. This inevitably leads to some compromises, but far fewer than in the less technologically advanced aircraft of the 1950s and '60s, where "multi-role" meant "does one thing well and phones the rest in."

So What Does All This Stuff Do?

The U.S. Air Force is all about controlling and exploiting air and space. The USAF prides itself on speed, flexibility, and the global nature of its reach and perspective. That manifests itself in six "competencies" that the Air Force develops and maintains:

♦ The USAF calls **Air and Space Superiority** "Job 1." If you're superior in air and space, everything else your force needs to do is easier. Without air superior-ity, you cannot land or operate surface forces without unacceptable losses. So dominating air and space is where it all begins.

♦ **Global Attack** means the USAF has the ability to put fire and steel on targets anywhere in the world, at any time. They "kick the door down," neutralizing enemy defenses so other kinds of forces can enter the theater.

♦ **Rapid Global Mobility** means that the Air Force can get places quickly. Not long ago, America—or any militarily equipped nation—could maintain bases and posts pretty much anywhere on the globe. Today, reduced military budgets, declining support in other countries for hosting foreign military, and a host of other factors mean that it is simply not profitable to station forces on a daily basis around the world. Combine Global Attack and Rapid Global Mobility, and you have a force well suited for operations in *immature theaters*.

Fighting Words

Immature theaters Places showing *101 Dalmatians*. Also Air Force-speak for areas where we really haven't done a lot of preparation for going to war.

♦ **Information Superiority** is the Air Force's ability to provide warning of an emerging crisis and, in combat, to develop a clear picture of the enemy's forces and operations. The Air Force maintains enormous information-gathering capabilities. Perhaps you've heard of AWACS, the Airborne Warning and Command System, which looks like a 707 with a flying saucer attached to the roof. These planes, along with airborne battlefield command, control centers, and other flying or orbiting information-seeking and collation devices, provide commanders the information they need in order to control a military situation.

♦ The Air Force prides itself on the "high kill probability" that comes when you have **precision engagement,** which is to say bombs that go where they are supposed to go. Such weapon systems allow the Air Force to reduce its overall size while maintaining a serious edge over potential adversaries. In other words, if you're going to Vegas during wartime, and the Air Force is on the board against some other "united military force," don't bet the under.

Precision engagement is also important because the world is less tolerant than ever before of civilian casualties. So it's vital that the Air Force can hit the target, and not the grocery store next door to the target.

♦ **Agile Combat Support** means getting materiel—food, gas, supplies—to Air Force units in a speedy way. Since we no longer have supply depots around the globe—and since you can't count on finding a 7-Eleven for all your military needs as you're headed into, say, Rwanda or Afghanistan, there's nothing like the ability to deliver stuff by air, and quickly. You can think of this part of the Air Force as its own FedEx system. When you can deliver logistics systems (stuff) quickly, you can deploy your planes in an effective and sustainable manner.

So They Get There. Then What?

A lot. You're probably sitting at home, scratching your chin and saying, "Gosh, I sure wonder what the Air Force does, given those six 'competencies' that Mike and Jeff so eagerly outlined for me only a moment ago."

The Air Force has five main air and space power functions, which is to say that there are five important things that it does after takeoff. And none of them have to do with the distribution of peanuts and soft drinks to passengers. We'll take a look at those five main functions right now, as long as your seatback is in the upright and locked position.

Just as we have an Air Force, so do the bad guys.

Counterair is the Air Force mission of destroying or neutralizing the enemy's air force, and surface-based air defense network. Without control of the air, it's tough to do things well on the ground. Flexibility in battle comes from the security that your air force has taken out their air force. That's counterair.

Offensive counterair (OCA) means we attack proactively, generally over enemy territory, against their ability to employ their airpower and defend against ours. What do we like to blow up in these circumstances? Airfields, command and control facilities, and munitions storage. Useful things like that.

In *defensive counterair* (DCA) missions, the enemy attacks us in the air, and we fight back. Hard. DCA generally means air-to-air engagements or defensive attacks against surface-to-air systems. In other words, if they come at us with a plane or a ground-based weapon, they've done a very bad thing—and we will make them pay.

Basic Training

One way the Air Force operates to minimize fratricide and stay out of its own way is to establish "kill boxes," areas from which our other forces are banished, and in which one pilot is told, "Anything that moves in this defined area, you kill." This was, for example, how the Iraqi army lost so many of its tanks during the Gulf War.

Counterland operations are all about attaining and maintaining superiority over the enemy on the ground. The tricky thing about counterland is that you probably have your own forces on the ground, which makes fratricide a problem. Detailed integration of the Air Force's role in the battle along with those folks on the ground is therefore highly recommended.

There are two traditional aspects to counterland operations. *Interdiction* means destroying, neutralizing, or delaying enemy military potential before they can bring it to bear against us. This means that we go in from above and knock out anything and everything that they've got on the ground that they could use against us. While some claim that "no one ever surrendered to an airplane," when the USAF drops their stuff on you, it sure puts the idea of surrender way toward the top of your to-do list.

The second traditional aspect of counterland operations is *close air support* (CAS). What we're close to is our own forces on the ground. This is the time for detailed integration of the Air Force mission with the mission of our friendly forces on the ground, because you've got Air Force planes operating against hostile targets in close proximity to our forces. That's where Air Force ground controllers come into play—people who speak air but serve among the Army. They proved invaluable in Afghanistan, getting to within eyesight of the enemy, then calling in orbiting fighters or on-call bombers with precise coordinates.

> **Pentagon Parables**
>
> Airpower critics like that line about how nobody ever surrendered to an airplane. Well, it isn't true. In fact, during the Gulf War, Iraqi troops surrendered not only to airplanes, but to helicopters, remotely-piloted drones, and CNN.

Close air support comes in two flavors: *preplanned* and *immediate*. The good thing about preplanned close air support is that you have a chance to take your time and plan the mission exactly the way you want it to go. You can coordinate with other services and, if appropriate, with your allies. You can put together the proper mix of weapons, given the targets that you'll be aiming for. You've got the time to review intelligence that will make your decisions easier and more accurate. You've got time to familiarize your aircrews with the situation, the weather, and the terrain.

Sounds great, but preplanned close air support also has some critical disadvantages. Not all battles go the way they're planned. If a plan is wrong, disaster may well ensue. Timing is critical—there may be some information that's simply not available until the last possible minute. Since we can't always preplan our close air support, which is to say we can't always figure out in advance where exactly Air Force planes will be flying, the Air Force has a doctrine of immediate close air support as well.

When those pesky enemies won't sit still and take their bombing like a man, or the weather changes, or the mission changes, or when an Air Force general just feels like beating the hell out of somebody's army to impress his date, it's time for what the Air Force calls immediate close air support. This means that instead of going in with a detailed plan, you respond to the situation as it unfolds.

> ### Pentagon Parables
>
> Thanks to technical advances and an unusual target list, the air war in Afghanistan provided an astounding example of immediate close air support. Over 40 percent of the aircraft that took off wound up being directed to a target of opportunity—one that wasn't on their mission plan, but became important or vulnerable. Some fighters and bombers were deliberately sent to fly around and wait for whatever target presented itself.

The advantages to immediate close air support are that you can react to the unexpected. You can use your planes at the decisive time and place—you're not locked into a prior plan. You can respond quickly to changes. You can take advantage of last-minute intelligence.

The down side of immediate close air support is that it's in some ways the equivalent of going to the Bahamas with nothing but a toothbrush and a Speedo. You may not have the proper mix of weapons, given the targets you suddenly discover you've got to destroy. Your aircrew may be unfamiliar with the situation. The original target that you had planned to take out may well survive, since you are distracted by the new targets that have presented themselves. So there's a time and a place for planning, and as they said in the movie *Fast Times at Ridgemont High*, there's a time and a place for spontaneity.

When do you turn to immediate CAS? Let's say that some events take place that were not anticipated during the planning process. A request for immediate CAS energizes all levels of the military to determine what sort of ground attack can take place to coordinate with this sudden, unexpected use of Air Force tactics. The Air Force thinks of immediate CAS as a "zero-sum" situation—in order to provide close air support on this sort of unexpected basis, resources have to be taken away from some of the other activities that the Air Force is engaging in at the same time, be it counterair (going against airplanes in the air) or other preplanned operations. Warfare requires flexibility; since you never know what's going to happen next, you've got to be ready to change your mind at the last minute.

Airlift means delivering people and things directly into a war zone, during the assault phase of an operation and afterward. When we're talking airlift, we're generally talking trans-oceanic. Ever wonder how we are able to deliver ground forces into places like Somalia, Kosovo, or Afghanistan? Chances are that an Air Force pilot delivered those people, places, and things to the hot spot.

Strategic Attack means going after an enemy target that will affect its ability to wage war overall. It's not about winning a particular battle. It's about creating a sense of destabilization and crippling the enemy in such a way as to induce a feeling that it's just not worth it to keep going. They don't call us the world's only remaining super-power for nothing.

Sure, two thirds of the earth's surface is covered by water. But 100 percent is covered by air. Using stealth and precision, the U.S. Air Force can attack anywhere on the planet on very short notice. With the coming F-22 and F-35, American superiority in the air is only likely to grow.

The Least You Need to Know

- In addition to fighters and bombers, the Air Force is responsible for interconti-nental missiles and transporting gear for all services.

- The Air Force is structured by commands, wings, and squadrons, but deploys in flexible Air Expeditionary Forces.

- Air superiority is job one.

Chapter 17

The Few, the Proud: The Marines

In This Chapter

- ◆ Through the Crucible
- ◆ Going on expeditions
- ◆ Khaki to the future

If you're dropping your son or daughter off at the Marine Recruit Depot at Parris Island, North Carolina, or San Diego to begin recruit training, take a picture, because you'll never see that kid again. For the next 12 weeks, he or she will learn to fight, to obey, to march and drill, to act with honor, and—more than anything—to function as part of a team. All of this is accomplished under the continuous observation, direction, and criticism of a Marine drill instructor.

A Breed Apart

The Marine Corps is part of the U.S. Navy, but don't tell that to the Marines. They see themselves as a separate, hard-charging, invincible corps. And are you going to tell them they're wrong?

Basic Training

Note that while this box is called "Basic Training," Marine training isn't. It's called recruit training, because the people taking it aren't Marines yet (and won't be unless they make it through recruit training) and because there's nothing basic about it.

The drill instructors, or DIs, are legendary, so much so that you can picture one in your mind right now. Ramrod straight, with recruiting-poster perfect uniforms, the DIs can shame recruits into wanting to be better Marines even if they never utter a word. Ask any Marine about his or her DI, and you'll get respect and fear even decades later.

Hardships, physical and mental, are a deliberate part of the training. If wars were easy or comfortable, we could fight them in rec rooms. The goal of Marine recruit training is to make every recruit a reliable Marine regardless of circumstances.

Every Marine a Rifleman

A large part of that 12 weeks is spent on the firing range. It doesn't matter if you want to be a Marine cook, pilot, or glockenspiel player, Corps lore dictates that every Marine is first and foremost a rifleman. You're there to fight. Everything else is secondary. So you shoot a lot and you learn to shoot well, or you're on the bus home to Mama.

Marine recruit training culminates in the "Crucible," a 54-hour exercise in which the recruits hike, solve problems, hike, surmount physical obstacles, hike, conduct infiltration and other exercises, shoot, and hike, all while receiving instruction on Marine Corps traditions and standards. The point is to get the recruits working and thinking as a team, especially while under stress. (Did we mention that the drill instructors are along, giving … ah … encouragement?)

After 40 miles, 2½ MREs and 8 hours of sleep (although not all at once), the recruits pin on the *eagle, globe, and anchor*, and are called "Marine" for the first time.

Fighting Words

Eagle, globe, and anchor As the symbol of the Marine Corps, the superimposed eagle, globe, and anchor symbolizes America, worldwide service, and naval traditions. We'll let you guess which symbol matches which. The Corps recently came up with a new camouflage pattern for its uniforms, and if you look really closely, you can see that it's made up of little colored eagle, globe, and anchor symbols. (This is true.)

Marine Corps Strategy

Like the Army, Marine Corps ground troops are organized into divisions, brigades, battalions, and so on for purposes of training and equipping. Like the Navy, air elements are organized by wing, but they don't deploy that way. A commander asking for Marines wouldn't get a division but a task force combining pieces of many units.

Some of the phrases that the Marines particularly like to use in describing themselves are:

- America's 911 Force

- A versatile, expeditionary force in readiness

- A balanced force for a Naval campaign and a ground and air striking force

- Always at a high state of readiness

- Ready to suppress or contain international disturbances short of war

> **Basic Training**
>
> The ceremonial sword that every Marine officer carries is called a Mameluke sword. They are patterned after the sword awarded to First Lieutenant Presley Neville O'Bannon after his heroic efforts in the battle for the fortress at Derne, Tripoli, in 1805, which took its pattern from swords of the Mameluke tribe of Egypt.

And perhaps the Marines' favorite description is "To be most ready when the nation is least ready."

The main purpose of the Marines, of course, is war fighting. Yet the Marines also see a vital part of their mission as imbuing young men and women who join with the core values of the Corps. Indeed, the Marine Corps likes to say that it wins battles and makes people. Those core values are honor, courage, and commitment.

Everybody knows the expression "Send in the Marines!" It is less well known that that call actually sounded over 200 times since the end of World War II—that is, an average of once every 90 days. The Marines pride themselves on their reputation for their ability to succeed any time, anywhere, and in any situation. The basis for that confidence, according to the Marines themselves, is what they call Marine Air-Ground Task Force Operations (MAGTF Operations). (Say "MAG-taff.")

MAGTF Operations is the Marines' way of describing its flexible response capabilities. Because Marines deploy as a combined air, sea, and ground force, they can provide decision-makers—diplomatic and military—with what the Marines describe as "an immediately available and programmable 'rheostat' of tailored cost effective crisis response capabilities across the conflict spectrum." Which means you can build big MAGTFs, little MAGTFs, or MAGTFs that are just right.

Because a MAGTF can be tailored, they are called upon for just about any kind of contingency, including:

♦ Disaster relief

♦ Humanitarian assistance

♦ Smaller-scale contingencies

♦ Evacuation operations

♦ Major theater war

All MAGTFs are made of four basic common organizational elements, which vary in size and composition according to the mission. They are:

♦ **Command Element.** This is MAGTF headquarters. The Command Element provides command and control for planning and execution.

♦ **Ground Combat Element.** A cohesive maneuver and combat team formed around a ground maneuver unit comprising infantry, tanks, or light armored vehicles, reinforced with the necessary artillery, transport, combat engineer, and reconnaissance assets to accomplish its mission. This is the ground striking power of a MAGTF.

♦ **Aviation Combat Element.** ACE, appropriately enough, has to do with the Marines in the air. We're talking helicopters, we're talking fixed-wing squadrons, we're talking surface-to-air missile units (SAMs). This provides the air striking power of, and air support to, the MAGTF.

♦ **Combat Service Element Support.** You've got to have fuel. You've got to have food. You've got to have bullets. The Combat Service Support people make sure that the supply lines stretch to wherever the Marines need to be, so that they can do their job, if necessary, over an extended period.

Put all these things together, and you have a scaleable fighting force that can come in with any combination of assets necessary in order to do the job. One of the reasons the Marines are so frequently called upon is the flexibility—and success rate—of the MAGTF's Operations approach.

The Marines like to say that MAGTFs are among the most versatile instruments of U.S. national military power. To quote the Marine Corps itself, "MAGTFs define a unique form of naval expeditionary operations that allow the Regional Commanders in Chief to employ Marine forces independently in a crisis role, as a sustainable first-on-the-scene enabling force for follow-on joint operations, or in support of a larger naval or joint war fighting campaign." *OO-rah!*

Fighting Words

OO-rah!   One of the fastest ways to expose yourself as a spy is to use the wrong cheer. You learned in Chapter 14 that Army soldiers say "HOO-ah!" Well, Marines say, "OO-rah," but not as often. HOO-ah is a cheer and a regular part of speech. OO-rah is a cheer, period.

Who Are the Marines?

Today, there are approximately 174,000 active duty Marine Corps members. Approximately two thirds are assigned to two different Marine Forces (MARFORs), called Marine Forces, Pacific and Marine Forces, Atlantic. The next level of organization in the Marines is the Marine Expeditionary Forces, or MEFs. They are the primary building block of the Marines. There are two Marine Expeditionary Forces attached to the Commander, Marine Forces, Pacific, and one under the command of the Commander, Marine Forces, Atlantic. The Pacific-based MEFs are located in Southern California; Okinawa, Japan; and Hawaii. The Atlantic-based MEFs can be found in North and South Carolina.

Let's Go MEFs!

There are three basic components of a Marine Expeditionary Force. And here they are:

♦ **The Marine Division.** This includes infantry regiments, an artillery regiment, a tank battalion, an assault amphibious vehicle battalion, a light armored reconnaissance battalion, and a combat engineer battalion. These guys can do anything from operations to major theater war.

♦ **The Marine Aircraft Wing.** These are your Marines in the sky. They offer a complete range of air operations including anti-air warfare, offensive air support, aero reconnaissance, and electronic warfare (including active and passive electronic countermeasures). The wing may also provide units based on navy aircraft carriers. But the primary function of Marine aviation is to support Marines on the ground in combat. The Marines are very determined to maintain control of their own air support.

Basic Training

Today, Marine air wings fly the F-18 Hornet and AV-8 Harrier fighters. The Harrier takes off and lands vertically, so it can accompany Marine ground units to places where there aren't airports. Both are scheduled to be replaced by the F-35 Joint Strike Fighter beginning around 2010.

◆ **The Force Service Support Group.** They deliver the goods: medical, dental, maintenance, supply, motor transport, and engineer capabilities are within the purview of the Force Service Support Group.

Put it all together and what do you have? A balanced, powerful armed force, with one commander that can do whatever it needs to do for 60 straight days. MEFs can handle sea-based operations, sustained operations ashore in almost any geographic location, either alone or with other branches of the military.

The beauty of the MEF is its unique ability to match weaponry, equipment, and tactics to the situation and terrain it faces. For example, if you're going into jungles or cities, you probably won't be deploying your heavier mechanized units. On the other hand, if you've got a high intensity operation to fight, you may need extra armored artillery and air units. You name the war, we'll get it done. That's what the Marines are all about.

There are two ways to think about the MEFs. On the one hand, they are the largest and only "standing" MAGTFs. Each one of them could serve as an entire MAGTF in wartime. So one way to deploy the Marines, when you send in the Marines, is to send in *all* of the Marines. It's doable. All three MEFs are located near major naval bases and excellent airports, road networks, and seaports. That's how the Marines can deploy rapidly worldwide. Location, location, location.

Let's say you've got a situation that doesn't require an entire Marine Expeditionary Force. Well, you can draw upon any of the three MEFs, whether in California, Japan, Hawaii, or the Carolinas, depending on where the problem is and what kind of assets you need. The Marines call this process "sourcing." As a crisis escalates, you can keep sending in additional MAGTFs until, if need be, the entire MEF is in place to support the battle plan.

How Many People Are We Talking About?

A Marine Expeditionary Force is approximately 46,000 personnel. About 4,000 are attached to the command element. These include the folks at headquarters, the intelligence-gathering people, and the communications folks. Below the command element are the three elements we just discussed: the Ground Combat Element, the Aviation Combat Element, and the Combat Service Support Element. How big are these groups? Count on about 18,000 for the Ground Combat Element. About 15,000 make up the Aviation Combat Element. Just under 10,000 are found in the Combat Service Support Element.

Typically, the Ground Combat Element of an MEF will contain 58 M1A1 tanks, 233 amphibious assault vehicles, 130 light armored vehicles, 72 howitzers, 151 short- and long-range mortars, 108 Dragon medium-range antitank missiles, and 186 TOW long-range antitank missiles.

What do the aircraft folks have? Try this: more than 160 fixed-wing aircraft, and approximately 180 rotary wing vehicles or helicopters. To round things off on the aviation side they also have, for air defense purposes, 12 Hawk launchers, 60 Avengers, and 30 Stingers. So the next time you hear that the Marines have been sent in somewhere, you'll know they aren't just sending a couple of *gunnies* in a gig.

Fighting Words

Gunnies Gunnery Sergeants. Remember that every Marine is a rifleman. Accordingly, the most revered rank in the Corps is Gunnery Sergeant, denoting a noncommissioned officer who instructs in the use of weapons.

Corps Competencies

MAGTF Operations are built on a foundation of six core competencies. As the Marines themselves say, these core competencies "define what Marines do and how they operate." Let's take a look at them now.

Quick Quiz

Where is the U.S. Marine Corps Academy?

❏ Pocatello, Idaho

❏ Ste. Therese, Quebec

❏ Across the street from the Marine War College

❏ Silly, the Marines are part of the Navy and don't have a separate academy or war college

◆ **Expeditionary Readiness.** The Marine mentality means that they are ready to respond instantaneously to worldwide crises 365 days a year. The Marines expect to win the first battles in any given situation. This requires a force that can transition from peacetime to combat operations at a moments notice, without having to call up reserves, and with certain success. The Marines like to say that they "flourish under conditions of uncertainty." They can handle whatever is "out there," improvising and finding unconventional solutions to unconventional problems. It also means preparing to fight the next war, as opposed to refighting the last war, which, as all military planners know, never comes back a second time.

♦ **Combined Arms Operation.** The Marines plan to be the first on the scene, so they have to be totally competent in ground combat, air combat, and combat service support capabilities. The Marines like to say, chiding the Army and the Air Force, "Other services practice combined arms operations. MAGTF Operations embody them." In other words, the Marines are well versed in all aspects of war-making. That's because Marines don't have to put together combined task forces; their land, air, and sea components are all *organic*.

♦ **Expeditionary Operations.** The Marines consider it a luxury whenever they get any sort of support from the host nation, where the battle is taking place. Rather, they view each mission as a potential expedition to hostile and unwelcoming terrain. They expect to find nothing there that they can count on as they win battles. So they bring everything with them they need to accomplish the mission—from individual equipment up to and including airfields and hospitals. (How do you pack a hospital in a backpack? If anybody can do it, the Marines can.)

♦ **Sea-Based Operations.** The Marine Corps, of course, is rooted in the Navy. Their competence with sea-based operations means that they can dramatically extend the reach of the U.S. military force into practically any part of the globe. The Marines command the seas.

♦ **Forcible Entry—From the Sea.** This is perhaps the trait for which the Marines are best known—the ability to land on a beach under enemy fire, establish a beachhead, build up combat power, and take the hill. Or do whatever they need to do. The Marines pride themselves on their ability to make forcible entry from the sea, which they define as "an uninterrupted movement of forces from ships located far over the horizon directly against decisive objectives."

♦ **Reserve Integration.** The nature of most Marine operations requires immediate deployment, without time to call up reserve forces. And yet, the Marines are uniquely able to call up a very high percentage of their reserves very quickly and integrate them into whatever operation is going on. The Marines like to point out that they activated 53 percent of their reserves during Operation Desert Storm, surpassing any other service reserve component activation by more than a factor of two. That's military-speak for saying that for every Naval Reserve or Army Reserve member called to service in the Gulf War, two Marines went to the Gulf, and folded themselves seamlessly into the Marine Corps fighting force to defeat Iraq.

Basic Training

The Marines use reserves differently from other services. In the Army or Air Force, reserves generally perform support functions for the regular troops, or form their own units that enter battle after they've been trained up. By contrast, Marine reserves are absorbed into regular units, doing the same jobs and fighting side by side with their full-time brethren. They are not so much "reserve Marines" as just more Marines.

What's Ahead for the Corps?

Big changes are coming for the Corps, and some are already here. The most significant is the change from a purely littoral force—one that wades ashore and works close to the ocean—to one that operates deeper inland. The deployment of Marines to establish and man Camp Rhino, over 800 miles from the ocean near Kandahar, Afghanistan, in 2002 was the clearest sign of that.

That brings with it, a need to go deep and get places fast. That's why the Marines are trying to acquire the V-22 Osprey transport aircraft, sort of a cross between a helicopter and an airplane, that can take off and land vertically but fly at 300 knots, or more than twice as fast as their current helicopters.

The Corps is also working with the Navy on experiments using high-speed ships designed to operate close to shore to move them from place to place.

A third challenge is to keep a definition of what the Corps is for. The light, mobile brigade combat teams we told you the Army was creating (in Chapter 14) look a lot like Marine ground forces.

But in these ways as always, the U.S. Marine Corps loves a good challenge. Semper Fi!

The Least You Need to Know

- The Marines are a corps within the Navy.
- Marine expeditionary forces and task forces feature combined arms, including land, sea, and air elements.
- Marines organize differently from how they deploy.
- You do not under any circumstances want to shout "HOO-ah" at a Marine.

Chapter 18

Also at Your Service: Coast Guard and SOCOM

In This Chapter

- A lot of coast to guard
- Smoke on the water
- Quiet but effective
- Return of the cavalry

Two other major military elements of Pentagon power aren't in the mold of traditional services. To be sure, the U.S. Coast Guard is a military service, but in peacetime, it's not even part of the Department of Defense. The Coast Guard is run by the Transportation Department, except when the President chops command to DoD. On the other hand, U.S. Special Operations Command (SOCOM) encompasses units from multiple services, primarily the Army and Air Force. Each has a distinct role in national defense.

Safety at Sea

The Coast Guard is the smallest of America's armed forces, and in many ways the least known. Yet it has always played a variety of significant roles in protecting our nation's coastline and ports. Its most visible roles recently were interdiction of drug smuggling and hollering at dorks fooling around in speedboats without life jackets. But they are—and always have been—much more.

The Coast Guard is very sensitive about its status as a military service. They take pains to emphasize at every opportunity that the legislation creating the service stated it was to be part of the military; in researching this book, it was an odd Coast Guard document indeed that didn't include some similar citation. That said, the Coast Guard is run by a commandant rather than a service chief. (But so is the Marine Corps, and we're not giving *them* any backtalk.) Unlike the Commandant of the Marine Corps, the Commandant of the Coast Guard is *not* a member of the Joint Chiefs.

Of all the military services, the Coast Guard may be in for the most change in the wake of the 2001 attacks on the United States. "Guarding the coast" took on new meanings and much more emphasis after September 11, and while the list of Coast Guard missions changed little, their priorities were fundamentally rearranged.

The Coast Guard likes to remind us that our future will remain "tied to the sea." Our presence in the world's waters guarantees our primacy among nations as a superpower, and allows us to project our power to assist and protect our friends across the globe. Free shipping lanes worldwide permit the United States to remain the leader in world trade. And yet, the seas also are a potential highway for terrorists and others bent on harming U.S. interests, at home and abroad. The Coast Guard can defend sea lanes with the best of them.

Defending free navigation of the seas, which is guaranteed by international law, is a big part of what the Navy and Coast Guard are about. From time to time, they will conduct "freedom of navigation exercises," which usually consist of sailing through an area of international waters that some country has claimed as its own and saying, "Oh, yeah?"

> ### ⏰ Changes Since 9/11
>
> With the establishment of the Cabinet-level Department of Homeland Security, the Coast Guard appears to be on the move again. Although details weren't final as we went to press, the Coast Guard is on the administration's list of entities to be folded into the new department.

> ### Pentagon Parables
>
> The Coast Guard describes itself as "America's maritime guardian," and in that position, it works as policemen, sailors, warriors, humanitarians, regulators, stewards of the environment, diplomats, and—oh, yes—guardians of the coast.

The Coast Guard is responsible for maritime security, maritime safety, the protection of natural resources, maritime mobility, and national defense. The Coast Guard likes to describe itself using the three m's: military, multi-mission, and maritime. Okay, that's four m's, but who's counting?

From Sea to Shining Sea

Since colonial times, America has relied on the seas for commerce, sustenance, and defense. We are, and always have been, a maritime nation. Our national forefathers founded a nation that would one day comprise more than 95,000 miles of shoreline, bordering nearly 3.4 million square miles of territory covered by ocean, which the United States claims as its own.

When we think about the area the Coast Guard patrols, we are most likely to think of the Atlantic and Pacific Oceans and the Gulf of Mexico, as they define the edges of the continent. It's easy to overlook the fact that the Coast Guard is also involved in a broad swath of ocean surrounding Alaska, and has many responsibilities for the rivers and other navigable waters inside our country.

The Coast Guard is also responsible for protecting the waters around Puerto Rico and the U.S. Virgin Islands in the Caribbean. In the Pacific, the Coast Guard's responsibility extends to Hawaii, the Northern Mariana Islands, Guam, Wake Island, American Samoa, and a number of smaller islands that are U.S. territories or possessions. Let's take a look at the specific responsibilities of the Coast Guard in these areas.

Basic Training

Where the Navy is organized by fleets aligned with ocean areas, the Coast Guard is organized into 10 districts, each with responsibility for a portion of the United States and the waters off it.

Maritime Security

The Coast Guard was founded as the Revenue Marine in 1790, and maritime law enforcement and border control are the oldest part of the Coast Guard's responsibilities, dating back to the seventeenth century. It was established by Congress to patrol coasts and seaports to frustrate smuggling activities. That role has broadened and enlarged over the centuries to include drug interdiction. The Coast Guard is the lead agency for maritime drug interdiction, and the co-lead agency with the U.S. Customs Service for air interdiction operations. So it's the Coast Guard's responsibility to try to stem or halt the flow of illicit drugs into the United States.

Changes Since 9/11

The port security mission, including the interception and inspection of every ship headed for a U.S. port, has increased dramatically since September 11, 2001. Other Coast Guard missions have taken a back seat, but that doesn't mean they've stopped; it does mean that far more Coasties are on duty, and working hard.

What kind of power does the Coast Guard have? A lot more than you may think. The Coast Guard has the authority to board any vessel in U.S. waters in order to make inspections, searches, and arrests. This is an extraordinarily broad police power; no agency on dry land can enter any home or business at will, without a warrant, to search and seize. (That isn't to say it doesn't happen, but it's not *supposed* to.)

The Coast Guard traditionally limited its use of this power to focus on issues of drugs, immigration, fisheries, and protection of environmental laws. It's now being employed to counter terrorism through inspection of ships entering U.S. ports.

Along these lines, part of maritime security for the Coast Guard involves the interdiction of alien migrants. Frequently, individuals attempt to smuggle migrants in the hulls of ships, often in inhuman conditions, into the United States. Similarly, the Coast Guard often intercepts illegal immigrants coming by sea from Cuba or Haiti. The Coast Guard is the first line of defense in seeing that our immigration laws are upheld.

National Defense

The Coast Guard has served alongside the U.S. Navy in critical national defense missions, going all the way back to a scuffle with France in 1798, through the Civil War, both world wars, Vietnam, and the Persian Gulf War. As part of national defense, the Coast Guard is involved with maritime interception operations, military environmental response operations, port operations, security, and defense, and many other roles. The Coast Guard is the only element of the U.S. military to operate polar icebreakers, which permit the U.S. ships to enter Arctic and Antarctic regions. These polar vessels also provide supplies to America's polar facilities and support the research efforts of the National Science Foundation. In short, the Coast Guard does much more than guard the coast. If it has anything to do with protecting or enhancing life, liberty, commerce, and freedom on the high seas, the Coast Guard is there.

The Coast Guard is also famous for its maritime search and rescue efforts. When other units are involved, whether they are Federal, State or local, the Coast Guard, both sea and airborne, is responsible for coordinating those search and rescue efforts. And when accidents do happen, the Coast Guard is there to determine what happened and why, whether laws have been violated, or whether changes should be made to improve safety.

Basic Training

The average citizen perhaps knows the Coast Guard best in its role as "National Recreational Boating Safety Coordinator." This means that when you get tanked up and hop in your power boat to go careening around the bay scaring the heck out of the canoers and water skiers, it's up to the Coast Guard to try to rein you in. To that extent, they provide public education programs, regulation on boat design and construction, approval of boating safety equipment, and free marine examinations of boats for compliance with Federal and State safety requirements.

Protecting Natural Resources

Protecting the marine waters is a vital aspect of the Coast Guard's mission. America's marine environment is an extraordinary ecosystem—actually, many different ecosystems, some linked together and others spread out around the world—containing one fifth of the world's fishery resources. America's coastline areas are also a region of extraordinary recreation, minerals development, and transportation. Since the 1820s, the Coast Guard has been protecting America's natural resources.

Today, the Coast Guard also works to protect the environment as a public service. The Coast Guard is actively involved in protecting sensitive marine habitats, marine mammals, and endangered marine species. If you discharge oil or other hazardous substances into America's waters, be prepared for the knock on the door from someone in a Coast Guard uniform, and he or she probably will not be smiling.

Pentagon Parables

The Coast Guard, at various times, has been responsible for the protection of whales, fur-bearing animals, and fish. Almost two centuries ago, its predecessor, the Revenue Marine, was charged by Congress with protecting Florida live oak, owned by the Federal government. Trees, that is.

Maritime Mobility

The Coast Guard is also responsible for four aspects of maritime mobility, which is to say, keeping the waterways functioning smoothly as highways for trade, recreation, and military purposes. The Coast Guard's responsibilities include aiding navigation, icebreaking services, bridge administration, and traffic management on waterways.

How important is this system? Well, more than 2 billion tons of America's foreign and domestic freight and 3.3 billion barrels of oil move each year through the maritime waterways protected by the Coast Guard. That includes the half tank of gas in your Honda.

Changes Since 9/11

The future of the Coast Guard is the Deepwater Project, an almost total remaking of Coast Guard hardware, operations, and training. Planned before September 11, 2001, Deepwater is meant to extend the Coast Guard's effectiveness farther from shore, while modernizing its ships, aircraft, and communications systems. How much of this will survive the reprioritization of Coast Guard missions after September 11 won't be known for some time.

Special Forces—"Without Equal"

To a generation of Americans, the picture of a burned-out helicopter in a desert is symbolic of military impotence. In 1979, when Iranian "students" took an embassy full of Americans hostage, the Pentagon was tasked to put together a rescue mission. The failure of that mission, at a remote rendezvous point called Desert One, led directly to the creation of Special Operations Command.

Fighting Words

Special Forces Units with unconventional tactics, training, and/or equipment that operate in hostile, denied, or politically-sensitive areas. They aren't spies, in that Special Forces aren't limited to information gathering. They often go in to make things happen, except you usually won't hear about it when they do.

To be sure, the services already had *Special Forces*— those mythologized warriors who carry out covert missions, sometimes when hostilities aren't even contemplated, to lay the groundwork for success. And they had a history of notable achievements. Here's what led up to Desert One, and what came after.

Rogers' Rangers

Well before the term "Special Forces" was coined, certain American soldiers were performing the heroic tasks that would bring glory to the military and victory to the young nation. Rogers' Rangers were named after their commander, Robert Rogers. They stalked the enemy in woods and swamps in the French and Indian Wars. They moved with stealth and modeled their tactics on Native Americans. Rogers told his men, "Move fast and hit hard," and "Don't forget nothing," both good advice today, especially if you're Yogi Berra.

Two other names stand out in early Special Forces history. During the Revolutionary War, R.R.R. Francis Marion, the "Swamp Fox" from South Carolina, led a small unit that harassed and frustrated the British. During the Civil War, John Singleton Mosby formed a band of Confederate raiders that terrorized Union generals, cutting off communications and supplies behind the lines.

The Special Forces in World War II

Special units saw combat and won great acclaim during the Second World War. Three American special ops units were of note. One was the Devil's Brigade, a Canadian-American venture from 1942 to 1944 that was organized to assist in a planned liberation of Norway, but when that operation was scrubbed, they went to the Aleutian Islands, Italy, and later France. (If you're taking that tour, that's the best sequence of stops.)

The first Ranger Battalion, known as Darby's Rangers for its commander, Major William O. Darby, fought throughout Europe, but is best known for scaling the cliffs at Point du Hoc as part of the D-Day invasion of Normandy. This was the source of their motto, "If it's impossible, let the Rangers do it."

> ### Pentagon Parables
>
> The Devil's Brigade lives on in American special operations: The knife shown on a Green Beret patch was carried by (and designed for) the Devil's Brigade.

The third American special unit that won great acclaim during World War II was Merrill's Marauders, a 2,000-man force that fought in the Burmese jungle. They challenged the Japanese regulars to fight, and the Marauders beat the Japanese in 5 major battles and 17 skirmishes. They are famous for a march through hundreds of miles of thick Burmese foliage in order to capture an important airfield.

At the same time, a new type of special operations group was coming into being. They borrowed the daring and courage from the three units we've discussed, and added in new techniques of airborne and guerrilla fighting.

In a world of devils and marauders, the new covert agency had a bureaucratically neutral name: the Office of Strategic Services, or OSS. President Roosevelt's friend "Wild Bill" Donovan, a World War I veteran, convinced the President that intelligence gathering would be a vital aspect of winning World War II. Donovan was given authority by Roosevelt in 1941 to create a new agency, Coordinator of Information. The agency was renamed the OSS in 1942, and Donovan became a major general.

The OSS fought behind enemy lines in Italy, France, Greece, Yugoslavia, and Norway, conducting raids, assisting resistance movements, and generally creating "the maximum amount of confusion." While the OSS was disbanded after World War II, its members formed the core of the Central Intelligence Agency, created in 1947. The other outgrowth of the OSS was Army Special Forces, better known as the Green Berets.

Not-So-Jolly Green Giants

The basic idea behind the Green Berets is that in many situations, conventional warfare would be too overt, or insufficiently *surgical*. At the same time, special operations could help larger combat forces achieve their goals by disrupting enemy efforts and infrastructure behind their lines.

That sort of covert operational force was considered a boon in the Cold War, where one might want to cause trouble for, say, Soviet forces occupying an Eastern European country without starting a global thermonuclear war. Indeed, many members of the early Special Forces teams in fact had fled Eastern Europe and Communist tyranny, seeking the freedom of the United States. As a result, they spoke the language, understood the customs, and could travel freely around Eastern Europe, blending in with the local citizens.

Fighting Words

Surgical Precise, or affecting only a particular target.

Special Forces would conduct guerrilla warfare operations where necessary, but only after enduring perhaps the hardest training any soldiers have ever had to face in the history of war. Special Forces in Europe was soon complemented by Special Forces divisions in Asia and the Pacific.

All the Way with JFK

President John F. Kennedy, who took office in 1961, was a Navy veteran of World War II, and a connoisseur of military history. He had a special interest in counterinsurgency—ways and means of defeating guerrilla movements. Kennedy developed a deep affinity for the Special Forces, which grew rapidly during his administration.

As a result of President Kennedy's support, Army Special Forces was finally permitted to make the green beret its official headgear. JFK told the Pentagon that the Green Beret was "symbolic of one of the highest levels of courage and achievement of the United States military." The terms "Green Beret" and "Special Forces" soon became interchangeable.

Special Forces had a noble career during the Vietnam War, although after the war ended for America in 1973, Special Forces were reduced in number. Many of the units were deactivated. Army Special Forces were not resurrected in number until the 1980s, when guerrilla movements in Central America arose, creating a need for more Special Forces-type services.

> **Basic Training**
>
> Under President Kennedy, Special Forces began what is today its most significant continuing mission: working with allied armies and nations, especially smaller ones, in peacetime; training their troops; and developing ways to coordinate operations should we need to work together in combat at some point. This constant effort and maintaining of contacts is part of how U.S. and allied forces were able to come together quickly in the fight against terror, and may have helped get use of bases in some countries not usually thought of as close U.S. allies.

Panama and Desert Storm

Army Special Forces teams served with valor in Operation Just Cause in Panama in December 1989, and certainly in Desert Storm. In Saudi Arabia, Iraq, and Kuwait, Special Forces teams conducted deep reconnaissance, performed direct action missions, helped rescue downed pilots, supported the Kuwaiti resistance, and trained coalition units. It is said that the 109 Special Forces teams accompanied virtually the entire range of forces into battle during the ground war, and they were the "glue" that held the coalition together and made it work.

Air Force Special Operations

They call themselves the "quiet professionals." They are the Air Force Special Operations Command, or AFSOC ("AFF-sock"). What the Army did on the ground, the Air Force (and its predecessor, the Army Air Corps) did from the air.

One typical mission during World War II was conducted by the 800 First Bombardment Group, the "Carpetbaggers." These bold flyers delivered supplies, agents, and leaflets behind enemy lines using highly modified, black painted B-24s. The Air Force Special Ops pilots flew 3,769 successful missions into the Balkans, dropping more than 7,000 tons of supplies to resistance groups. Nearly 1,000 landings behind enemy lines brought in another 2,000 tons of supplies to those in need. Special Ops units also assisted in the evacuation of allied airmen and wounded partisans toward the end of the war.

Flying below the radar, Special Operations crews developed great proficiency at long-range navigation, often in poor weather and mountainous terrain. During early June 1944, six teams landed in Brittany, France, where they developed and provided vital intelligence that led to the success of the Normandy invasion.

When General Patton, moving fast across Europe, outran his fuel trucks, the Carpet-baggers were there. When highly mobile British ground forces needed resupplying in mountains and jungles in Burma, the First Air Commando Group of the Special Operations Command was there, earning the motto, "Any Place, Any Time, Any Where."

After the War

Special Operations, including AFSOC, were not perceived as necessary in the years immediately following World War II, as the nuclear balance of terror was expected to deter wars. That illusion was punctured to Special Ops' benefit when Communists began an insurgency in the Philippines in the late 1940s. The Korean War was also a time for the skills that the Air Force Special Operations embodied capabilities, most notably deploying intelligence teams and bringing in supplies in short- and long-range low-level penetration into both North and South Korea. Special Ops was revitalized and has grown in strength up to this day.

During the 1950s and 1960s, Air Force Special Forces were used in secret operations in Tibet, in Iran, behind the Iron Curtain, Vietnam, and at the Bay of Pigs in Cuba. The Soviet Union adopted the tactic of supporting "wars of liberation" throughout the Third World, using unrest in small capitalist nations to destabilize neighbors. That gave Air Force Special Operations a new job: counterinsurgency training for allied nations. As the Vietnam War expanded, so did the role of Air Force Special Ops. Indeed, it continued to grow in importance and success throughout the '60s, '70s, and '80s—with one vital exception, which we'll dwell on because it changed everything.

Operation Rice Bowl

The hostages taken by Iran in 1979 were draining the very lifeblood of the Carter administration and, day after week after month, presenting a continuing embarrassment to the world. A rescue attempt was planned … or perhaps "planned" is the wrong word.

Thanks to poor coordination and rehearsal, the rescue mission resulted in the deaths of eight Americans and a terrible black eye for the American military. It had suffered terrible problems throughout the entire planning stages. Air Force Special Ops pilots were asked to fly unfamiliar Navy helicopters in conditions for which they hadn't been designed. The Army Special Ops people worked for a different boss than the Air Force pilots who were to get them into Tehran, and the Navy maintainers for another boss yet.

> **Pentagon Parables**
>
> Another of the more significant problems identified in after-action studies of the Iranian rescue mission was that it had never been practiced with more than half the number of assigned aircraft—and complexity goes up faster than the number of aircraft.
>
> Even if there had been adequate coordination, one still wonders how it would have been possible to land helicopters or other airborne vehicles in what was essentially downtown Teheran, load them up with the hostages, and somehow get out without being assaulted by Iranian weaponry.
>
> Actually, the story of and problems with this mission could (and have) made their own fascinating books.

Perhaps the most important problem was the fact that, due to equipment and doctrinal incompatibilities, the different services involved in the mission couldn't agree on a single radio frequency for communications. As a result, there were no adequate means of communicating among the various airborne and land-based units that were supposed to assemble in the desert outside Tehran and fly into the city.

A special commission was convened to examine this mission failure and recommend changes. This began a reorganization and rebirth for all U.S. Special Forces.

There's No U in Team

The answer was to create a single command in charge of planning and executing special operations, leaving each service to its core competency. AFSOC would fly the aircraft, Army Special Forces would execute the land missions, and the Navy SEALS would laugh and eat everyone's lunch.

The mix worked. Special Forces served with great success in the 1983 rescue of Americans from the Caribbean nation of Grenada, in the reestablishment of democracy in Panama during 1989 and early 1990, and in Desert Storm and the Gulf War itself. During the Gulf War, Special Forces performed direct action missions, combat search and rescue, infiltration, exfiltration, airbase ground defense, air interdiction, special reconnaissance, close air support, psychological operations, and helicopter air refuelings. SOCOM units led the helicopter assault on radars, which blinded Iraq at the onset of hostilities. They also suffered the greatest single Air Force loss in the entire coalition—the shooting down of an AC-130 and the death of all 14 crew members aboard.

Changes Since 9/11

The war on terror is uniquely suited to SOCOM. Small unit and covert operations are exactly what's needed when going house to house and cave to cave tracking al-Qaeda leaders in Afghanistan. Training and coordinating with multinational forces is even more important in a time of global war.

Yet even as SOCOM reached an unprecedented rate of activity, with units spread across Afghanistan and elsewhere in support of the war, its future became less and less certain. As we write, DoD is considering proposals to reduce SOLIC from an ASD to a deputy assistant secretaryship, or even to transfer it to the new Department of Homeland Security.

In the 1990s, SOCOM provided support in the Balkans, in Somalia, and in the Rwandan civil war. At the close of the twentieth century, SOCOM forces were extremely involved in Kosovo, both in military operations and in humanitarian operations as well. They also play an important role today in homeland defense.

But special operators really kicked some posterior in Afghanistan. Some units were in country weeks before shooting commenced, establishing relations with Afghan tribal leaders, identifying targets, and locating Taliban and al-Qaeda leadership. (This has all been in the newspaper, so we're not blowing anybody's cover here. We may be idiots, but we're not stupid.)

Special Forces also fought and rode with tribal forces. One of the lasting images of the Afghan incursion was that of American troops fighting on horseback, over 100 years after the last great cavalry charge, while carrying GPS locators and digital communications gear to call in air support. Truly, special operators are masters of war in all its forms.

The Least You Need to Know

- The Coast Guard is part of the Transportation Department, but comes under the Pentagon in time of war or when designated by the President.
- Coast Guard OPTEMPO has soared since September 11, 2001.
- SOCOM was created in the wake of the Desert One disaster, to provide truly joint special operations capabilities.
- SOCOM oversees Special Operations Forces from all the services and provides them to CINCs.

Part 5 The Future

Where is the Pentagon going? So far, we have looked at the Pentagon today and yesterday. Now let's look at the challenges of a new century and a very new world.

Chapter 19

After September 11: The Pentagon in the Twenty-First Century

In This Chapter

◆ The attack on the Pentagon

◆ All change

◆ Construction time again

◆ The armed forces' information highway

The twentieth century saw the United States become the world's leading power. Much of that power was due to military strength and prowess, particularly as demonstrated in the middle of the century.

But it's hard to be number one, and the hardest part is realizing when the old songs and dances just aren't going to make it anymore. The end of the Cold War meant that the Pentagon had to adapt to a number of new realities, from coping with new alliances to finding justifications for some of the jobs they continued to do. And just when the kinks were getting worked out of the new process, everything changed again. The Pentagon is faced, once again, with the following question: Where does the American military go from here?

The Day It All Changed Again

On September 11, 2001, American Airlines Flight 77, a Boeing 757 leaving Washington Dulles Airport for Los Angeles, was taken over by hijackers. At 9:38 A.M., it was deliberately crashed into the Pentagon midway between the fourth and fifth corridors.

The airplane actually landed short of the building, striking the helipad outside the southwest side of E ring. It bounced and partly cartwheeled into the Pentagon, which may have helped dissipate the impact's energy. But the fuselage pierced the E, D, and C rings, and came to rest with its nose against the B ring.

Flaming jet fuel burst into the E ring, sending fireballs from the crash site toward the Mall entrance. Fortunately, the fourth and fifth floors remained intact above the crash site until 20 minutes or so after the impact, allowing people in those spaces precious time to crawl through the smoke and flame to freedom.

The Pentagon, September 12, 2001. At the top center, just below the helipad, you can see the gap where a portion of the E ring has collapsed following the impact of American Airlines Flight 77. The plane struck the helipad, then pierced the building almost perpendicular to the outside wall. The blackened areas show where fire lingered in the roofing long after the main blaze had been extinguished. Some emergency equipment is on the helipad side and blocking Route 27; note also the tents already set up in South Parking.

(spaceimaging.com)

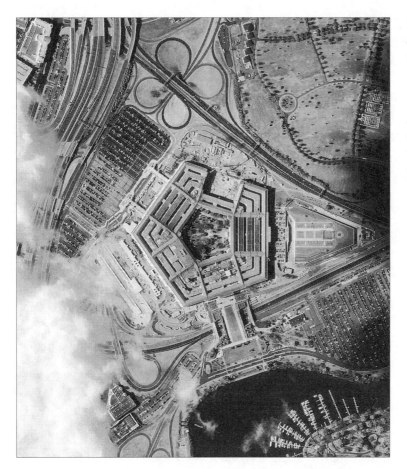

On November 20, 2001, you can see that the E, D, and C rings have been completely torn down between Corridors 4 and 5. The emergency equipment has given way to construction trailers beginning Project Phoenix, the round-the-clock rebuilding of the Pentagon.

(spaceimaging.com)

Inside, the destruction matched the diverse nature of Pentagon business. The Navy's new command center was destroyed. So, too, were cubicle offices of civilians working on the Army budget. So were the offices of the Army Deputy Chief of Staff for Personnel, and many more. Officers, enlisted, civilians, and contractors all work together, and some of each died.

The fire that began at the crash site spread to the roof of the E ring and persisted there well after fire at the crash site was under control.

> ### Pentagon Parables
>
> One person counted as both an airliner casualty and a Pentagon loss. Top budget analyst Bryan Jack, traveling aboard American Airlines 77, was the lone Pentagon casualty from aboard the aircraft instead of in the building.

The Pentagon, June 3, 2002. The exterior walls of all three damaged rings are in place and roofed. Aside from the construction equipment and the completed transit and delivery centers, it's not clear that much has changed from before the attack. But everything did.

(spaceimaging.com)

In the crash, subsequent fire, and partial collapse, 125 Pentagon workers lost their lives, along with all 59 passengers and crew aboard the airplane (we choose not to count those who acted to cause the deaths). While the toll is horrific, with 23,000 people working in the building, to have lost only 125 is almost miraculous.

And the NMCC never closed.

The attack didn't change how the Pentagon does business. However, it dramatically focused and energized the people who work in the Pentagon. Just as September 11 created a new spirit of unity across the country, it rededicated the people of the Pentagon. And because of the state of war, it made resources much easier to get, both to prosecute terrorists and to protect the people who protect America. Physically, much of the building's first renovated wedge was destroyed. Offices far from the crash site suffered smoke damage. Most visibly, the exterior of the E ring wall was charred along almost its entire southwestern face.

Yet the building is so large that people working on the other side, near the Metro entrance, were so unaware that anything had happened that when alarms were sounded to evacuate the building, many thought it was just a fire drill.

Close-ups of the attack damage.

(DoD photos by Tech. Sgt. Cedric H. Rudisill)

Pentagon security today is much tighter than on September 10, 2001, in ways both visible and not. Changes were made to how deliveries are handled to the subway and bus systems near the Pentagon. Public tours were discontinued, and photography in and around the building is now restricted. OSD did set up a podium and backdrop in the public areas outside the security gates, so you can pretend to give your own press conference.

Transformation Station

Although it began before September 11, all of the services have discovered a new buzzword for the twenty-first century: *transformation*. They're looking for ways to do their jobs more efficiently, to leverage new technology, and, frankly, to stay relevant. Aside from cutting back in numbers, the services haven't changed very much since the end of the Cold War. Transformation is the first real effort to size and shape the forces for the twenty-first century.

Fighting Words

Transformation Hard to define in the Pentagon context, but like Justice Potter Stewart said about pornography, you know it when you see it.

(The joke is that in the Army, transformation means changing their equipment; in the Air Force, it means changing operations patterns; and the Navy, it means using a slightly different shade of gray for the ships. But that's unfair to the Air Force.)

Transformation, though, is very much like the parable of the blind men and the elephant: It's different to everyone who touches it.

The Army looked at the end of the Cold War and saw a reduced probability of having to fight a major tank battle on an open plain. They took a lesson from peacekeeping operations in the former Yugoslavia, and particularly from the experience of the 82nd Airborne in Operation Desert Storm. They decided that the Army needed to be lighter, more mobile, and able to fight in smaller units. The goal of their transformation is the Future Combat System we described in Chapter 14, which includes not only weapons but also new ways of operating that maximize quickness, firepower, and networked sensors.

Pentagon Parables

When Saddam Hussein deployed his forces into Kuwait, the Army sent the ready brigade of the 82nd Airborne and elements of the First Marine Division into northern Saudi Arabia to protect that kingdom. To get the troops there quickly, they were sent without armored vehicles, as the Army didn't have readily deployable light armor. That meant that, had Iraqi forces continued into Saudi Arabia, they would have faced only dismounted infantry. The Americans were thus little more than—as they called themselves— a "speed bump." The new light armored vehicle, called the Stryker, will be able to deploy quickly with troops and provide at least some protection.

The Air Force chose a different path to transformation. While they are bringing in a new generation of fighter aircraft, with the new F-22 and F-35 fighters in development, the bigger change is in how the Air Force manages its deployments. In the old days, when a situation arose, the Air Force would send the most ready units. This meant that some units were getting sent over and over again, while others stayed mostly at home. It's hard for a unit on deployment to keep up training, morale, and see to their families.

So the Air Force took a page from the Navy's book. Navy battle groups rotate on a regular basis. They go to sea for six months; then home for six months; and prepare for their next employment for six months. Crises aside, a sailor can look at a calendar and know when he will be home and when he will be away.

Looking at that model, the Air Force created what it calls Aerospace Expeditionary Forces, essentially aerial battle groups that rotate to forward areas on a regular schedule. That way, it's more likely that the Air Force will have airpower near any contingency that occurs, and they improve their *PERSTEMPO*. The Air Force is also defying its fighter jock culture and making much more use of unmanned aerial vehicles (UAVs) to carry out missions that would previously have required a pilot and maybe crew.

> **Basic Training**
>
> The emergence of UAVs led to a warm discussion in the Air Force: Do the remote controllers "flying" UAVs have to be pilots? Do they even have to be officers? So far, the answer is no and no, but the discussion continues.

> **Fighting Words**
>
> PERSTEMPO (short for "personnel tempo")   How hard you're making your forces work. A high PERSTEMPO, as in wartime, gets a lot done but wears out your people.

Now let's be nice to the Navy. They do have transformation plans, much of which involves taking advantage of networking to make their forces work better. They are looking at how smaller, high-speed ships might bring a new dimension to operations. And they are refitting ballistic missile submarines to carry conventional weapons, making them more relevant to today's challenges. The challenge for naval leaders is less in dealing with the old threats than staying relevant to the new ones. After all, terrorists tend to fight on land. If your weapons and platforms are based at sea, how do you help deal with them?

The Navy looks to two simple but key attributes that distinguish their efforts: access and persistence.

Water covers two-thirds of the earth's surface. Almost all of that is international waters, where the Navy can operate. So they have access to much of the world, where other forces need bases, and thus the cooperation of other countries. As any Navy official will tell you if you so much as mention water, a carrier is sovereign American territory that happens to move from place to place. That's access.

That same idea contributes to persistence. Sure, long-range bombers can go any-where in the world. But they hit and run. The Navy can sit there 24/7, or until the rum runs out.

The Marines have a little tougher time transforming, in part because they start a little ahead of the other kids and don't need to transform as much. The Corps already fights lean, which means they are efficient. And because air and fire support are packaged with their infantry, Marines can communicate within service channels to do things that other services have to coordinate through joint means.

Pentagon Parables

A hot Pentagon buzzphrase, *network-centric warfare*, started with Navy thinkers. Network-centric warfare differs from platform-centric warfare, in which your carriers and other major weapons systems define how you fight. Network-centric warfare is all about getting the right piece of data to the right place at the right time. That way, you can have a cheap and easily hidden unmanned sensor tell you what the enemy is up to, and you can send one airplane, ship, or missile to take care of the job. Instead of having your sensors tied to the platform that actually does the shooting and bringing a whole battle group in to see what needs doing.

So the Marines are transforming their notion of their battlespace. Whereas they used to fight as far inland as they could walk after storming the beach, operations in Afghanistan saw the Marines 800 miles inland. And their goal for the future is to get there faster, with a new half-helicopter, half-airplane called the V-22. (Whether going farther and faster while doing the same job are evolutionary or transformational, we leave to the less nuance-challenged.)

The common vision across the services is of globally accessible, free-flowing data. Commanders used to dole out information on an as-needed basis; the systems and doctrines of the twenty-first century now emphasize the ability of even individual sol-diers to see the whole battle, not just their part in it. That gives them the ability to better understand their situation and what really needs to be done.

It creates a tremendous challenge for the services, too. Information has always been used as a command mechanism. By keeping troops in the dark, commanders helped assure that their forces would go where and when they were ordered. Individual initiative is a good thing in the military, but not when it involves making up your own orders. So the services will have to find ways of commanding and controlling forces who have as much knowledge of the battle as the commander does, and who may reach different conclusions about the best course of action.

But there's no question that information can be empowering. In what was billed as a preview of the Army 15 years ahead, early in 2001, the Army ran an exercise at the National Training Center using an armored brigade fitted with systems that showed each crew the position of every unit in the field, friendly and—as far as was known—hostile. This awareness, coupled with the ability to communicate through digital networks without voice radios, allowed the visiting units to surprise and decisively defeat the in-house "enemy."

Everybody Row

One of the toughest remaining jobs is to make sure all these transformations work together. We've shown how the services have different words for the same idea. But they also have different ideas for the same word. Let us illustrate with a joke going around on the building e-mail network, which will also show you just what passes for humor in the Pentagon:

A Navy lieutenant and captains from the Army, Marine Corps, and Air Force are asked to outline how they would secure a building. Here's what they turn in:

Navy

- Unplug the coffeepots
- Turn off the computers
- Turn out the lights
- Lock the doors and leave the building unoccupied

Army

- Assemble the company
- Appoint Sergeant of the Guard
- Take control of all exits
- Make sure no one gets into the building without a pass

Marine Corps

- ◆ Assemble the platoon and supplies
- ◆ Approach the building along three axes
- ◆ Assault the building under covering fire
- ◆ Sequester surviving prisoners
- ◆ Repel counterattacks

Air Force

- ◆ Contact real estate agent
- ◆ Negotiate one-year lease
- ◆ Be sure to get option to buy

In the Navy, the verb "secure" means quit. You've probably heard "Secure from general quarters!" in a Navy movie or two. In the Army, it means "protect," or make it secure. In the Marine Corps, it means "take," and in the Air Force, "acquire." (This is important when one of the services wants to give you a ride someplace, because if the Air Force says they secured transportation, they scheduled a limo. But if the Marines say they secured transportation, it means they tossed some guy out of his Toyota at gunpoint.)

This represents in a very small way the kinds of cultural differences that challenge OSD in coordinating any transformation of the services. It's hard for a service to adopt new ways of operating without impinging on another service's *rice bowl*. And the services are themselves not all on the same page internally. That leaves service chiefs telling OSD, "I'm with you, but hang on a minute while I put out some fires."

Fighting Words

Rice bowl Pentagon term for an area of interest. An Army move to make its forces lighter and more mobile could be seen as eating from the Marine Corps' rice bowl. Efforts to reorganize the services or OSD may require breaking rice bowls.

Transformation has affected the Pentagon, too. You've already read about the Directorate of Force Transformation bringing OSD-wide oversight to service transformations. But OSD is changing as well.

One initiative—discussed in Chapter 11 (of the book, silly, not bankruptcy)—was streamlining acquisition. Another was to reduce oversight and auditing, both internally and from outside. A third sought to combine the services' legislative affairs shops with OSD's, ostensibly for efficiency, but many in the building suspected the real agenda was to minimize deviation from the OSD message. And there were many more. Although not all of these have been fully implemented, the message from SecDef Rumsfeld was clear: There's a new sheriff in town.

Free Housing! Free Guns!

As the Pentagon entered the twenty-first century, leaders expected to face another major challenge—filling the ranks. Although the services usually meet their goals for bringing new people into uniform and convincing those already in to reenlist, recruiting tends to be counter-cyclical. When the economy is good, private sector advantages in pay make recruiting a real challenge. In less prosperous times, the military's promise of a secure and interesting job with free training in technical disciplines and a clear career path has greater appeal.

The economic boom of the 1990s, coupled with well-publicized reductions in the size of the military, made life very hard for recruiters. That was especially true in high-skill specialties, like aircraft pilots and information systems specialists, where civilian demand was very high and the pay scale off the charts. The military doesn't have much flexibility when it comes to salary and benefits. It wasn't unusual for college graduates talented in data systems to make more as starting pay than the Secretary of Defense ($161,200 in 2001, and free helicopter rides).

When the dot-com bubble burst and the economy started to go south, things started looking better for recruitment. But the attacks of September 11, 2001, changed the equation completely. Recruiting offices were swamped, often with people who'd retired from the service but felt motivated to go back. Even more dramatic was the effect on reenlistment, which soared.

With Congress actively considering increasing the number of personnel authorized to the services, keeping the military filled with good people may get a bit tougher. Today, the Pentagon faces problems with certain specialties, but the pessimism of 2000 has passed.

Basic Training

The services count on a certain amount of disenchantment in the ranks. Resignations and retirements give them room under their manpower caps to bring in new blood, and to allocate those new people to specialties that may be needed more than the jobs being done by the existing folks. Also, there are fewer slots in each higher rank, so—particularly in the officer ranks—it's up or out.

Show Me the Money

A similar pattern applies to military funding. Funding tends to run in 20-year cycles, not least because that's about how long it takes for major weapon systems to wear out.

Spending was high in the 1940s because of the Second World War. After the war, the forces shrank, and in the '50s (as you read in Chapter 12) the nuclear deterrent provided defense on the cheap. Spending surged again in the '60s because of the Vietnam War and a need for modernization. In the '70s, a number of systems went into development in order to incorporate lessons learned from Vietnam. Those systems became ready in the 1980s, leading to another spending peak.

A public insistence on a "peace dividend" following the Cold War, coupled with relatively few demands for American forces in combat roles (albeit a high demand for other kinds of missions) led to limited growth in the 1990s. But the confluence of new technologies, aging of weapons bought in the 1980s buildup, and the need to adapt forces to new missions indicated that the cycle would continue. The September 11, 2001, attacks snapped public opinion solidly behind defense increases, and the FY2003 budget being debated as we write contains the largest increase in—well, the usual 20 years.

Fighting Words

Train wreck Government—and budgeteer-speak—for what happens when something you plan to do either goes badly awry or collides with something else you plan to do.

That increase and its consequences lead to perhaps the most difficult problem facing the Pentagon today—the *train wreck* of FY07.

Don't Show Me *That* Much

In Chapter 11, when we went through the military hardware procurement process, we saw that systems happen when the available technology matches a current need. However, just as people sometimes conceive more than one child at a time (hence, twins, triplets, quintuplets—you get the idea) sometimes technologies meet several different needs simultaneously.

The train wreck of FY07 comes about because technology has met every service's needs at once, and because the post-September 11, 2001, expansion of defense spending comes on top of what was already an ambitious defense budget. We were set for the upswing of the 20-year cycle; then we went to war on top of that.

The unexpected nature of the attacks on America caused the G.W. Bush administration to violate an established Washington budgeting practice. Usually, an administration gets aggressive about defense toward the end of its first term, or early in its second.

That way, the administration can say "Look at all the stuff we're buying for defense!" while the real costs—the outyear bills—are left to the next president to deal with. The urgent need to replace platforms fielded en masse in the 1980s, along with the imperative to devise new ways of meeting new threats, however, means that the outyear bills really start to mount in FY07 and FY08, in what the administration hopes will be its second term.

The train wreck happens when a whole bunch of procurement programs that are in development now go into production, which is when the real money starts to get spent. Look at just part of the list of programs set to expand dramatically in the 07–08 timeframe:

- The Air Force's F-22 will have just started full-rate production.

- The joint service F-35 will also be well on its way to being produced.

- The Navy's F/A-18E/F fighter—yes, that's three different fighters at once—will still be in production.

- The Army's Crusader, or whatever replaces it, is supposed to appear in FY08, which means big money in FY07. So is the first iteration of the Future Combat System.

- The Air Force will be in the midst of multiyear production of C-17 and C-130J cargo planes. Throw in a couple of KC-130 tankers for the Marines.

- Ballistic Missile Defense will start going from the drawing board to metal and circuits.

- The Navy is behind on shipbuilding and wants to increase ship numbers. They expect to build a new aircraft carrier, CVN(X), around that same time. The DD(X) destroyer will be turning into a real ship about then, too.

- The SSGN ballistic missile submarine conversions will be underway.

- The V-22 for the Marine Corps and Air Force may be hitting full production.

The Pentagon will be trying to squeeze all of those systems, and a lot more, into the FY07–FY08 budgets, and that's just the weapons systems. We haven't even discussed paying the troops or building base housing or starting other research projects. Just this above list represents tens of billions of dollars more than the procurement portion of the FY02 budget.

Every one of these programs has a reason to exist. But the question going around the building is how to make them all work at once. The easy answer is to raise the defense topline. But whether the administration will be able to do that, and whether Americans will want to foot the bill, are open questions right now.

Another question keeping the SecDef and his advisors up at night is whether any of the technology listed previously will help in a war against terrorism. We'll tackle that question in the next chapter. (We just wanted to make sure you came back after the commercial.)

As the Pentagon enters the twenty-first century, it has a lot to think about.

The Least You Need to Know

◆ Of approximately 23,000 Pentagon employees, 125 perished in the attacks of September 11, 2001.

◆ Services are looking for ways to do their jobs more efficiently, to leverage new technology, and to stay relevant.

◆ Recruiting and retention have become easier since September 11, 2001.

Chapter 20

W(h)ither Warfare?

In This Chapter

- ◆ Potential elements of the next war
- ◆ Unforeseen dangers
- ◆ The sum of all fears
- ◆ Civilian casualties

If a strategist wants to insult a colleague, the most offensive slander is to accuse the other of planning to fight the previous war. That's because military strategists always need to plan for future contingencies, future developments, and future enemies.

America's last major war was in the Persian Gulf in 1991. Many allied systems and tactics used during the Gulf War were developed for a war that never happened, the superpower confrontation in Europe. It's good that these preparations proved more than adequate to meet the challenge of Iraq. Unfortunately, it may be a poor lesson for future wars. It would be a mistake to look back in smugness.

What Is the Next War?

America did well in the Gulf War, and our forces demonstrated in the desert the useful effects of six months' preparation to engage a specific enemy, courtesy of Saddam Hussein. A cautious planner should nonetheless ask two questions:

◆ What is the *next* war?

◆ For what are we *not* prepared?

Armed with the answers to those questions, Pentagon planners and budgeters and others in a position to establish defense priorities can make the tradeoffs necessary to ensure that America can and will prevail against the next threat. And remember, the standard isn't victory in a test of arms, because—as September 11, 2001 proved—many new threats to the United States don't involve military versus military ("force-on-force") engagements.

Traditional defense planning designs forces to meet the most taxing possible contingency, the big one. It's rational to assume that being ready for the greatest challenge will automatically allow us to respond to what the department calls "lesser included contingencies." But in fact "lesser" contingencies—like Desert Storm or the Afghan campaign—are not necessarily "included."

Changes Since 9/11

Although not related to the attacks, SecDef Rumsfeld put forth a new basis for sizing the force that differed from the two-major-war guidance of the past. His "4-2-1" construct recognized the drain placed on the military by large operations other than war. By his lights, the U.S. military should be able to deter challenges in four key regions and fight two major contingencies at once, holding the line in one while winning the other, then moving forces over to win the second. At the same time, they should be capable of defending the United States.

Just as a world-class marathon runner may do poorly in sprints, so being prepared for the most difficult threat to American national security doesn't mean that U.S. forces are thus ready to meet every lesser challenge. Today's greatest threats to American security and interests may come in forms for which we are utterly unprepared.

Remember, until recently, the Defense Planning Guidance required that American forces be able ultimately to prevail in two major regional contingencies. Broad as it is, that guidance nonetheless risked overlooking three salient features of some significant threats to the United States and its interests:

♦ They aren't major

♦ They aren't regional

♦ They aren't contingencies

If history is a guide, some elements of the next war are clear.

Element 1: The Next War Will Put Civilians Directly at Risk

One of the clearest trends in the evolution of armed conflict is that noncombatants will be targets.

War has steadily progressed, from tribal days through 1990s Bosnia, to include civilian casualties not as incidental to war but a goal of it.

> **Basic Training** _____
>
> Nobody has a patent on the idea of violent organized forces that don't represent a country. The Middle East has been full of them: Today's Hezb'ollah and al-Qaeda; the Israeli Irgun of the 1940s; the 1970s' factions of the Palestine Liberation Organization (notably Black September, Al Fatah, and the Popular Front for the Liberation of Palestine). In fact, the '60s and '70s were full of them. Vietnam had the Viet Cong, Italy the Red Brigades, Germany the Baader-Meinhof gang, and Japan the Red Army. The Provisional Wing of the Irish Republican Army and Sri Lanka's Tamil Tigers carry the banner today. And the United States isn't left out; remember the Weathermen in the '60s or today's Michigan Militia.

That's an especial threat to a militarily strong state. The U.S. military is without question the best equipped, best prepared, and most powerful on the face of the planet. It would thus be foolhardy for an opponent to go force-on-force with us. Threatening the civilian population, though, gives an opponent great leverage.

This is true regardless of the opponent in that next conflict. There is, after all, little difference between a terrorist group and a nation that chooses to operate like one. Were a weapon of mass destruction (WMD) placed on a civilian ship and sailed into New York harbor, it would scarcely matter whether it was placed there by the government of Libya or the stateless al-Qaeda.

This kind of scenario threatens the United States populace directly, yet it isn't major, regional, or—because it isn't amenable to a direct military solution—a contingency in the classic sense.

The United States populace is unaccustomed to being directly threatened. Although fallout shelters and duck-and-cover drills proved there was some perceived threat to the United States during the nuclear stalemate of the Cold War, America's civilian populace hasn't been directly in the sights of a foreign army since the Second World War, when U-boats operated within sight of the Atlantic coast and the Japanese sent fire balloons to the Pacific Northwest. Apart from terrorist acts like the Oklahoma City bombing and September 11, 2001 actions, the last combat operations on the American mainland came at Appomattox Courthouse in 1865.

It's reasonable to believe that, should large-scale violence occur, the American public would demand protection and wonder why an appropriate defense had not been in place. Many of these questions were asked after September 11, 2001. The answer may well be that without advance knowledge of a given threat, there is no highly effective defense. Returning to the previous example, the ship in New York harbor could have been stopped en route, but once it is there, no defense policy or weapons system can prevent someone from detonating its weapon.

Element 2: The Next War Might Not Be Force-on-Force

The United States has traditionally sized its force against opponents' capabilities. In the current world, though, other countries' capabilities are less and less relevant. No nation or faction today poses a credible conventional challenge to the U.S. military. The more pressing problem is unconventional or *asymmetric* warfare, both against civilians (as just mentioned) and the use or threat of use of WMD.

Fighting Words

Asymmetric Having capabilities or tactics the other side just doesn't possess. The United States has an asymmetric capability at sea over al-Qaeda. They, on the other hand, are more willing to create civilian casualties and thus have an asymmetric advantage on that front.

All the advanced fighter aircraft in the world won't deter an opponent fighting unconventionally, particularly if they're threatening something (say, U.S. civilians) we hold dear while not exposing similar vulnerability themselves. Because the United States global interests are so broad, while other groups and nations have a much narrower focus, it's possible for potential adversaries to pose a threat to us with little corresponding leverage on our part.

Almost by definition, nonnational groups offer little opportunity for leverage. Military force is effective against buildings, facilities, equipment, and populations. (This is often expressed in the Pentagon with the phrase "We know how to break things and kill people.") Non-national groups, though, don't have infrastructure we can threaten; they often don't represent a particular populace. Even when they do, reprisals against a populace (such as, arguably, the failure of Israeli operations in refugee camps to affect PLO policy) may have little effect on a foe who values its goals more than human life itself.

The late Formula One racing champion Ayrton Senna, a devout Christian, believed that the next world would be infinitely better than this one. Many of his rivals admitted that Senna's beliefs often kept them from trying to pass him, as Senna had nothing to lose by taking life-threatening risks. They feared for their safety in this world when close to someone who was eager to get to the next.

That same calculus applies to those willing to give their lives to inflict harm upon the United States. As we discussed in Chapter 12, the Cold War calculations of nuclear deterrence were based on the notion that the opponent was a rational person who valued his life and those of his countrymen. No amount of American force structure or military expertise will deter an opponent who doesn't share those values, and who has no regard for the opinions of the international community or life itself.

Element 3: WMD Greatly Expands the List of Possible Threats

U.S. defenses are traditionally planned against adversary states, many of which have well-developed military forces. In an age of easily obtainable weapons of mass destruction, the focus on the largest threats may miss the more likely threats.

> ### Pentagon Parables
>
> Another recent change at the Pentagon is the shift from "threat-based" to "capabilities-based" planning. Previously, force structure and strategic-level planning had been based on looking at a limited set of specific adversaries and making sure we could beat their forces. Capabilities-based planning looks at what weapons or technologies are available to whomever might fight us, recognizing that we may not know where the threat will come from, and that these days, anybody can buy almost anything.

Neither national wealth nor even defense spending is a reliable guide to which opponents pose the greatest challenge to U.S. interests. Economically benighted nations can threaten us as well. For many years, the Soviet Union was bitterly impoverished, with little better than a Third World economy. It was nonetheless an international player due to the strength of its military, and particularly, its possession of nuclear, chemical, and biological weapons. Size is irrelevant: *One man with WMD and a delivery system is a superpower*.

Element 4: Military Engagements Will Be Fought as Part of a Coalition

Historical trends also indicate that, should an opponent not learn from the Iraqi example and engage the United States in a traditional military battle, it's likely that the United States will not fight alone.

Despite an impressive and heroic military history, the United States taking on an opponent solo is the exception, rather than the rule. The First and Second World Wars, Korea, Desert Storm, and even the Revolutionary War were all fought with the United States in a leading role, but as part of multinational coalitions. (Panama and Grenada were, for all intents and purposes, solo.)

Rarely a military necessity, the coalition approach has become politically essential. Administrations of both parties have sought UN approval before taking military action and have volunteered U.S. forces to be part of UN initiatives. The most recent National Security Strategy of the United States specifies that in war, fighting "combined with allies and friends" is a basic principle, coming ahead even of joint operations.

Fighting Words

Bottom-Up Review (BUR) A major study of force sizing and strategy initiated under SecDef Les Aspin, the BUR was the forerunner of today's Quadrennial Defense Review.

Basic Training

The way administration insiders keep the two President Bushes separate is to call them "41" and "43," indicating where each falls in the history of the Presidency. Of course, author Douglas Adams said the answer to the ultimate question of life, the universe and everything is 42. So they're close.

Indeed, the United States has come to rely on combined operations to a degree that may lead one to question our ability to operate autonomously in many contingencies. The scenarios used in the 1994 *Bottom-Up Review* (BUR) to size American forces assumed some measure of allied assistance.

The first Bush administration's levels, called "Base Force," similarly assumed allied assistance. Indeed, President G.H.W. Bush's characterization of Desert Storm as "the first conflict of the post-war era" was a reference not to tactical innovation or advanced systems but because it was fought as an international collective.

Relying on coalition warfare serves two political purposes and one strategic purpose.

- It helps legitimize U.S. operations in the international community by showing broad multinational support. This short-circuits claims that the United States is simply attempting to impose an American order on other nations.

- It undercuts domestic criticism of overseas operations by showing other nations putting their national blood and treasure on the line. This is particularly important following what was perceived as unilateral American sacrifice in Vietnam.

- It builds America's credibility with other nations, so that arrangements for access to their facilities may be easier to make should the United States care to initiate a unilateral action in the future.

- Coalition partners can also take on valuable roles in logistics and combat support, freeing American units to focus on the fight.

In sum, of the four attributes possibly characterizing the next war, coalition operations are the only one with which U.S. forces have current experience. While we cannot know the shape of the next war, history suggests that it is likely to include at least some elements for which our military may not be prepared.

What Are We Least Prepared For?

First, let's understand that a lack of preparation isn't necessarily a problem. It's no drawback to be unprepared for events that are unlikely to occur. We aren't prepared to keep alien spaceships from blowing up the White House, but that probably isn't a serious deficiency, as such an attack, while not impossible, has a low likelihood of occurring this week. A prudent planner probably wouldn't spend much to develop a defense against such an attack.

On the other hand, an open and current question, as discussed in Chapter 13, is how intensively the United States should develop and deploy defenses against ballistic missiles. That's a question of the probability of that threat (and our vulnerability to it) against the other demands on defense resources. Some of those vulnerabilities follow, in no particular order.

Attack from Within

Domestic terrorism or insurgency falls into a crack in the national security structure. The FBI and conventional law enforcement agencies are tasked with detecting this class of threat, but their organic resources to deal with it are few and relatively inexperienced. And although servicepeople are sworn to defend the Republic against enemies foreign and domestic, our military forces are heavily oriented toward defeating external threats.

Changes Since 9/11

When this book went to print, debate was underway as to whether powers granted to the Director of Homeland Security, a post created following the September 11, 2001 attacks to coordinate the Federal response to all threats to the nation, could be used to fill the gap between the military's externally focused capabilities and the new demand for domestic defense.

That situation arises largely because the threat posed by militias or domestic groups sympathetic to outside terrorists has traditionally been small and ineffective. With foreign terrorists now known to be operating inside the United States and the domestic militia movement increasing in virulence and sophistication, America may need to adjust its national security structure so the intelligence assets devoted to domestic threats are integrated with the forces likely to respond to them.

Information War or EMP

Information warfare refers to the sabotage or interruption of computer networks and communications. Think hacking on a large and organized scale.

EMP stands for "electromagnetic pulse." When a nuclear weapon goes off, it emits a strong wave of electromagnetic energy. Some scientists and strategists argue that the EMP from a nuclear weapon detonated just above the atmosphere spreads out many types of electronic circuits across a wide swath of territory.

These two forms of attack on the information flow infrastructure result in many of the same effects.

While information warfare attacks data systems with computer viruses and the like, and EMP "fries" circuitry with a raw surge of electrons, each results in communications paralysis and inaccessibility of data needed for the proper functioning of industry, the nation's financial system, and, most importantly, for response to the assault.

Absent countermeasures, this vulnerability will only grow with the explosion of computer networking capabilities and reliance on distant resources. Communications networks allow companies to rely on telecommuting workers and government agencies to retrieve research data from the Internet rather than maintaining hard copies, but add a new level of vulnerability to these enterprises. A nation that increasingly receives its news and official information over cables rather than through broadcast is more vulnerable to disruption or confusion.

America is well along the way to building a society based on "just-in-time" data. Those who speak of an "information superhighway" boast of the benefits to a societies ability to retrieve news, research, or any data from distant sources whenever it's needed. The problem with this system, as with "just-in-time" manufacturing, is that output becomes susceptible to small perturbations of input. The society that depends on a free flow of information must also defend it.

> **Pentagon Parables**
>
> For examples of why it's important to defend networks, look at the satellite failure that killed thousands of ATMs and cell phones in 1998, or the 1996 strike at one General Motors brake plant that shut down most of the company's North American operations within a few days. A problem at one point crippled those networks over a wide area.

Missile Attack

A radio advertisement that aired in the Washington area a few years back pointed out that for $50 million, a terrorist group could purchase SCUD-class missiles against which the United States would have no defense. Apart from the question of from where the missiles would be launched (Canada? Mexico? Alabama?), the weakness described is real; as you read in Chapter 13, the United States possesses essentially no defense against missile attack. Many high-value targets, both civilian and military, are within range of sea-launched tactical or cruise missiles, and the entire nation can be targeted by ICBMs.

One is, however, compelled to ask why an aggressor would buy a $50-million missile to deliver a nuclear bomb when a panel truck will do as well.

Irrationality

As discussed in Chapter 12, defense planning has long assumed that the opponent is a rational human being. Our military could defeat Saddam Hussein's forces, but it couldn't locate Saddam, nor predict that he would fire missiles against noncombatant nations. Who is willing or able to predict what villainy the current Osama bin Laden or a successor will do next? And how do you defend against an unpredictable threat?

America's Advantages

That we are unprepared for some threats is not to say that the United States is without advantages in the military arena. They are considerable. The question is, in the next war, will America's advantages matter?

Advantage 1: Relative Spending on Defense

Nobody can match America's ability to design, build, and procure defense hardware. No other country can raise and train a ready force while equipping them to our standard. (Even we couldn't, which is why we cut back in the 1990s.) Note that the next nine biggest spending nations are either allies or reasonably neutral.

Total defense spending in dollars, from the CIA World Factbook, 2000. Who's the big dog?

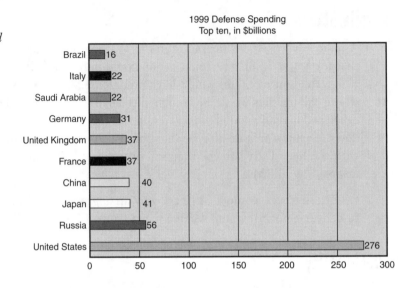

The picture changes a bit if one considers defense spending as a percentage of a country's Gross Domestic Product (GDP), which evens the playing field.

Percentage of GDP spent on defense, from the CIA World Factbook, 2000. Things that make you say, "Hmm ..."

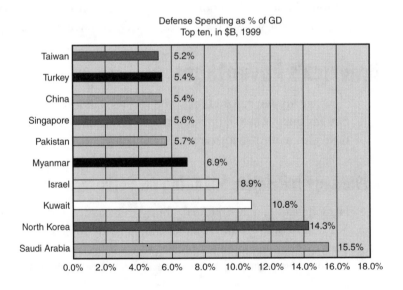

Although more hostile nations spend a high percentage of GDP on defense, two factors ameliorate that:

◆ The high ranking of these nations is primarily a function of their small GDPs, and;

◆ You can't buy a fighter with GDP percentage; it takes raw cash.

So while percentage of GDP provides a useful measure of the *strain* defense spending provides on a nation, defense spending proves a more relevant measure of the scope of possible threats. On that scale, threats are few.

Of course, it costs us a lot more to fight than other countries, because we have to get to where the fight is, we take better care of our people, and the technology that makes the United States a winning force isn't cheap.

The drawback to this measure is that many current threats aren't from countries, and therefore aren't captured by measures of national defense spending. Further, some weapons of mass destruction are relatively inexpensive to manufacture, and (as discussed earlier in this chapter) can yield high *leverage*.

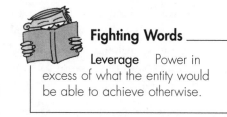

Fighting Words

Leverage Power in excess of what the entity would be able to achieve otherwise.

The United States was able to win the Cold War in large measure by spending the Soviet Union into Chapter 11. (A CPA might actually argue that it was Chapter 7, liquidation, rather than 11, reorganization, but you get the idea.) But the Soviets courteously agreed to play by our high-technology, high-procurement rules. The next opponent might threaten targets of high value to the United States with a few, simple, inexpensive weapons. The rules in such a case don't favor the sole superpower.

Advantage 2: U.S. Technological Excellence

Of all the United States' advantages, its technological know-how is the one best suited to fighting unconventional warfare. Paradoxically, though, it's not the edge in weapons technology that helps most. Our technological leadership in weapons systems yields clear dividends in a straight-up shooting war like Iraq. It is technology's application to intelligence systems, though, that also allows us advance warning of most conventional and many unconventional forms of attack, although the warning period varies with the type of threatening forces.

Advantage 3: Training, Morale, and Professionalism

The superior preparation and discipline of American forces is a tremendous asset *once a conflict begins*. It is less likely that they will *deter* a conflict. The intimidation factor of a military is a combination of its discipline and equipment, the resources available to it, and its nation's commitment to the conflict, which in the United States is often uncertain in advance. That last factor gives an adversary reason to question our commitment. (After all, the French Foreign Legion has plenty of training, morale, and professionalism, but we don't lose sleep over them.)

Where Do We Go from Here?

Let's not be vague: The U.S. military is ready to fight and win most of the nation's wars. The challenge is to ensure that this stays true as the nature of war changes. Historical trends are clearly moving us toward threats and conflicts that are less and less amenable to traditional types of military solution.

The threat of retaliation, however massive, is no longer sufficient to deter actions against the United States, its people, and its interests. An entire class of threats has emerged that can be defeated only through relentless pressure on their operations and foreknowledge of opponents' intentions and likely actions. Yet, while U.S. intelligence capabilities are not to be underestimated, it is impossible to know of every threat in advance.

The challenge for the defense planner, then, is to identify those technologies, systems, and programs able to find potential threats and to remedy U.S. vulnerabilities where they exist (or may reasonably be expected to). That could, for example, lead one to the conclusion that intelligence programs, special operations forces, foreign training and advisory teams, and law enforcement specialists may today be more relevant to the defense of our nation than advanced fighter aircraft, or that language training may take precedence over combat simulators.

Whatever the answer, some in the national security structure will be unhappy. But the nation as a whole may sleep more soundly. And the Pentagon will be, as it is today, at the center of the action.

The Least You Need to Know

- Over time, wars have involved civilians to an increasing degree.

- The elements of future wars are not cut and dry, nor can they be predicted.

- The policy of coordinating operations with allies, once a nicety, is increasingly a requirement.

- The threat of retaliation, however massive, is no longer sufficient to deter actions against the United States.

Appendix A

Fighting Words

8th and I Colloquial name for Marine Barracks, Washington, D.C., located at 8th and I Streets Southeast. Home of the Marine Band, ceremonial details (including the Marines who work at the White House) and the Commandant's home.

A-76 The process by which the government decides between public and private bidders for the same work.

AAFES See *Army and Air Force Exchange Service*.

ABL See *Airborne Laser*.

ABM See *anti-ballistic missile*.

Airborne Laser (ABL) A large ray gun mounted in a Boeing 747 airframe to be used in boost-phase missile defense.

alliance Two or more countries that work together under treaty arrangements; compare with *coalition*.

amphibious ready group Fleet of ships centered on one or more LHAs, LHDs, or other Marine ships designed to support amphibious operations.

anti-ballistic missile (ABM) Defense to protect against ballistic missiles.

AOR Area of responsibility. That realm in which a geographical CINC is king.

apportionment Prioritizing a set of tasks.

architecture   The overall design of a system, including how the components work together and share tasks.

Army and Air Force Exchange Service (AAFES)   The agency that runs the post and base exchanges (PXs and BXs) for the Army and Air Force.

ARPAnet   A rudimentary predecessor of the Internet that linked together government research labs.

Arrow   An Israeli midcourse antimissile program, partially funded by the United States, with a capability similar to THAAD.

ASD   Assistant Secretary of Defense.

aviators   The people who fly airplanes in the Navy.

Ballistic Missile Defense Organization (BMDO)   Former name of the Missile Defense Agency.

Beltway bandit   A firm that makes its living by supplying analytical or other support services to OSD or the services. The name is derived from the location of many top firms along the Washington Beltway in Virginia.

Berry Amendment   A section of law which states that the textiles and food products DoD buys must be grown or produced in the United States.

black   See *white*.

blue-on-blue   See *fratricide*.

blue water/brown water   The high seas are "blue water"; areas close to shore are brown.

BMDO   See *Ballistic Missile Defense Organization*.

BMEWS (Ballistic Missile Early Warning System)   A system of radars offering early warning of missile attack.

bolt from the blue   An unexpected, unwarned attack. The phrase refers to a lightning strike.

Book of Honor   Glass-encased book at CIA headquarters listing the names (those that can be told) of those who died while serving their country.

Bottom-Up Review (BUR)   A predecessor to the Quadrennial Defense Review, under SecDef Aspin, looking at the needs of the American military from the bottom up.

branch   The area of the Army you serve in, defined by the general career area you seek (like engineers, armor, artillery, or communications).

brigade   A subset of an Army division, usually about 10,000 soldiers.

The Building   How Pentagonites usually refer to the Pentagon in casual conversation, as in "I have to get back to The Building," or "The Building is going crazy today."

BUR   See *Bottom-Up Review*.

bus   The upper portion of a MIRVed missile that the warheads ride on while waiting to be released to go to their individual targets.

BX (base exchange)   On-base, government-owned department store. Formerly PX, for post exchange.

CAD   See *Component Advanced Development*.

carrier battle group   A Navy force centered on one or more aircraft carriers, but including destroyers, cruisers, or other ships.

chemical and biological weapons   Chemical weapons are things like nerve gases, or poisons that cause injury or death. Rudimentary chemical weapons were used in the First World War. Biological weapons are diseases or viruses that occur naturally, but are used as weapons.

Child Development Center   Military terminology for "daycare center."

CINCdom   A simple way to refer to the territory overseen by a regional CINC. Also refers to the CINC's near-total power in the region.

CINCLANT   Navy Commander in Chief, Atlantic.

CINCPAC   Navy Commander in Chief, Pacific.

classified annex   Part of many Pentagon reports made unclassified so they can be released to the public, the classified annex includes the more interesting parts.

coalition   A set of different countries acting together in wartime. Compare with *alliance*.

collateral secret   Something that combines unclassified information in such a way that the result is deemed classified.

COMINT   Communications Intelligence. Information learned through listening in on somebody else's conversation.

CONFIDENTIAL   The least respected of classifications, just a step above *FOUO*. Controlled like SECRET, but why?

CONPLAN   Contingency plan for how the United States might respond to different situations.

CNWDI   Classified Nuclear Weapon Design Information.

comms   Slang for "communications."

Component Advanced Development (CAD)   An interim phase of developing a new system.

Cooperative Threat Reduction   Program between the United States and Russia to provide alternate uses for the former Soviet defense establishment.

counterair   The Air Force mission of destroying or neutralizing the enemy's air force and air defense network.

counterforce strike   An attack aimed at destroying the opponent's strategic weapons.

counterinsurgency   Ways and means of defeating guerrilla movements.

counterland   Operations involving attaining and maintaining superiority over the enemy on the ground.

countervalue targeting   Aiming your weapons at an enemy's cities or economic targets.

Crucible   The final exam in Marine recruit training, a 54-hour exercise in which the recruits hike, solve problems, hike, surmount physical obstacles, hike, conduct infiltration and other exercises, shoot, and hike, all while receiving instruction on Marine Corps traditions and standards.

Current News Early Bird   See *Yellowbird*.

customs and courtesies   The rules that govern military conduct, such as who salutes whom, how to act when the flag is displayed, and how one addresses fellow personnel of various ranks.

CVBG   Carrier Battle Group.

DAB   See *Defense Acquisition Board*.

DACOWITS   See *Defense Advisory Committee on Women in the Services*.

DARPA   Defense Advanced Research Projects Agency.

DASD   See *Deputy Assistant Secretary of Defense*.

DCI   See *Director of Central Intelligence*.

DCS   Deputy Chief of Staff.

DCSOPS   See *Deputy Chief of Staff for Operations*, pronounced "dessops."

DCSPER   Deputy Chief of Staff for Personnel, pronounced "dessper."

DDR&E   See *Director of Defense Research and Engineering.*

declassify on   The date or event on which documents are no longer classified. Sometimes, they will say "Declassify on OADR," which stands for Originating Agency's Determination Required.

Defense Acquisition Board   The senior review panel for all DoD acquisitions. The DAB (pronounced "dab") includes the USD for Acquisition, the Vice-Chairman of the Joint Chiefs, the service acquisition chiefs, and more.

Defense Advisory Committee on Women in the Services (DACOWITS)
A board established by George C. Marshall to increase the number of women in the armed services and to enhance their roles in the military.

Defense Commissary Agency   The agency overseeing military grocery stores.

Defense Finance and Accounting Service (DFAS)   The Pentagon's bookkeepers.

Defense Information Systems Agency   The department in charge of monitoring computer and communications needs for the Pentagon.

Defense Logistics Agency   Department in charge of military purchasing.

Defense Planning Guidance (DPG)   The basic document by which the SecDef prescribes the priorities and parameters around which DoD components are to prepare their budgets.

Defense Support Program (DSP)   Satellite-based infrared sensors that search out unusually large amounts of heat concentrated in small space, like that of a rocket launch.

Defense Threat Reduction Agency   The Pentagon agency dedicated to reducing threats without resorting to military action, often through treaties.

defensive counterair (DCA)   Fighting back against enemy attacks in the air.

DepSecDef   See *Deputy Secretary of Defense.*

Deputy Assistant Secretary of Defense (DASD)   The next level below ASD, usually with responsibility for a subject area. The ASD for Personnel and Readiness has a DASD for Readiness, for example.

Deputy Chief of Staff for Operations   The General in charge of all operations. In the Army, it's abbreviated DCSOPS; in the Air Force, AF/XO, on the Joint Staff, J3.

Deputy Secretary of Defense (DepSecDef)   Number two in name, but in many ways number one in the life of the Pentagon. Although his role varies from administration to administration, the DepSecDef usually runs the building and acts as the chief doorkeeper for the Secretary.

DESRON   Destroyer Squadron.

destabilizing   Making war more likely.

detailer   The officer who makes assignments for your specialty.

DEW (Distant Early Warning) Line   A series of radar stations in very cold places, aimed at detecting incoming bomber raids. See also BMEWS.

DFAS   See *Defense Finance and Accounting Service.*

DI   See 1. *Directorate of Intelligence.* 2. *drill instructor.*

digitized brigade   An Army brigade with communications and other equipment allowing information to be shared digitally among all units.

Director of Central Intelligence (DCI)   The director of the CIA.

Director of Defense Research and Engineering (DDR&E)   Sponsors the development of new ideas, whether by contractors, by services, or in-house.

Directorate of Intelligence (DI)   The analytical branch of the CIA.

Directorate of Operations (DO)   The branch of the CIA that gathers some of the information that DI analysts put together.

Directorate of Science and Technology (DS&T)   The branch of the CIA that collects information in ways both traditional and new.

division minus   Army division in which one or more of the brigades comes from the reserve component.

DLA   See *Defense Logistics Agency.*

DO   See *Directorate of Operations.*

DoD   See *Department of Defense.*

downselect   The point when a winner is chosen in a competitive procurement.

DPG   See *Defense Planning Guidance.*

DSP   See *Defense Support Program.*

DS&T   See *Directorate of Science and Technology.*

eagle, globe, and anchor   As the symbol of the Marine Corps, the superimposed eagle, globe, and anchor symbolizes America, worldwide service, and naval traditions.

electromagnetic pulse (EMP)   A strong wave of electromagnetic energy emitted by a nuclear weapon.

ELINT Electronic Intelligence. Tells you where a signal is coming from and what its characteristics are (if it's a radio, a radar, etc.).

EMP See *electromagnetic pulse.*

Federally Funded Research and Development Center (FFRDC) A nonprofit organization with a contract that lets them be treated as an extension of the service that is their client.

FFRDC See *Federally Funded Research and Development Center.*

fire control Aboard ship, the fire control party is the guys with hoses who try to put out fires. In the missile world, fire control is the system that helps you target and launch a missile. Some ships have both.

fiscal year An accounting term for the year-long period over which you budget. The federal government's fiscal year runs from October to the following September; fiscal year 2003 (or FY03, as it's abbreviated) started on October 1, 2002.

flight profile The speed, direction, and altitude of a particular missile or aircraft.

former Marine There are no retired Marines. In keeping with a Corps dictum, "Once a Marine, always a Marine," members no longer on duty are referred to as "formerly active."

FORSCOM Army Forces Command.

FOUO (For Official Use Only) Documents that are not classified but that contain sensitive information. Usually drafts, decision memoranda, or other working papers.

fratricide Shooting at someone from your own team.

frock To authorize an officer to wear one rank higher than he or she actually has earned, if promotion to that grade is forthcoming.

Future (or Five) Years Defense Plan (FYDP) The future budget projections presented with each year's defense budget.

FYDP See *Future Years Defense Plan.*

geospatial intelligence Looking at features of the earth.

Ground Zero The point on the ground immediately under a nuclear explosion. Called that because measurements of a bomb's effects begin from that point. The Trinity site near Los Alamos, New Mexico, was the world's first Ground Zero. Also the unofficial name for the Pentagon courtyard.

guidance Pentagon euphemism for an order.

guidon   A pole bearing multicolored ribbons, bearing the name of a battle a unit was in.

gunny   Gunnery Sergeant, a noncommissioned Marine who instructs in the use of weapons.

Hogan's Alley   A mock town in which troops can train for house-to-house warfare and the kinds of surprises that can await indoors. More formally called a MOUT (Military Operations in Urban Terrain) site.

homeport   Where a ship lives when it isn't deployed, like a base for the Army. The crew's families usually live at the homeport.

horseholder   The aide who sits outside or silently in the back of the room while his or her star-emblazoned boss meets and plans.

HUMINT   Human Intelligence. Information collected from people.

IBCT   See *Interim Brigade Combat Team.*

ICBM   Intercontinental ballistic missile.

ID   See *infantry division.*

IMINT   Imagery Intelligence. Gathering information by looking at pictures.

immature theatres   Air Force-speak for areas where we really haven't done a lot of preparation for going to war.

Independent Research and Development (IR&D)   Corporate research subsidized by DoD with the hope that what they come up with might be militarily useful.

indications and warning   Ways to detect when an attack might be coming. Indications are things like recalling certain units to duty or refueling of missiles that give you the idea something might be up. Warning is when you see unmistakable proof that an attack is about to begin, or just has. The United States has a National Intelligence Officer just for warning.

infantry division   A basic Army fighting unit consisting of approximately 20,000 soldiers.

infiltration/exfiltration   Getting people or things into denied areas (infiltration) or out of them (exfiltration).

intel   Slang for "intelligence."

intelligence community   The 14 organizations that gather or analyze intelligence information: Central Intelligence Agency; Defense Intelligence Agency; National

Security Agency; the intelligence operations of each of the branches of the military the Army, Navy, Air Force, and Marines; the National Imagery and Mapping Agency; the National Reconnaissance Office, and then five other intelligence-gathering organizations under the direction of the President of the United States: the Federal Bureau of Investigation, and the Departments of Treasury, Energy, Justice, and State.

Interim Brigade Combat Team (IBCT)   An experimental Army unit combining infantry with easily transportable armored vehicles.

Intermediate-Range Ballistic Missile (IRBM)   A ballistic missile with a range of around 1,000 miles.

International Security Affairs (ISA)   The department of OSD charged with managing programs providing military assistance to other countries.

International Security Policy (ISP)   A department of USD policy that helps formulate America's security treaties, decides on technology transfer rules, and represents DoD in negotiations with other countries.

interoperable   Able to work together, such as radios for different services that use a common frequency.

IRBM   See *Intermediate-Range Ballistic Missile.*

IR&D   See *Independent Research and Development.*

ISA   See *International Security Affairs.*

ISP   See *International Security Policy.*

Jammer   See *Joint Monthly Readiness Review.*

JCS   Joint Chief of Staff.

JFACC   See *Joint Forces Air Component Commander.*

JMETL   A joint METL.

joint   The ability to operate together with other services.

Joint Chiefs briefing room   A two-story tall auditorium with floor-to-ceiling rear-projection displays that show everything from the inevitable PowerPoint slides to maps and live video.

Joint Chiefs of Staff   The group of heads of the military services.

Joint Forces Air Component Commander (JFACC)   The air boss of a joint task force, with operational authority over all air forces regardless of what service or country they're from.

Joint Monthly Readiness Review ("Jammer")   Monthly meeting where services and OSD readiness types look for shortfalls in training, equipment, or any factor that would keep units from being able to carry out their missions, and attempting to find and fix patterns across the services.

Joint Operations Planning and Execution System (JOPES)   The process by which major operations are planned.

Joint Requirements Oversight Council (JROC)   A review group, made up of the service vices and chaired by the vice-chairman of the Joint Chiefs, that approves hardware programs to reduce overlap among the services.

Joint Strategic Capabilities Plan (JSCP)   The plan, issued by the Joint Chiefs of Staff, that assigns tasks to the CINCs and apportions major forces.

Joint Task Force (JTS)   The structure the supported CINC assembles in wartime.

JOPES   See *Joint Operations Planning and Execution System.*

JROC   See *Joint Readiness Oversight Council.*

JSCP   See *Joint Strategic Capabilities Plan.*

JTS   See *Joint Task Force.*

key performance parameters (KPP)   A list of how well systems in development are required to do different tasks.

KPP   See *Key Performance Parameters.*

lessons learned   After each major conflict—and, in some cases, any major engagement—a "lessons learned" team goes over the action to prepare a formal report on what happened, what didn't, and how the results could be improved upon. The findings are incorporated into service training and planning.

LIMDIS   Notation on a classified document indicating Limited Distribution. This has always confused us, because all classified is by definition limited distribution.

local time   The time wherever the person being talked to is.

logistics   The science of supply. Every service has logisticians whose whole job is to figure out how to get the forces what they need, where they need it, and when they need it there.

MAGTF   See *Marine Air-Ground Task Force.*

major theater war (MTW)   An all-out war involving a substantial commitment of forces, money, and time.

Mameluke   The ceremonial sword that every Marine officer carries.

man-in-the-loop   A system that is not automatic, but requires a real human to make a real decision.

maneuvering reentry vehicle (MaRV)   A missile that is steered in erratic paths to confound defenses.

MARFORs   Marine Forces.

Marine Air-Ground Task Force (MAGTF)   How Marines deploy for combat. A MAGTF combines air, sea, and ground forces.

Marine Expeditionary Forces (MEFs)   Geographical Marine commands including air, sea, and ground assets.

Marshall Plan   The program designed by SecDef George C. Marshall to help restore the nations of Europe after World War II.

MaRV   See *maneuvering reentry vehicle.*

MASINT   Measurement and Signatures Intelligence. Telling what a thing is by the way it reflects light, the gases it emits, or other technical characteristics.

materiel   Stuff.

MDA   See *Missile Defense Agency.*

MEADS   See *Medium Extended Air Defense System.*

mechanized infantry division   Division armed with tanks and helicopters.

Medium Extended Air Defense System (MEADS)   A U.S.-German cooperative development that started out as a way to put missile defense assets at the corps level using the Patriot missile and a simpler fire control network; pronounced "mee-adds."

MEFs   See *Marine Expeditionary Forces.*

megaton   The equivalent of a million tons of TNT. The bomb dropped on Hiroshima was about 12.5 kilotons, or 12,500 tons of TNT. That flattened every-thing in a 1.5-mile radius.

METL   See *Mission-Essential Task List.*

metric   The measurement relevant to a particular decision. At Disneyland, your height is a metric to decide whether you can ride Space Mountain.

military-industrial complex   A phrase often used by critics of defense spending to describe the combination of contractors, Congressional supporters, and Pentagon personnel they perceive as driving excessive spending.

Military Occupational Specialty (MOS) A code that designates what profession you've been trained to do.

Military Specifications (MILSPECs) The guidelines which items procured by the Department of Defense must meet.

MILSPECs See *Military Specifications.*

MIRVs See *Multiple Independently-Targeted Reentry Vehicles.*

Missile Defense Agency (MDA) The OSD organization in charge of creating both theater and national missile defenses.

Mission-Essential Task List (METL) Your unit's jobs.

MOS See *Military Occupational Specialty.*

MOOSEMUSS Acronym for the principles of war: mass, objective, offensive, simplicity, economy of force, maneuver, unity of command, security, surprise.

MOOTW Military operations other than war.

MREs Meals, Ready to Eat. The standard combat ration, which typically includes an entrée, side dish, crackers, fruit cup, and utensils, all individually sealed and encased in a waterproof plastic pouch.

MTW See *Major Theater War.*

Multiple Independently-Targeted Reentry Vehicle (MIRV) A missile with several warheads, each of which could go to a different place. See also *maneuvering reentry vehicle (MaRV).*

mutual assured destruction The idea that neither the United States nor the Soviet Union would ever use nuclear weapons on each other, because each knew that the other superpower could retaliate by destroying the other country as well.

National Imagery and Mapping Agency (NIMA) The department whose job it is to provide "timely, relative, and accurate geospatial intelligence in support of national security."

National Military Command Center (NMCC) The room, full of monitors, printers, and busy coffeepots, where the Pentagon keeps a 24-hour eye on the world.

National Military Strategy (NMS) A document the SecDef is required to produce each year showing how the military will support the National Security Strategy.

National Security Agency (NSA) The "nation's cryptologic organization," which means essentially that it studies coded information.

National Security Council (NSC)   Where defense and foreign policy issues are hashed out before going to the President; comprised of the President, Vice President, and the Secretaries of State, Treasury, and Defense.

National Security Strategy (NSS)   An annual report, signed by the President, outlining the goals of America's national security structure, both military and diplomatic.

Naval Air Systems Command (NAVAIR)   The part of the Navy responsible for developing new airplanes.

Naval Exchange Command (NEXCOM)   The command that runs BXs on navy bases.

NEXCOM   See *Naval Exchange Command.*

Naval Sea Systems Command (NAVSEA)   The part of the Navy responsible for developing new ships.

NCO   Noncommissioned officer.

NDU   National Defense University.

New Look   The defense concept developed in the 1950s that emphasized greater reliance on nuclear weapons, the elevation of strategic air power as the major means to deliver nuclear weapons, and a cut in conventional ground forces.

NMCC   See *National Military Command Center.*

NMS   See *National Military Strategy.*

NOFORN   Marking on a classified document that means it cannot be shown to foreigners, even allies.

NORAD   See *North American Air Defense Command.*

North American Air Defense Command (NORAD)   The joint U.S.-Canadian command charged with securing the skies from enemy attack.

NSA   See *National Security Agency.*

NSC   See *National Security Council.*

NSS   See *National Security Strategy.*

NTC   The Army's National Training Center, located at Fort Irwin, California, where units come to practice against an opposing force trained in enemy tactics.

Nuclear Cities Initiative   A U.S. effort to find useful pursuits for the Russian nuclear industrial base, in part so they don't sell knowledge or technology elsewhere.

Nunn-McCurdy A law passed in 1982 that says if a system increases in cost by 25 percent or more, the SecDef has to certify, among other things, that continuing the program is essential to the national security of the United States, and that there are no other ways to do the same job.

offensive counterair (OCA) Attacking proactively, generally over enemy territory, against their ability to employ their airpower and defend against ours.

Office of Management and Budget (OMB) The White House budget office.

Office of the Secretary of Defense (OSD) The civilian leadership of the Pentagon.

OMB See *Office of Management and Budget.*

OODA loop The process of making a decision; stands for "Observe, Orient, Decide, Act."

operational contract An arrangement in which the Pentagon hires a firm to make decisions and run a particular area. See also support contract.

operational control (OPCON) Having the authority to issue orders. An Army unit may be under the operational control of the regional CINC, which means he can assign them missions, but he isn't responsible for paying them or deciding their promotions. He only has control over the unit's operations, and has to give them back to the Army when he's finished with them.

Operations Deputies (OPSDEPS) The service generals in charge of operations, or "3s."

OPFOR Opposing force.

OPLAN Operational plan; a CONPLAN with details filled in.

OPSDEPS See *Operations Deputies.*

OPSDEPS room Conference center in the Joint Staff area where the service 3s (or OPSDEPS) meet to discuss and plan operations. Also the meeting room for the JROC.

organic A capability that's part of the organization, and doesn't have to be added on.

OSD See *Office of the Secretary of Defense.*

out of hide Paying from the existing budget.

oversight Congressional review of government operations.

Pave Paws A ground-based missile- and air-defense radar system.

PDD See *Presidential Decision Directive.*

peace enforcement   Inserting forces between warring parties to create peace where none exists. Compare with *peacekeeping*.

peacekeeping   When combatants agree to have a force separating them. Compare with *peace enforcement*.

Pentagon Officers' Athletic Club (POAC)   Now officially just the Pentagon Athletic Club, although it is still referred to as the POAC (say "POE-ack").

Pentagon Papers   A secret history of the Vietnam War prepared during McNamara's time as Secretary of Defense and published in *The New York Times* and the *Washington Post*, despite the fact that they had never been declassified.

PERSTEMPO (short for "personnel tempo")   How hard you are making your forces work. A high PERSTEMPO, as in wartime, gets a lot done but wears out your people.

Pk   The capital P stands for "probability"; the small k for "kill." The probability of kill for any weapon system. Pks of weapon systems are among the more closely guarded secrets in the Pentagon.

plus-up   The amount added by Congress to a budget.

POM   See *Program Objective Memoranda*.

post exchange (PX)   See *base exchange*.

PPBS   See *Program Planning and Budgeting System*.

Presidential Decision Directive (PDD)   An order from the President.

Program Objective Memoranda (POM)   Each service's take on how it will follow the DPG, and how much it will cost. Essentially, a draft of the new budget.

program office   A group of people dedicated to getting a particular system through the procurement process.

Program Planning and Budgeting System (PPBS)   The arcane system by which the Pentagon decides what it will buy and how much it will spend.

PX (post exchange)   See *base exchange*.

Q   Classification level requiring a separate clearance from the Department of Energy.

QDR   See *Quadrennial Defense Review*.

Quadrennial Defense Review (QDR)   A top-to-bottom Department study, done every four years, of the military's missions, how they'll go about meeting them, and whether the planned forces are up to the task.

radius of effects   The area affected by a detonation. Nuclear weapons have two primary kinds of effects: blast and prompt radiation. The blast radius, where things get knocked down or vaporized, is much smaller than the area subjected to intense radiation and heat.

redundant   Systems that have more than one way to get a job done, so if one fails or is knocked out, the system should still work.

reserve component   The Guard and Reserves.

Revenue Marine   The original name for the Coast Guard.

rice bowl   Pentagon term for an area of interest.

ROE   See *rules of engagement.*

rules of engagement (ROE)   The guidelines on who may use force, when, and how much.

SALT   Strategic Arms Limitation Talks, conducted between the United States and the Soviet Union in the 1970s.

SAP   See *Statement of Administration Policy.*

SBIRS   See *Space Based Infra Red System.*

SBL   See *Space-Based Laser.*

SCI/SAP   Sensitive Compartmented Information, often intelligence data; Special Access Programs, or things we do that are quite secret.

SCIF   See *Secure Compartmented Information Facility.*

SCUD   A silly name for a nasty Russian short-range missile.

SDI   See *Strategic Defense Initiative.*

SecDef   See *Secretary of Defense.*

SECRET   The second category of "real" controlled material.

Secretary of Defense (SecDef)   The senior civilian in the Pentagon and, with the exception of the President, in the entire national security structure. He is appointed by the President and confirmed by Congress.

secure   To protect (Army); to take (Marine Corps); to acquire (Air Force); to quit or leave (Navy).

Secure Compartmented Information Facility (SCIF)   A safe, access-controlled room for classified materials and personnel. Say "skiff."

Secure Internet Protocol Router Network (SIPRnet)   The DoD's own secure, classified global Internet.

Secure Telephone Unit (STU)   A phone from which classified information may be discussed. Say "stew."

Senior Executive Service (SES)   Senior civilians, roughly equivalent to military general officers.

sensor-to-shooter time   The period required from detection of a target to firing on it, whether in missile defense, artillery, or torpedoes.

SES   See *Senior Executive Service.*

SIGINT   Signals Intelligence. Information gleaned through communications intelligence (COMINT) and electronic intelligence (ELINT).

Single Integrated Operations Plan (SIOP)   A series of plans for employing the United States' nuclear force.

SIOP   See *Single Integrated Operations Plan.*

SIPRnet (Secure Internet Protocol Router Network)   DoD's own secure, classified global Internet.

six-by   Usually written 6x6, the standard medium military truck for years and years.

skunk works   A small, efficient, secretive organization.

SLBM   See *submarine-launched ballistic missile.*

SNAFU   Such a common term in American vernacular that it's usually not capitalized anymore, SNAFU originally stood for Situation Normal, All (Fouled) Up.

SOLIC   See *Special Operations and Low Intensity Conflict*

sortie   A single flight by a single plane.

SORTS   See *Status of Resources and Training System.*

Space-A (space available)   The military benefit of being able to ride along free on a military flight as long as they have a spare seat.

Space Based Infra Red System (SBIRS)   Pronounced "sibbers," a system under development to provide warning of missile attacks.

Space-Based Laser (SBL)   A proposed constellation of satellites in space with large lasers capable of knocking out missiles.

Special Operations and Low Intensity Conflict (SOLIC)   A department of USD policy that focuses on the unique needs of smaller military conflicts (not wars).

special operations forces (SOF)   Forces that perform unconventional combat missions, and to work with foreign militaries, helping to train them or to aid in coordinating their efforts with the United States.

spin up   To generate, or excite. The phrase comes from aviation, where you have to wait for the gyroscopes in a navigation unit to get to operating speed, literally to spin up, before using the navigational device.

SPN   A code placed on the discharge papers of every individual separated from the service.

standing down   Closing. Units are *stood up* and *stood down*.

START   See *Strategic Arms Reduction Talks*.

Statement of Administration Policy (SAP)   A document issued by the White House defending their budget and pointing out disagreements with committee changes or proposed amendments.

Status of Resources and Training System (SORTS)   System that communicates unit readiness, along with the factors that may be causing shortfalls, through the chain of command to the Pentagon, where it's reviewed by the JROC.

status quo ante   Latin for "the way it was before." Most statements of goals of a war include at least returning the situation to where it was before the bad guys attacked.

Strategic Arms Reduction Talks (START)   A series of negotiations between the 1970s and 1980s that resulted in smaller nuclear forces.

strategic attack   Going after an enemy target that will affect its ability to wage war overall.

Strategic Defense Initiative (SDI)   Original concept for a space-based anti-missile system to provide a comprehensive defense against enemy missiles; nicknamed "Star Wars" by its detractors.

submarine-launched ballistic missile (SLBM)   A missile fired from beneath the ocean.

support contract   An arrangement in which contractors help with planning, force structure, and other headquarters functions while OSD or the service retains decision authority. See also *operational contract*.

surgical   Precise, or affecting only a particular target.

T for C   "Termination for convenience of the government." A contract provision that allows the government to cancel at any time.

tail   1. The money that a new program will cost in the outyears. 2. The people required to support the current fighting force.

Tank, the   Where the Joint Chiefs meet to plan operations and, often, to settle differences out of public view.

TEMPEST   A set of rules that controls how much radiation a piece of equipment puts out.

THAAD   See *Theater High Altitude Area Defense.*

Theater High Altitude Area Defense (THAAD)   An Army anti-missile defense system.

Time-Phased Force Deployment Data (TPFDD)   A list of what forces the CINC needs to carry out an OPLAN and when they need them.

topline   The total amount of a budget, with everything added up.

TOP SECRET (TS)   Like secret, only more so.

Total Force   Including active and reserve component forces as a single fighting force.

train wreck   Government- and budgeteer-speak for what happens when something you plan to do collides with something else you plan to do, and there's not enough money for both.

triad   The three possible means of delivery (missiles, submarines, and manned bombers) of nuclear weapons.

TRICARE   The medical benefit program for military dependents and retirees.

TS   See *TOP SECRET.*

type commanders   The admirals in charge of each element of naval power. Each geographical commander will have type commanders for ships, aircraft, and submarines.

UJTL   See *Universal Joint Task List.*

Under Secretary of Defense for Personnel and Readiness (USD [P&R])   The Pentagon's corporate human resources department.

Universal Code of Military Justice (UCMJ)   The laws of conduct in the military, and how violations are to be adjudicated and punished.

Universal Joint Task List (UJTL)   A list of everything a joint force should ever be able to do.

USD (P&R)   See *Under Secretary of Defense for Personnel and Readiness.*

vice   When most of the world would say "versus" or "against," the military says "vice." Can't begin to tell you why.

Weapon of Mass Destruction (WMD)   Weapon designed to inflict damage on a large area, and against all persons in that area.

weaponized   Turned into an effective military weapon. Weaponization can be making a virus that exists in one climate survive in another, finding a way to make it even more lethal, or to design a warhead that spreads toxic substances.

white/black   Some Pentagon agencies and activities are "black" which means secret. Black agencies have classified or partially classified budgets, and their specific activities aren't listed in the Secretary's annual report. There are, of course, varying degrees of blackness; some "white," or public, agencies have black compartments, while some agencies could be so black that the agency itself doesn't officially exist.

WMD   See *Weapon of Mass Destruction.*

Yellowbird   A collection of news items of interest from around the world, once distributed around the building in early morning as hard copy but today via Internet.

Zulu time   Greenwich Mean Time.

By the Book

For those of you whose appetites have been whetted for more Pentagonia, or who just couldn't get enough of this stuff in the first place, we've put together a list of books you might find interesting.

Well, actually we put some of it together, but we let the pros do most of it. Each of the service chiefs maintains a reading list, books of professional interest that are recommended reading in the ranks. They tend to group the books by ranks for whom they'd be appropriate; we kept the ranking, but changed the labels.

Interestingly, some titles are so good that several of the chiefs list them. That's not just the classics, like Clausewitz' *On War*, either. Michael Shaara's tale of the Civil War battle of Gettysburg, *The Killer Angels*, is a chiefs' choice, as is Harold Moore and Joe Galloway's Vietnam memoir *We Were Soldiers Once and Young*.

The one liberty we took was to pare down the lists a bit while maintaining a diversity of books about the services yesterday, today, and tomorrow, academic and practical. Chiefs sure read a lot.

Army   General Eric Shinseki

Basic

Band of Brothers, Stephen Ambrose

The Long Gray Line, Rick Atkinson

The Face of Battle, John Keegan

We Were Soldiers Once and Young, Harold Moore and Joe Galloway

The Killer Angels, Michael Shaara

Intermediate

Citizen Soldiers, Stephen Ambrose

Company Commander, Charles B. MacDonald

Men against Fire: The Problem of Battle Command in Future War, S. L. A. Marshall

General George C. Marshall: Soldier-Statesman of the American Century, Mark A. Stoler

Buffalo Soldiers (Black Saber Chronicles), Tom Willard

Advanced

East of Chosin, Roy Appleman

Jomini and His Summary of the Art of War, Antoine Henri Jomini

Supplying War, Martin Van Creveld

The American Way of War, Russell F. Weigley

Real Pro

On War, Carl von Clausewitz, Ed. by Paret and Howard

Command Decisions, Kent Greenfield

Thinking in Time, Richard Neustadt and Ernest May

On Strategy, Harry Summers

Navy   Admiral Vernon Clark

Basic

All Quiet on the Western Front, Erich Maria Remarque

American Caesar: Douglas MacArthur, 1880–1964, William Manchester

Command of the Seas, John Lehman

Everything We Had: an oral history of the Vietnam War, Al Santoli

The Killer Angels, Michael Shaara

On Watch: a memoir, Elmo R. Zumwalt

Run Silent, Run Deep, Edward L. Beach

Two Ocean War: a short history of the United States Navy in the Second World War, Samuel Eliot Morison

The United States Navy: 200 years, Edward L. Beach

Intermediate

Admiral Arleigh Burke, E. B. Potter

At Dawn We Slept: the untold story of Pearl Harbor, Gordon W. Prange

Assignment Pentagon: the insider's guide to the Potomac puzzle palace, Perry M. Smith

A Bright Shining Lie: John Paul Vann and America in Vietnam, Neil Sheehan

Bull Halsey, E. B. Potter

Eagle Against the Sun: the American war with Japan, Ronald H. Spector

The Face of Battle, John Keegan

First to Fight: an inside view of the U.S. Marine Corps, Victor H. Krulak

From Hiroshima to Glasnost: at the center of decision, a memoir, Paul Nitze

The Future of Sea Power, Eric Grove

The Guns of August, Barbara W. Tuchman

Makers of Modern Strategy: from Machiavelli to the nuclear age, Peter Paret

The Price of Admiralty: the evolution of naval warfare, John Keegan

Sea Power: a Naval history, E. B. Potter

The Second World War, John Keegan

Silent Victory: the U.S. submarine war against Japan, Clay Blair

Vietnam: a history, Stanley Karnow

Advanced

The Art of War, Sun-tzu

Cold Dawn: the story of SALT, John Newhouse

The Geopolitics of Super Power, Colin S. Gray

The Influence of Sea Power upon History, 1660–1783, Alfred Thayer Mahan.

On War, Carl von Clausewitz

Seapower and Strategy, Colin S. Gray and Roger W. Barnett

The Soldier and the State: the theory and politics of civil-military relations, Samuel P. Huntington

Strategy: the logic of war and peace, Edward Luttwak

U.S. Defense Policy in an Era of Constrained Resources, Robert L. Pfaltzgraff, Jr. and Richard H. Shultz, Jr.

The U.S. Navy: the view from the mid-1990s, James L. George

Air Force   General Mike Ryan maintained a reading list for interested civilians. (His successor, General John Jumper, hadn't published a reading list as we went to press.)

Basic

10 Propositions Regarding Air Power, Philip Meilinger

Makers of the United States Air Force, John L. Frisbee

Winged Victory: The Army Air Forces in World War II, Geoffrey Perret

This Kind of War: The Classic Korean War History, T.R. Fehrenbach

The Killer Angels, Michael Shaara

Intermediate

Winged Shield, Winged Sword: A History of the USAF, Bernard C. Nalty, Ed.

The Right Stuff, Tom Wolfe

Hostile Skies: A Combat History of the American Air Service in World War I, James J. Hudson

A Few Great Captains: The Men and Events That Shaped the Development of U.S. Air Power, DeWitt Copp

Thud Ridge, Jack Broughton

Advanced

Air Power: A Centennial Appraisal, Tony Mason

Beyond Horizons: A Half Century of Air Force Space Leadership, David N. Spires

Over Lord: General Pete Quesada and the Triumph of Tactical Air Power in World War II, Thomas Alexander Hughes

The United States Air Force in Korea, Robert Futrell

Rise of the Fighter General, 1945–1982: The Problem of Air Force Leadership, Mike Worden

Storm Over Iraq: Air Power and the Gulf War, Richard Hallion

Real Pro

Dereliction of Duty: Lyndon Johnson, Robert McNamara, The Joint Chiefs of Staff, and the Lies That Led to Vietnam, H.R. McMaster

Ideas and Weapons, I.B. Holley

... the Heavens and the Earth: A Political History of the Space Age, Walter A. McDougall

Hoyt S. Vandenberg: The Life of a General, Philip Meilinger

Strategy for Defeat: Vietnam in Retrospect, U.S. Grant Sharp

Joint Air Operations: Pursuit of Unity in Command and Control, 1942–1991, James Winnefeld and Dana Johnson

On War, Carl von Clausewitz

Airpower Against an Army: Challenge and Response in CENTAF's Duel with the Republican Guard, William F. Andrews

The Air Campaign [Desert Shield / Desert Storm], John Warden III

Marine Corps   General James Jones

(We left the following label because it's just so … Marine.)

COMMANDANT'S BEDROCK FOUNDATION

A Bright Shining Lie, Neil Sheehan

Gods of War, John Toland

The Forgotten Soldier, Guy Sajer

Citizen Soldiers, Stephen Ambrose

My American Journey, Colin Powell

Breakout, Martin Russ

Black Hawk Down, Mark Bowden

Marines Of Autumn, James Brady

Other Areas of Interest

Intelligence

Deep Black, William E. Burrows

Body of Secrets, James Bamford

The Book of Honor, Ted Gup

The Wizards of Langley, Jeffrey Richelson

Think tanks

The Wizards of Armageddon, Fred Kaplan

Arms control and nuclear strategy

Endgame, Strobe Talbott

Deadly Gambits, Strobe Talbott

Preventing World War III, David Abshire

Military and the Pentagon in the Gulf War

(Good studies of joint warfighting and the challenge of operating with Washington looking over your shoulder.)

The Generals' War, Bernard Trainor and Michael R. Gordon

The Commanders, Bob Woodward

Crusade, Rick Atkinson

It Doesn't Take a Hero, H. Norman Schwarzkopf

General

Thinking About National Security, Harold Brown

Masters of War, Michael Handel

The Joint Staff Officer's Guide, available online at www.au.af.mil/au/awc/awcgate/pub1/index2000.htm

Websites of Interest

Army

www.army.mil/aps/aps_toc.htm
Where the Army spells out what it is and where it's going, at great length.

www.army.mil/cmh-pg/
The Army's historian, and there's a lot to see.

www.army.mil/A-Z.htm
Has links to all the unit and fort websites.

Navy

www.chinfo.navy.mil/navpalib/organization/org-over.html.
Lays out of the organization of the Navy.

www.chinfo.navy.mil/navpalib/factfile/ffiletop.html.
Other fascinating Navy facts.

www.history.navy.mil.
The Navy's comprehensive historical website.

Air Force

www-cgsc.army.mil/ctac/refpubs/ST100-3/c9/9sect1.htm
A broad overview of the Air Force, written by the Army (go figure).

www.airforcehistory.hq.af.mil.
A lot of history.

www.af.mil/lib/taf.pdf
A view into how the corporate Air Force thinks, and what they think about.

Index

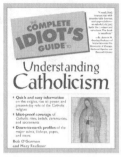

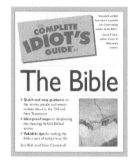
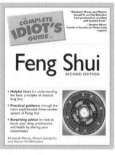

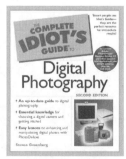
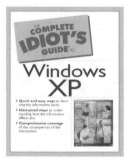